COLLECTING
JEWELLERY

JOHN BENJAMIN

COLLECTING JEWELLERY

ACC ART BOOKS

CONTENTS

Interior of Cameo Corner, 26 Museum Street, London. Note the cabinets on the right filled from top to bottom with antique parures.

INTRODUCTION

I began my career in the jewellery trade in 1972 when, after leaving school, I started work as an apprentice at Cameo Corner, an antique jewellers in Bloomsbury, London. The shop was situated some fifty yards from the gates of the British Museum and was just a stone's throw from University College, Lincoln's Inn and Covent Garden. The area was jam-packed with antiquarian booksellers, antique shops, academics who daily occupied the Reading Room at the Museum, artists, writers and a fair number of eccentrics who seemed to gravitate towards what was then a rather bohemian area of London. It was certainly the ideal environment for a young and keen junior shop assistant to learn about such a strongly aesthetic subject as antique jewellery.

Cameo Corner was established in the 1920s by Mosheh Oved, a Polish Jew who had started with next to nothing – although by the time of his death in 1953 the shop could boast a list of celebrated and significant clients including the sculptor Jacob Epstein, several foreign princesses and our own Queen Mary (who enjoyed the exclusive use of her own armchair). The shop specialised in a broad spectrum of rare and beautiful jewels and gems from Ancient Rome to Victorian England and, naturally, we always kept a large stock of cameos mounted into rings, brooches or even complete sets in their original fitted cases. One cabinet contained a group of Renaissance enamels and another an assortment of Italian Revivalist collars and bracelets jostling with Regency amethyst and garnet diadems. Our incomparable collection of Greek and Roman gold torcs and ancient artefacts was lodged in a safe at the back of the shop. In 1974 much of this irreplaceable stock disappeared in an armed robbery, never to be seen again.

I believe that there are four principal differences between the jewellery industry in the 1970s and that of today. Firstly, availability. In those days, Victorian gold – particularly low-carat pendants and bangles – was so abundant that it sold for negligibly more than scrap. Today, a gold collar with locket or a pair of revivalist teardrop earrings are scarce, highly sought and correspondingly expensive.

Secondly, value. Whatever the item, be it a Giuliano pendant, a piece of Imperial jade or a Victorian silver sweetheart brooch, the price has shot up reflecting rarity, collectability and demand. How many times have I heard a veteran dealer bemoan the fact that the pretty Belle Époque ring which has just cost him £5,000 could be bought for £500 thirty years ago!

Thirdly, fashion. In much the same way that unfashionable 'estate' jewels, diamonds and old gems were routinely broken up for re-cutting and re-setting, so much period jewellery has undergone several phases of reassessment, often experiencing surges and losses in popularity and associated value. A few years ago, Post-War 'Retro' jewellery was proving difficult to sell and currently Victorian diamond flower sprays are in low demand. No doubt in ten years' time 9-carat gold charm bracelets will be the ultimate in chic. Now they sell at auction for little more than scrap.

Fourthly, knowledge. This factor has had an enormous impact upon how we understand and value jewellery today. When I first joined the business very few people knew about Mughal jewellery, fancy diamonds or 'obscure' 19th-century goldsmiths like Jules and Louis Wiese. Today, access to the internet, erudite books and auction house catalogues supply lengthy descriptions and biographies accompanied by state-of-the-art colour photographs. Lectures, courses and workshops are held all over the world by acknowledged specialists and exhibitions display rare and neglected pieces previously locked away, undiscovered, for generations. Together with popular television programmes like the *Antiques Roadshow* and the accessibility of the Internet, there has never been a time when information about jewellery has been so universally available.

The aim of *Collecting Jewellery* is to provide the sort of fundamental information which will enable the collector, student and enthusiast to recognise and identify many of the varieties of antique and 20th-century jewellery readily available on the market today. The scope of the book embraces early times to the Millennium and several important single topics such as gemstones, mourning jewellery, revivalist jewellery and paste are explored, as well as practical information on repairs and valuations. *Collecting Jewellery* is, however, not a price guide. In my opinion the best method of understanding how goods are valued – and constructed – is to adopt the 'hands on' approach and spend time inspecting jewellery at specialist auctions in the U.K. and overseas.

A colourful Georgian multi gem-set gold demi parure comprising necklace and earrings set with ruby, pink topaz, yellow topaz, opal, turquoise, amethyst, emerald and pearl. It is worth noting that the top sections of the earrings were removed in the 19th century and converted into a double-headed tiepin. Later modifications are rarely recommended where antique jewellery is concerned; an experienced workshop should, however, be able to restore this particular pair of earrings back to their original construction.

Chapter 1

Gemmology and Gems in Antique Jewellery

Gemmology is the science of gemstones. In Britain a two-year course in the theoretical and practical study of gemmology leads to an internationally recognised qualification: F.G.A. or Fellow of the Gemmological Association. The equivalent course in the U.S.A. results in the successful applicant achieving the status of Graduate Gemologist or G.G.

The fact that you are an F.G.A. will give you a visible advantage over unqualified competitors simply because you will have the knowledge and confidence of examining a piece of jewellery and being able to differentiate between any number of valuable gems and their less valuable or worthless counterparts. Once qualified, an F.G.A. can choose to go on and take a further year's Diploma course in the study and examination of diamonds (D.G.A.).

In the world of gemstones, confusion frequently reigns supreme. Antique jewellery compounds the problem perfectly since many old gems which *appear* to be one thing are found to be something quite different. Here are some examples. A late Victorian diamond brooch with a 'coral' drop is found to be a rare and costly pink conch pearl. A Regency necklace of graduated pink 'topaz' is actually foil-back rock crystals worth a fraction of the price. An aquamarine ring priced at £3,000 is found on testing to be man-made synthetic blue spinel worth £50 and a 1950s gold brooch set with a 'fine harlequin black opal' is actually an opal triplet, a 'sandwich' of modest opal and crystal. Probably one of the most notorious of these man-made stones masquerading as the real thing is synthetic corundum. Possessing the ability of changing colour in natural or artificial light, these near-valueless gems are sold on as alexandrite, a highly sought and extremely expensive variety of chrysoberyl. It is indeed very easy to come unstuck where gems are concerned and, therefore, a basic knowledge of gemstones and their simulants can help to make – or save – you thousands of pounds.

Gemstones are invariably divided into several distinct categories based upon a variety of factors of which beauty, durability, rarity and value are the dominant characteristics dictating in which 'column' the gem tends to be listed. These categories are highly subjective and the cause of endless debate. Take jade as an example. An Imperial jade bead necklace can sell internationally for millions of dollars whilst a crude nephrite jade modern carving may be worth less than £100. Similarly, a 19th-century gilt-metal and deep red Bohemian garnet star brooch may fetch only £100 whilst the rare green Russian demantoid garnet can achieve as much as £8,000 *per carat* at auction. Some gems can achieve prices which even astound industry professionals. In 2024 Bonhams sold in Hong Kong a cushion-shaped 5.44-carat Brazilian blue Paraiba tourmaline – a relative newcomer to the gemstone pantheon. Estimated at US$40,000-60,000 it fetched $533,900 – more than thirteen times its lower estimate.

The following tables are a personal – and by no means exhaustive – categorisation, chosen within the context of identifying those gems and materials most commonly encountered in antique jewellery.

Table One: Precious Stones

Diamond
Corundum (Ruby and Sapphire)
Emerald
Precious Black Opal
Imperial Jadeite
Alexandrite

Table Two: Semi-Precious Stones

Amethyst	Peridot
Aquamarine	Rock Crystal
Chrysoberyl	Spinel
Citrine	Topaz
Garnet	Tourmaline
Moonstone	Turquoise
Opal	Zircon

Table Three: Ornamental Hardstones

Agate	Labradorite
Bloodstone	Lapis Lazuli
Chalcedony	Malachite
Chrysoprase	Nephrite Jade
Cornelian	Non-precious jadeite
Fluorspar	Onyx and Sardonyx
Jasper	Rose quartz

Table Four: Organic Materials

Pearl	Jet
Amber	Shell
Coral	Tortoiseshell
Ivory	

PRECIOUS STONES

DIAMOND

Diamond is carbon in its purest state. Appropriately enough, its name is taken from the Ancient Greek word ***Adamas*** meaning 'unconquerable.' Diamond is the stuff of legends, intrigue, romance, betrayal and greed. Of all gems, it fulfils the necessary criteria for being considered a truly precious stone. It is the hardest and most durable natural substance on earth. Its beauty is arguably unsurpassed. It is phenomenally difficult to mine and extract and is unrivalled in value.

Diamonds are assessed using four basic factors – the so-called '4 Cs' – and each of these factors will play a critical role when calculating the value of any given stone.

(i) *Colour.* The vast majority of diamonds found in jewellery are almost colourless or exhibit a slight tint of yellow. The degree of yellow is actually extremely subtle and difficult to judge, especially when comparing two stones at the 'colourless' or top end of the range. The jewellery industry uses an alphabetical scale to differentiate colour where 'D' is totally colourless and 'Z' is visibly yellow, so telling the difference between, say, a G colour and an H colour diamond requires skill and experience. Many jewellers and diamond merchants own sets of specimen diamonds of a known colour so they can compare two stones and make a confident judgement. The difference in price between diamonds which ***appear*** identical may actually be several thousands of dollars per carat.

A diamond may frequently be such a good colour that it requires certification at one of the world's internationally recognised laboratories. This is particularly relevant when dealing with larger stones or antique diamonds where significant numbers of crystals are celebrated for their exceptional lack of colour – and fine clarity.

(ii) *Clarity.* It is extremely rare to find a diamond which is totally free of impurities or 'internally flawless.' The impurities in a diamond are known as ***inclusions*** and range from black spots of carbon to white crystals, cracks, fractures, stress lines and surface imperfections which must all be visible under 10x magnification. As with colour, an internationally recognised scale of clarity has been adopted ranging from Internally Flawless (IF) to Third Piqué (I3). Diamonds worse than piqué are usually referred to as spotted and are, frankly, so poor as to render them unsuitable for setting in jewellery. Diamonds which are so heavily flawed that they appear almost opaque are set aside for use in the industrial sector, where their supreme hardness means they are eminently suitable for more robust tasks such as drill heads, grinding wheels and the optical industry.

(iii) *Cut* refers to the shape of a diamond and how it is polished. The most popular and, therefore, highest value shape for diamond is the round ***brilliant***, consisting of fifty-eight perfectly proportioned facets to allow maximum brilliance. This is the so-called 'make' of the stone and a well-made diamond will command a considerable premium in price whilst a poorly made stone will in turn lose some of its value. Modern diamonds are cut into many diverse shapes with ever-increasing numbers of complicated facets. Popular traditional shapes include the rectangular emerald-cut, the marquise (boat or torpedo shape), the heart, the oval, the baguette (small emerald-cuts used extensively in jewellery from the 1930s), and the ***briolette*** (diamond faceted beads). Antique diamonds were often cut from crystals which came from long dried-up alluvial deposits in countries such as India and Brazil. These old stones retain a 'soft' purity and beauty which is often why antique diamond pieces are broken up for repolishing into modern stones – more valuable and desirable because of their historical origin than many stones from 'modern' mines.

Impressive pair of modern diamond earrings, the cushion-shaped top stones suspending pear-shaped diamond drops weighing 4.14 carats and 4.11 carats respectively. G.I.A. graded – Colour: E; Clarity: VS2.

Fancy cushion-shaped vivid yellow diamond ring weighing 5.26 carats set between fancy-shaped white diamond shoulders.

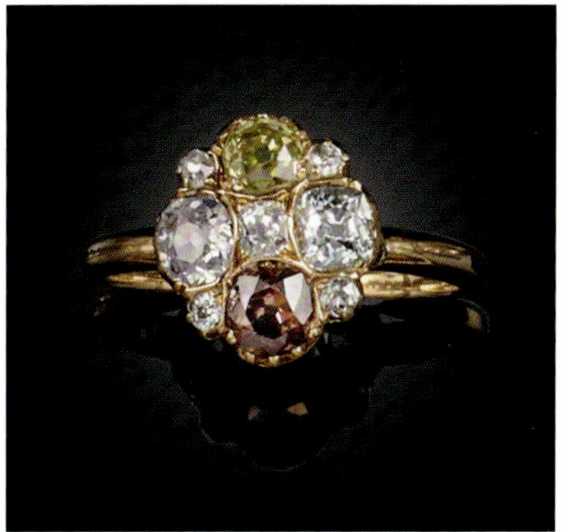

Unusual late Victorian gold ring set with a medley of fancy coloured specimen diamonds including light blue, pinkish brown, greenish yellow and near-colourless examples, c.1900.

(iv) *Carat* is the unit of weight for all diamonds and gemstones and is equal to one fifth of a gram. The word 'carat' is taken form the Greek ***keration*** or 'little horn.' It was discovered by pearl merchants in ancient times that the dried seeds of the carob tree were extremely reliable units of weight due to their uniformity of size; these seeds were contained in bean pods which closely resembled little horns and, thus, the name carat gained common usage. A diamond which, say, weighs three and a half carats is described as '3.50 carats' and one of half a carat as '0.50 carats'. The second decimal point is an important criterion when differentiating the weight of two diamonds of apparently similar size.

Coloured Diamonds

The extraordinarily high price which is paid at international auction for fancy coloured diamonds is actually a relatively recent phenomenon. Certainly, prior to the 1970s, the beauty and rarity of a pink or blue diamond may have been recognised, but prices were nothing like as astronomic as they are today. In Victorian times coloured diamonds were collected as curiosities but 'white' diamonds were commercially more desirable and invariably dearer in price.

Diamonds are found in all colours of the rainbow, although the rarest is red. In 1987 a purplish-red diamond weighing 0.95 carats fetched $880,000 – $926,000 per carat – at auction. It is the purity and intensity of colour which determines its value; a yellow diamond graded as 'vivid' is far more expensive than a lighter yellow 'intense' diamond, whilst a 'greyish blue' diamond is far less desirable than, say, a 'deep blue' stone. This is why fancy diamonds are always sent to an international laboratory so their precise colour can be scientifically assessed. Generally speaking, brown is the least expensive fancy colour and black is surprisingly affordable in price, although the recent trend for setting numerous small black diamonds in contrasting clusters with colourless diamonds has increased their popularity and value.

It is possible to find beautiful coloured diamonds in antique brooches and pendants. Invariably, these stones are removed from their settings for repolishing into modern, perfectly proportioned gems with enhanced value. An excellent method of collecting fancy coloured diamonds is to search for Victorian tiepins where it was reasonably common to set a single specimen stone into a simple claw setting of gold. These diamonds are usually too small to be of great commercial merit and it is perfectly possible to build up a reasonable spectrum of colours for a not unrealistic outlay.

Diamond Cutting Through History

Diamonds have been set into jewellery since Roman times and throughout history have been prized for all sorts of properties and powers including magical, medicinal and talismanic. In medieval times wearing diamonds could apparently prevent the plague and powdered diamond was reliably considered to be a potent poison. During the Middle Ages, and well into the 16th century, unpolished diamond crystals were set into gold rings and were used

Splendid rose-cut diamond and old-mine cut diamond lyre brooch, c.1800.

Old-mine brilliant-cut diamond chandelier earrings with antique Indian briolette diamond drops, c.1850.

for writing messages on window panes. Known as 'pointed' diamonds, these octahedral crystals were set with the point of the natural unpolished, four-sided pyramid above the top of the gold mount and possessed one unrivalled property – they never wore out.

The most basic method of faceting a diamond was the ***table-cut*** – quite simply an unpolished octahedral crystal with its top ground down into a square. Sometimes the opposing point of the crystal was also removed, creating a smaller facet at the back of the stone, known as the ***culet***. The table-cut reigned supreme throughout the 16th and 17th centuries – unsurprising, considering the technical difficulties in polishing a diamond with the primitive tools available.

Diamond polishers in Amsterdam and Antwerp experimented with more complex methods of cutting as early as the 15th century and it was in Holland that a new style of faceting gradually emerged. Known as the ***rose-cut***, the crown or top of the diamond was cut into a series of geometric triangular facets, whilst the pavilion, or bottom of the stone, was left flat. Rose diamonds became extremely popular throughout the 18th and 19th centuries, although they tend to appear rather grey in comparison with diamonds of more complex cut. They were invariably set in silver in tightly enclosed bands known as ***collets***. They lent themselves beautifully to the many designs of jewellery fashionable during this period – aigrettes, collet rivières, girandole earrings and naturalistic cluster rings. Sometimes rose diamonds were backed with silver tinfoil to intensify their sparkle.

By the middle of the 18th century society was beginning to enjoy the benefits of increasing wealth. Socially, this prosperity meant that ladies and gentlemen of the nobility and a burgeoning middle class were keen to dress up and meet one another at balls, the theatre and at receptions held in their splendid new houses and country estates. Here they could show off to one another the latest gown from London and Paris complemented by ravishing tiaras, corsage jewels and chandelier earrings mounted with ***brilliant-cut*** diamonds – the new style of polishing which, for the first time, showed diamonds off to their best effect. A modern brilliant is composed of fifty-eight perfectly proportioned facets but antique brilliants are often rather ill-proportioned and cushion in shape. Nevertheless, the impact of a Georgian faceted diamond brooch worn in the twinkling light of chandeliers and candelabra was breathtaking and made the diamond the most desirable and valuable of all gemstones in the 'Age of the Faceted Stone.'

The discovery of diamond deposits in South Africa in the 1870s – notably at Kimberley and subsequently in South West Africa (Namibia) – led to hundreds of thousands of carats being brought into Britain and Western Europe. In a boom economy where a more prosperous society possessed the necessary disposable income to buy jewellery, most of the principal towns and cities in Britain boasted several family jewellers catering for the needs of the public. In the 1890s diamond jewellery could be fairly modest – simple cluster brooches, crescents, stars, line bangles and half-hoop rings selling for considerably less than £100 – or far grander, such as the Goldsmiths & Silversmiths Company selling diamond crowns and necklaces for well over £1,000. The underlying theme was *availability.* Diamonds were both affordable and plentiful; by the end of the 19th century it was possible to buy a rivière of graduated diamonds from one London supplier in no less than twenty-three different sizes.

Mass production inevitably led to improvement in diamond cutting and by the start of the 20th century the introduction of platinum revolutionised both jewellery design and the technical accomplishment of mounting stones with the minimum of setting visible. Diamond cutters experimented with many different shapes – baguettes, emerald-cuts, marquises and briolettes, to name but a few – and the brilliant evolved into the perfectly proportioned symmetrical round stone exhibiting the unique adamantine lustre so familiar to us today.

CORUNDUM

Corundum is an oxide of aluminium which has two distinct varieties – ruby and sapphire. Although ruby is only found in shades of pale pink to deep red, sapphire is found in an entire spectrum of colours.

Impressive late Victorian diamond tiara composed of five graduated sunburst clusters mounted in gold and set in silver, c.1890. Note the irregular cushion-shaped diamonds which lack the perfect symmetry of modern cut stones.

Janesich platinum ring, c.1920, mounted with a polished sugarloaf-cut certificated Burmese ruby weighing 12.30 carats mounted between diamond and calibre-cut ruby shoulders. Burmese rubies contain chromium which causes them to fluoresce, so enhancing their vibrancy and commercial appeal.

Art Deco Ceylon (Sri Lankan) ruby and baguette-cut diamond ring, c.1935.

Siamese (Thai) ruby and diamond three-stone ring. Due to the presence of iron, Siam rubies usually exhibit a characteristic 'purplish' or 'brownish' red undertone. They invariably lack the pleasing bright red or pinkish red colour of commercially desirable Burmese and Ceylon varieties.

Ruby

An extremely fine precious ruby will compete in price with the costliest of diamonds whilst a poor colour ruby filled with an abundance of flaws rendering it opaque may only be worth £50 a carat. Rubies gained particular prominence and recognition during the Renaissance, when richly coloured specimens were brought into Western Europe along the Trade routes from the Orient and were set into magnificent pendants and stomachers with diamonds and pearls. The most important stones were mined in Burma (Myanmar) and the very best Burmese examples are described as ***pigeon's blood***. These rubies are characteristically a deep rich red colour due to the presence of chromium and are rarely found in sizes above four carats. Other sources for ruby include Ceylon (Sri Lanka) which produces paler stones of pinkish tone, Siam (Thailand) where the rubies are invariably purplish-pink or brownish due to the existence of iron, also Africa, Afghanistan and Vietnam.

Ruby was an important gemstone in 18th- and 19th-century jewellery. Its versatility meant that it could be set into contrasting lines or clusters with diamonds, half pearls or exclusively in elaborately chased gold mounts. In the period of mass production at the end of the 19th century, rubies were routinely set with diamonds in crescents, floral sprays, hinged gold bangles and modest cluster rings. These stones were usually of cushion shape and the quality was quite variable, although fine 'old-mine' Burmese stones are highly prized today. As stone cutting techniques advanced, ruby was cut into several new and interesting shapes including square, calibré (baton) and triangular. A popular design in the 1920s and 1930s was the line bracelet, where a channel of square-cut rubies was set in articulated side-by-side formation in a gold or platinum mount.

Fabergé used rubies, indigenous to Russia, which were an ideal accompaniment to the objects of function popular with his wealthy and sophisticated clientele; thus, bell pushes, photograph frames, gold brooches and cigarette cases were set with rubies polished *en cabochon* into domes. The cabochon was the only possible method of cutting suitable for exhibiting the distinctive six-pointed star effect known as ***asterism***. Star rubies and star sapphires were mounted in architectural diamond settings during the Art Deco period and were particularly popular in the U.S.A. Star rubies are less common than star sapphires and sell for significant sums dependent upon their quality and size.

Sapphire

Although we tend to think that sapphires are blue, they are actually found in many lovely colours, of which one in particular – the padparadscha – can be as rare and costly as some of the best blue examples.

The finest sapphires were mined in the Kashmir region of India and are a singular shade of warm, velvety blue. The Kashmir mines are now exhausted so antique stones are prized not just for their colour but their rarity. Burmese sapphires are also rare and expensive and are a deeper, clearer royal blue. The majority of good quality Victorian

Exceptional 22.13-carat yellow Ceylon sapphire and diamond cluster ring.

Ring mounted with a 3.51-carat Kashmiri sapphire set between trapeze-cut diamond shoulders. This stone exhibits the characteristic velvety blue of the rarest sapphires found only in this inaccessible region of India.

1920s star sapphire cabochon diamond and platinum ring.

Art Deco pendant mounted with a 13.10-carat Ceylon sapphire in an architectural diamond and calibré-cut sapphire frame. Ceylon sapphires are invariably found in tones of light to medium blue. This cushion-shaped example exhibits the irregular proportions of 'native-cutting'.

sapphires are, like ruby, of Burmese origin – a classic brooch might be designed as a crescent of graduated cushion-shaped Burmese sapphires within a border of old-mine cut diamonds.

Ceylon sapphires are considerably paler and less valuable than the Burmese variety. Sometimes called 'corn-flower blue', they are quite easy to identify as they invariably contain needle-like inclusions called 'silk' which reflect the light in a rainbow-like effect. Ceylon sapphires were used in late Victorian fringe necklaces, aesthetic jewellery in which a subtle tone of colour was considered appropriate and Art Nouveau jewellery. These sapphires were frequently 'native-cut' meaning that they were both poorly proportioned and fashioned to exhibit the best direction of colour. It is worth-while to examine a Ceylon sapphire through the side of the stone – it is sometimes totally colourless.

Other sources for blue sapphire include Siam (Thailand), Australia – where the stones are so deep a blue as to appear black – and Montana, where bright blue examples were often set in Edwardian pearl pendants. Other desirable colours include pink – where a deep shade of magenta is highly prized – purple, green, yellow and brown. Colourless or 'white' sapphires are often set in Eastern jewellery where they contrast with blue sapphires, citrines, zircons and low-grade emeralds. They are modestly priced and difficult to confuse with valuable diamonds.

Padparadscha sapphires are hard to define. The trade describes their colour as 'peach' and certainly paler, cheaper examples do seem to have a 'peachy' tone. However, a really top grade padparadscha sapphire will exhibit a vibrant orangey-pink colour, a case of once seen never forgotten. Seldom encountered, a price of $97,000 per carat was achieved for an 8.01-carat specimen stone in 2019.

Irregular polished rubies and sapphires were set in Roman gold rings and simple part-faceted examples appear in rings and brooches from the 13th and 14th centuries onwards. The rarity and quality of these jewels meant that their use was undoubtedly confined to bishops and high churchmen, wealthy merchants and the nobility. During the 18th century rings were frequently foiled to enhance the colour and intensify the lustre of the sapphire (or any coloured gem come to that); this technique lapsed with the development of open-back settings, advances in stone cutting and the discovery of new mine deposits.

Sapphires were the perfect accompaniment to diamonds in the 19th century and, along with rubies, were extensively set in flower spray brooches, tiaras, earrings

Superb Victorian emerald and diamond hinged gold bangle convertible to be worn as a pendant, c.1860. This emerald, weighing 5.66 carats, exhibits the finest colour and transparency seen in the very best stones which were sourced from the Chivor and Muzo mines in Colombia in the 19th century.

and endless half-hoop and floral cluster rings, universally popular from the 1880s onwards. Like ruby, sapphire was the ideal contrast to diamond in Art Deco platinum and white-gold jewellery and after the First World War large, pale Ceylon sapphires were set in broad bracelets and bold yellow-gold flower brooches enhanced by gems of unusual colour such as turquoise, zircon and rubies cut into rectangular batons.

EMERALD

It is an interesting paradox that although jewellery set with emeralds is reasonably common – especially in items manufactured after the Second World War – antique jewellery mounted with top quality 'old-mine' emeralds is extremely scarce.

Emerald is the green gem variety of beryl and has fairly widespread distribution. By far the most desirable antique stones originated in Colombia from the Chivor and Muzo mines. Their highly prized 'blue-green' colour is due to chromium and, internally, Colombian emeralds frequently contain characteristic 'three-phase inclusions' composed of a cavity filled with liquid, a gas bubble and a crystalline cube. Other sources of emerald include Russia (Siberia), Egypt – where mines can be traced as far back as Queen Cleopatra – Pakistan, Afghanistan and Africa. Emeralds from the Sandawana mines in Zimbabwe produce small stones of intense colour and fine clarity whilst less desirable pale and flawed stones were extracted from the old Habachtal mines in the Austrian Tyrol. Many of the semi-opaque, poor colour emeralds found in Renaissance revival jewellery at the end of the 19th century originated from this source.

As expensive as fine, old Colombian and Siberian emeralds may be, indifferent emeralds containing an abundance of cracks, flaws and assorted imperfections are not. Poorer stones are often polished *en cabochon* into domes which tends to mask internal defects better than the faceted varieties. Today emeralds are treated with caution by buyers because of the large number of stones on the market which have been 'improved' with oils, resins and artificial materials which strengthen colour and conceal defects. The problem has become so widespread that shops and auction houses publish disclaimers to protect themselves from legal dispute. Significant stones are thus sold at auction with an accompanying certificate stating natural, untreated colour and, ideally, country of origin.

Emerald was highly prized by the Ancient Egyptians and subsequently by the Spanish, who brought Colombian emeralds to India during the 16th century. Jewellery

Art Deco platinum jabot pin mounted with a polished and fluted melon-shaped emerald in a surround of diamond-set ruby beads with red and black enamelled highlights and matching diamond-set enamelled finial. Cartier, c.1930.

Modern emerald and diamond cluster pendant. Weighing approximately 24 carats, this substantial size stone is heavily flawed and has been subjected to significant clarity enhancement.

Edwardian 'Lightning Ridge' black opal and diamond pendant, c.1910. Due to their water content opals tend to dry out and crack. Opals exhibiting tell-tale cracks or fissures cannot be repaired and should thus be avoided.

Art Deco platinum ring mounted with a fine oval-shaped black opal between diamond-set shoulders.

originating from this period tends to be of religious design; crosses, rosaries, crowns and vestment ornaments were invariably mounted with large table-cut emeralds which were frequently foiled to enhance their colour. Old Indian emeralds of 17th- and 18th-century origin were highly prized by the Mughal emperors, who set huge pebble-like stones in armbands, collars and head ornaments known as *sarpechs*. These stones were sometimes engraved with complicated calligraphy and flowers; a fine 217-carat inscribed example sold at auction in September 2001 for a hammer price of £1.4 million.

Emerald and diamond jewellery was highly prized by European aristocracy during the 18th and 19th centuries. Complete parures of necklace, earrings, corsage brooch and tiara were lavishly mounted with Indian and Colombian stones, set in gold collets within diamond and silver frames of sévigné (tied bow), cluster and floral drop design. During the early 19th century foil-back emeralds were set in highly elaborate cannetille work gold frames and the gem was popular in sentimental jewellery of the period, such as padlocks, hearts and serpents. The scarcity of emeralds during the 19th century is probably due to the fact that much of the output from the Colombian mines was snapped up by Eastern potentates; certainly, Victorian emerald jewellery is hardly abundant, although by the 20th century the gem enjoyed a visible revival. Poorer, flawed gems (more beryl than emerald) were popular in Arts and Crafts jewellery due to their gentle, subtle colours, whilst in the 1920s and 1930s fine-quality stones were cut into rectangles and set in platinum as line bracelets, architectural pendants, double clip brooches and earrings contrasting with lines of baguette diamonds or the eternally popular three-stone ring.

PRECIOUS BLACK OPAL

Opal is a non-crystalline material composed of hardened silica gel and up to 20% water. Opals which exhibit several different colours of the rainbow within a deep grey, blue or black background are described as harlequin black opals and the unique 'play' of colour is known as the gem's 'pinfire'.

The majority of black opals are mined at Lightning Ridge, Queensland, Australia in conditions which are both arduous and exceedingly inhospitable, where subterranean labyrinthine tunnels have been carved out by hand. It is extremely unusual to find black opal jewellery before the end of the 19th century, although the material was used extensively in Arts and Crafts necklaces and pendants and Art Nouveau jewels where the highly individual and colourful gems were ideal for carving and shaping into naturalistic forms such as butterfly wings or imaginative figurative shapes such as sails.

Opal was popular in Edwardian and 'Belle Époque' platinum and diamond jewellery, usually taking the form of a simple oval plaque or domed cabochon in a border of brilliant-cut diamonds. Occasionally rubies, emeralds or green demantoid garnets were used as an effective contrast in colour. Black opals are exceptionally expensive today and it is unusual to find specimen gems in modern European manufactured jewellery. Opals which exhibit only blue and green pinfire are also, somewhat confusingly, known as black opals; however, these are usually correspondingly less valuable. Whatever the colour, care should be taken to ensure that any opal you may consider buying is free of chips, cracks and fractures.

Colour change in an alexandrite. The most sought-after examples came from the Russian Urals and are watermelon-rind green when viewed in natural light and raspberry red in artificial.

IMPERIAL, OR PRECIOUS, JADEITE

Like black opal, jadeite was seldom used in European jewellery before the 20th century although Imperial jade, mined in Burma (Myanmar) and carved in China, has been carved into amulets and pendants for 3,000 years. The colour of jade varies enormously, ranging from white to black, as well as yellow, brown and lavender, although the term 'Imperial jade' describes a rich emerald green tone, almost glass-like in its translucency and polish. Jade symbolises eternity and longevity and carvings frequently depict symbols associated with good luck such as bats, monkeys and dragons. Peaches and peonies represent happiness, whilst pomegranates symbolise fertility and children.

Chinese Imperial jade carved pendant suspended from a pink tourmaline and pearl ball, c.1910.

Polished jadeite ring mounted in platinum between diamond-set shoulders. Care should be taken to ensure that jade has not been treated to improve its appearance. This example was certificated as 'exhibiting no indications of artificial impregnation'.

To a great extent the West barely understands or appreciates the subtleties and potential value of jade which is why the major international auction houses hold their sales in the Far East where polished cabochons set into rings, carved earrings, hoop bangles and, especially, rows of graduated beads can easily fetch hundreds of thousands or even millions of dollars. Nevertheless, it is perfectly possible to purchase quite reasonable ***non-precious*** jade at auction or in the retail sector closer to home, although examples are unlikely to be particularly old and may exhibit irregularities in colour, clarity and quality.

ALEXANDRITE

Discovered in the Russian Urals in 1830, this singular gem was named in honour of Tsar Alexander II. A variety of chrysoberyl, it exhibits one fascinating property which makes it eminently desirable and correspondingly expensive – it changes colour depending upon the prevailing lighting conditions. The very finest 'old-mine' Russian stones alter from a deep bluish-green tone in natural light to raspberry-red in artificial and are usually found as small cushion-shaped stones in 19th-century Russian pendants and brooches. Alexandrites of five carats or more are extremely rare although occasionally specimen gems do appear in fine diamond 'Belle Époque' settings. Ceylon alexandrites are less pronounced in colour change and recent finds in Brazil of excellent quality have been appearing on the market, although these stones do not have quite the desirability of their antique Russian counterparts. Synthetic corundum, which changes colour from purplish-blue to red, is practically worthless and has been sold as 'alexandrite' since the 1950s. Cheap stones described as 'alexandrite' should thus be treated with great caution and scepticism.

SEMI-PRECIOUS STONES

AMETHYST

A transparent variety of crystalline quartz, amethyst ranges in colour from very pale mauve to deep purple. Versatile and distinctive, amethyst was used by ancient Romans and Greeks for intaglio seal stones and was favoured by the Church for bishops' rings and pectoral crosses. The finest stones originated from Siberia although the majority of amethysts used in 19th-century jewellery were from Brazil and Uruguay. Amethyst was particularly effective when mounted in yellow gold and was frequently accompanied by half pearls, diamonds and enamel. Scottish 'pebble' jewellery contained amethysts cut into the shape of thistles and late Victorian fringe necklaces were popular where the amethysts were set in graduated lines accompanied by compatible gems such as aquamarines and peridots. In the 1940s and 1950s amethyst was used in large-scale gold brooches and bracelets cut into rectangles and mounted with unusual gem combinations such as turquoise and citrine.

AQUAMARINE

The pale transparent blue variety of beryl, aquamarine was the ideal accompaniment for elaborate early 19th-century cannetille or floral work parures where the gem's subtle tone contrasted perfectly with fashionably delicate and feminine gold frames. The majority of these earlier aquamarine pieces were backed with foil to enhance their colour and brilliance and it was only in the 20th century that it was discovered that the blue colour could be intensified by heat treating. This resulted in large and bold rectangular aquamarines being mounted in Art Deco diamond and platinum architectural frames, a theme which extended through the 1950s when the gem often appeared in gold 'Retro' style settings.

Although world distribution is widespread, the finest quality gems originate from Brazil where fairly massive crystals have been discovered. Aquamarine is frequently confused with blue topaz and synthetic blue spinel and it is recommended that pieces made after the 1950s are tested for authenticity.

Impressive Victorian gold necklace mounted with large oval-shaped and circular amethysts in cut-down collet settings with pear-shaped drop, c.1845.

Unusual amethyst cameo and diamond pendant, c.1900.

Belle Époque aquamarine and platinum diamond-set pendant, c.1910. This aquamarine is especially appealing because of its excellent colour.

Art Deco ring mounted with emerald-cut aquamarine between diamond-set shoulders.

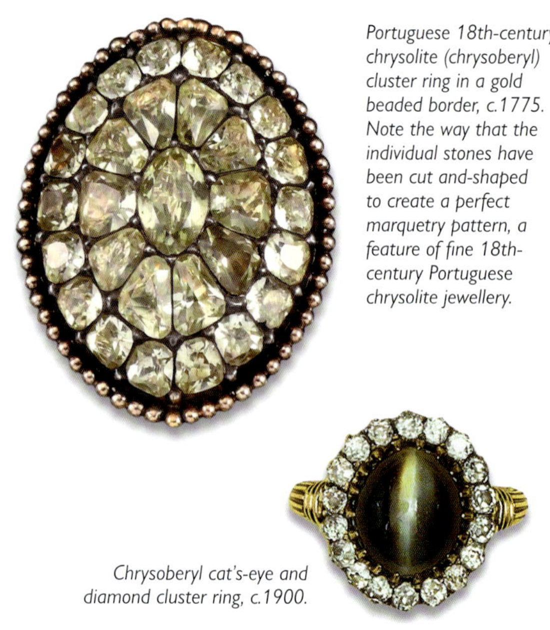

Portuguese 18th-century chrysolite (chrysoberyl) cluster ring in a gold beaded border, c.1775. Note the way that the individual stones have been cut and-shaped to create a perfect marquetry pattern, a feature of fine 18th-century Portuguese chrysolite jewellery.

Chrysoberyl cat's-eye and diamond cluster ring, c.1900.

CHRYSOBERYL FAMILY

Chrysoberyl is a confusing gem since it comprises a family of three totally different stones of disassociated appearance and value – alexandrite (see page 18), chrysoberyl and chrysoberyl cat's-eye.

Chrysoberyl

Although large pale yellowish green gems were used occasionally in mid-19th-century gold pendants and brooches, smaller clusters of the stone were more commonly used in 18th- and early 19th-century English and Continental jewellery where it was known as *chrysolite*. In Spain and Portugal, pavé-set clusters of chrysolites were fashioned as large navette-shaped dress rings or incredibly long bow and drop earrings whilst the gem enjoyed something of a revival in the 1870s, when it was set in colourful Neo-Renaissance enamel and cabochon garnet necklaces and pendants inspired by the paintings of Hans Holbein.

Chrysoberyl Cat's-Eye

Historically known as cymophane, chrysoberyl cat's-eyes are always polished *en cabochon* to exhibit their singular optical effect known as *chatoyancy* – a sharp band of light running from the top to the bottom of the centre of the stone. The finest stones are either honey green or olive green and originated in Ceylon (Sri Lanka) and India. They were thought to ward off the evil eye and were thus highly prized. Chrysoberyl cat's-eyes should not be confused with quartz cat's-eyes which are coarser and far cheaper.

CITRINE

A variety of crystalline quartz ranging in colour from the palest lemon through orange and brown, citrine has been used extensively in 19th- and 20th-century jewellery and ornamentation due to its abundance and modest value. The stone is often confused with *topaz*, but citrine lacks the brilliance of topaz and, when examined under a magnifying lens, often exhibits varying patches of colour. Citrine was widely used in gold and silver necklaces and bracelets and was so popular in Victorian Scottish jewellery that it was known as 'Cairngorm'. Early Victorian desk seals were sometimes made with faceted citrine handles which are desirable today; however, care should be taken to ensure that what is thought to be citrine is not actually paste. Like amethyst, citrine was popular in the 1940s and 1950s when large, rectangular stones in contrasting shades of yellow, gold and brown were set into architectural mounts.

Early 19th-century citrine and gold cannetille work girandole-style brooch, c.1825.

Art Deco tawny-brown citrine and diamond ring attributed to Cartier, c.1935.

Impressive Victorian pyrope garnet cabochon and gold parure comprising necklace, earrings and brooch, c.1845.

Smoky Quartz

A common dark brown transparent quartz principally used in Scottish jewellery and cheaper late 19th-century necklaces, brooches and bracelets where it was usually mounted in silver. Smoky quartz was also fashionable for accessories such as desk seal handles, vinaigrettes and snuff boxes.

GARNET

Once upon a time garnet jewellery was abundant and modestly priced, but prices for good antique pieces have resulted in a rapid and justifiable reassessment of their status.

Garnet is found in several colours although red is by far the most common. There are two distinct red varieties found in antique jewellery:

Pyrope Garnet

Blood red garnet used extensively in the 18th and 19th century. Georgian pyrope garnets were invariably flat cut and oval in shape, set in gold and frequently foiled to improve their appearance. Common Georgian designs included cushion-shaped brooches with half pearl decoration and hair locket centres, flower spray brooches, graduated collet rivières and necklaces of foliate design sometimes suspending a Maltese cross pendant convertible to a brooch.

Nineteenth-century pyrope garnets were used abundantly during the 'Grand' period of mid-Victorian opulence and were ideal gems for the extravagant effect. A popular fashion involved cutting garnets *en cabochon* and hollowing out the backs to 'lighten' the look of

Regency naturalistic gold bracelet set with foil-back garnets, c.1815.

Elegant late Victorian gold, hessonite garnet and enamel pendant on matching necklace by Giuliano, c.1895.

the stones. Cabochon garnets are often referred to as 'carbuncles'. Pyrope garnets were used in late 19th-century Czechoslovakian and German jewellery in pavé-set clusters of multi-faceted stones. Known as Bohemian garnets, they were usually mounted in low-grade gold or gilt metal in hundreds of different designs, from modest brooches to elaborate teardrop necklaces.

Almandine Garnet

Claret or purplish-red garnet, more commonly used in 19th-century 'carbuncle' jewellery such as French enamel and gold Neo-Renaissance 'Holbeinesque' pendants and necklaces where it was often accompanied by chrysolites.

The other principal varieties of garnet are:

Hessonite Garnet

A deep reddish-orange variety of grossular garnet. Hessonites were used in 19th-century earrings, pendants and fringe necklaces in which they were fashionably known as 'jacinths'. They are distinctive for their unusual treacle-like inclusions.

Demantoid Garnet

By far the most valuable member of the garnet family, demantoids are a beautiful leaf-green variety of andradite garnet discovered in the Ural mountains and used predominantly in late 19th-century figurative jewellery such as butterfly and lizard brooches, usually accompanied by diamonds, opals, half pearls or white enamel. Fine Russian demantoid specimens above 3-4 carats are seldom seen and can fetch several thousand dollars per carat. They contain characteristic inclusions of hair-like asbestos known as 'horsetails.'

Late Victorian diamond bee brooch set with three Russian demantoid garnets in its abdomen, a red spinel in its thorax and a sapphire in its head, c.1890.

Late Victorian gold necklace of scrolling design set with an upper gallery of circular moonstones and lower fringe of graduated oval moonstones, c.1900.

MOONSTONE

A variety of feldspar, moonstone is appropriately named as it displays a bluish-white sheen effect known as adularescence. The stone is still extensively mined in Ceylon and India and was rarely used in jewellery before the end of the 19th century when the subtle, understated property of the stone was found to be ideal for naturalistic silver and gold brooches, pendants and necklaces. Moonstone is practically always polished *en cabochon* to exhibit its unique lustre. When cut into figurative designs, such as the head of an Egyptian Pharaoh or a 'man in the moon', the value increases sharply, especially when enhanced by settings of diamonds.

OPAL

Milky Opal

Milky opals were commonly used in late 19th-century jewellery when their sheer versatility resulted in a wide assortment of designs such as bangles, set as a line of graduated cabochons with diamonds in between, cluster rings, fringe necklaces and crescent brooches. Superior examples exhibit an attractive play of red, green and blue colours whilst inferior milky opals are almost completely white with minimal flashes. Milky opals were also set with rubies, emeralds and demantoid garnets in naturalistic designs such as butterflies and lizards. Mid-Victorian opals exhibiting a softer play of colour were sometimes set in scrolling gold brooches and necklaces enamelled in royal blue.

Mexican Fire Opals

These vibrant gems were used in Art Nouveau and Art Deco diamond jewellery. Fire opal is usually deficient of any 'play' of colour but exhibits a singular shade of translucent mid- to deep orangey-red.

Opal doublets and triplets are fairly common in jewellery manufactured after the 1950s and were occasionally set in Arts and Crafts silver jewellery. The setting often concealed the fact that the opal was actually a 'sandwich' of two or three different materials and care should be taken to ensure that what appears to be a fine opal is not actually a composite.

Late Victorian hinged gold bangle mounted with a milky opal and diamond oval cluster between diamond scrolling shoulders, c.1890.

Late Victorian (c.1890) gold salamander brooch studded with graduated opal cabochons, diamonds and set with a demantoid-cut garnet in the head and rubies in the eyes. Opals were an ideal choice of gem for this kind of Victorian novelty jewellery and were often combined with bright green demantoids, echoing the colour of the reptile in nature.

Edwardian fire opal and diamond negligée pendant, c.1910.

PERIDOT

Formerly known as olivine, peridot is routinely confused with chrysolite, the yellowish green variety of chrysoberyl. The finest peridots are a deep lime-green colour and originated from the island of St John in the Red Sea. The stone has been set in jewellery since the time of the Romans although practically all the material on the market today is either Victorian or later. Peridots were sometimes used in 18th-century fob seals and in the 1840s were mounted in elaborate gold scrolling settings and sold as parures complete with tiara, necklace, pair of bracelets and very long pendant earrings. The stone is particularly common in late 19th-century openwork pendants, bar brooches and fringe necklaces invariably accompanied by half pearls in 9 or 15-carat gold settings. Peridots can be identified by their characteristic 'doubling of the back facets' when viewed under a magnifying lens; modern examples are often rather pale and insipid.

Edwardian gold brooch/pendant mounted with two fancy-shaped peridots in a half pearl-set scrolling frame, c.1910. Peridots were one of the most popular semi-precious gems used in the Edwardian era and are frequently seen in this kind of affordable naturalistic jewellery.

ROCK CRYSTAL

The colourless variety of quartz used since earliest times as an ornamental stone in large-scale objects of vertu such as vases, ewers and caskets and extensively in small-scale jewellery and decorative accessories. Usually polished *en cabochon,* rock crystal formed the back covers of jewelled lockets or were engraved and painted from behind with naturalistic subjects such as insects, birds and domestic animals. These 'reverse crystals' were mounted in gold as pendants or brooches and are highly collectable today. Other Victorian rock crystal jewels included gold fringe necklaces in which rock crystal cabochons were decorated with diamond and ruby 'flies', necklaces mounted with pink foiled rock crystal imitating pink topaz and butterfly brooches where rock crystal plaques covered real butterfly wings.

Rock crystal was used widely in Belle Époque and Art Deco diamond jewellery, cut into architectural shapes and mounted with sapphires, rubies and – most effectively – coral and onyx. The stone was favoured by Fabergé in accessories such as bell pushes, vases of flowers and photograph frames, and in the 1950s and 1960s, frosted rock crystal was popular in Austrian flower brooches in which the petals were sometimes stained in a variety of different colours.

Reverse rock crystal and gold locket-back pendant depicting a heron by the waterside.

Cluster ring mounted with 5.60-carat cushion-shaped red spinel and diamonds. In recent years the value of the finest red spinels has truly rocketed. This example was certificated by the Swiss Gemmological Institute (SSEF) as 'Burmese origin; no indications of treatment'.

Fine pink Burmese spinel taveez pendant suspended from an Oriental pearl and fluted emerald bead necklace.

SPINEL

Spinel is a gemstone which is surprisingly obscure in Western European jewellery but conversely was liberally used and highly valued in India where it was set into marvellous and flamboyant necklaces, bangles and earrings by the Mughal Emperors.

Seventeenth- and 18th-century Indian spinels are rare and costly and were usually cut into irregular pebble-like drops or were mounted in settings of gold as flat, table-cut stones accompanied by pearls, enamel and mirror-back diamonds. The principal colour of spinel is a bright fiery-red which is often confused with ruby; the huge 'Black Prince's Ruby' mounted in the Imperial State Crown is actually a red spinel. Indeed, in earlier times spinels were routinely described as 'Balas rubies'. Spinels in 18th- and early 19th-century European settings are usually pinkish-red in colour and originated in Burma and Ceylon. In 2015 Bonhams sold a splendid octagonal-shaped 50.13-carat deep purplish-pink spinel and diamond jewel. Named after its original owner Henry Philip Hope, a collector of rare gems who died in 1839, the Hope spinel was thought to have originated in the ancient mines of Tajikistan. Estimated to sell for around $300,000 it went on to fetch $1.4 million. Other colours used in antique jewellery include blue, purple and near-colourless.

Synthetic blue spinels appear deceptively like aquamarines but are usually a deeper blue tone. They were used in Continental jewellery after the 1950s and should be tested for authenticity.

TOPAZ

A beautiful transparent gemstone of which the three best known colours are golden brown, pink and blue. Precious or 'Imperial' topaz is a distinctive 'sherry' colour and was used in 18th-century and later gold and diamond set jewellery in which the stone's naturally bright and glittery appearance was often further enhanced by foiling. The finest topaz originated in Brazil and examples of good size and colour are extremely expensive today. Early 19th-century sherry topaz was sometimes set in graduated rivières or in parures of necklace, bracelets and earrings in elaborate gold cannetille work settings. Pink topaz were

Late 19th-century Continental 'Empire style' gold pendant mounted with a fine oval sherry topaz, the foliate frame set with diamonds and suspending an Oriental pearl drop.

Edwardian pink topaz, diamond and platinum demi-parure, c.1910.

Eighteenth-century Portuguese topaz girandole brooch, c.1775. Portuguese jewellery of this period was invariably fully backed in silver, while the individual stones were foiled to enhance their appearance. The variations in colour of the topaz in this example are caused by discolouration of the foiling.

set in a similar fashion, sometimes with cruciform-shaped gold pendants suspended below the necklace. Pink topaz was used sympathetically in early 19th-century sentimental heart and padlock jewels where its pretty, pastel colour formed the perfect partnership with half pearls.

Topaz has a characteristic 'greasy' or slippery feel quite unlike stones of similar colour such as citrine or zircon. In the 19th century much citrine was erroneously called 'citrine topaz', especially in Scotland. Blue topaz has become a common and liberally used gemstone in modern gold and silver jewellery, although much of the material on the market today is heat treated.

Victorian gold hinged bangle pavé-set with a domed cluster of turquoises and with rose-diamond points in between in a turquoise-studded surround, c.1870.

TOURMALINE

A multi-coloured gemstone of which the two most popular shades are deep green and deep pink. As with several semi-precious gemstones, tourmaline gained widespread popularity at the end of the 19th century in gold pendants, necklaces and brooches of naturalistic design set with half pearls, aesthetic Arts and Crafts jewellery and subsequently in 1940s and 1950s gold brooches and bracelets. Pink tourmaline, more commonly known as ***Rubellite,*** was used in Chinese carvings such as scent bottles and pendants suspended from jade balls. Care should be taken not to confuse the material with paler and more modestly priced rose quartz. 'Watermelon' tourmaline is an appropriately named variety exhibiting both green and pink colours, while ***indicolite*** is rarely seen blue tourmaline.

Finally, by far the most valuable and highly sought variety of tourmaline on the market today is paraiba tourmaline, a vivid and intense 'electric' neon blue caused by the presence of copper in its crystal structure.

TURQUOISE

A prominent gemstone from the 18th century onwards, turquoise is well known for its opaque, waxy lustre and unique sky-blue colour. The best examples originated in Persia and Egypt. During the 19th century, turquoise cut *en cabochon* was used extensively in sentimental brooches, pendants, bracelets and rings due to its association with forget-me-nots; gold settings in several colours were often highly embellished and decorated with turquoise half pearls or rubies. Turquoise was widely used in early Victorian serpent jewellery although many of the stones seen today are badly discoloured and need replacing. Mid-Victorian turquoises were ***pavé***-set in side-by-side formation and mounted into locket-back gold brooches and earrings with tassel fringes below. In the 1870s it became fashionable to mount oval gold lockets with turquoises cut into simple pyramids and set in geometric lines with rose diamonds or half pearls in between.

Of all gemstones, turquoise is probably the one

Gold Murrle Bennett Arts and Crafts brooch mounted with a turquoise matrix plaque and a pearl suspension drop, c.1905. Turquoise was an extremely popular gem in Arts and Crafts jewellery, used by leading firms such as Murrle Bennett and Liberty & Co.

Diamond-set white-gold stylised bow brooch mounted with a large step-cut green tourmaline weighing approximately 20.00 carats, c.1960.

Edwardian platinum and gold shamrock brooch mounted with three heart-shaped pink tourmalines, a diamond trefoil accent and diamond stem, c.1910.

which is most closely associated with the Arts and Crafts Movement. Designers including C.R. Ashbee at the Guild of Handicraft and Archibald Knox for Liberty & Co. produced many simple and uncomplicated gold and silver pendants and necklaces mounted with gem turquoise or turquoise matrix – turquoise with natural veins of limonite rock left visible. Indeed, the Anglo-German firm of Murrle Bennett & Co. became synonymous with turquoise matrix and gold jewellery at the very end of the 19th century. Today, turquoise matrix is produced in large and irregularly shaped pebble-like forms used in Navajo and New Mexican silver jewellery.

ZIRCON

Another 'aesthetic' late 19th-century gemstone used by Revivalist jewellers such as Giuliano, zircon was mounted in commercial quantities after the 1920s in Art Deco diamond architectural settings and particularly finger rings. In 19th-century Indian jewellery, colourless zircons, known as *jargoons,* were set in silver and mounted in turban ornaments or brooches. Most of the zircon on the market today has been heat treated and sometimes a treated stone will revert to its original colour, such as blue turning brown.

The majority of zircons are brownish-green, orange, blue or colourless. The availability of the stone after the Second World War led to many large three-dimensional brooches and bracelets being made with a combination of several different shades of orange and brown, whilst blue zircons from Ceylon were set into graduated lines in low-grade white gold or silver.

Zircon exhibits a natural fire and brilliance which has frequently resulted in colourless zircon being sold as diamond. Examination under a 10x lens will reveal strong double refraction of the back facets and a feature practically unknown in a real diamond – abrasions and chips on the stone's surface.

Unusual 1940s diamond-set white-gold brooch mounted with a colourful medley of vari-cut zircons. This example displays the sheer range of colours in which this versatile gem can be found. Zircon grew in popularity at the end of the Victorian era as well as the 1930s when the bright blue variety was often mounted in dress rings. It is far less fashionable today.

(Above left) Early 19th-century white chalcedony elongated teardrop earrings.

(Above right) Fine George III gold bracelet composed of a series of colourful specimen hardstone plaques including jasper, agate, malachite and lapis lazuli, c.1800. Probably a souvenir purchased in Italy on the Grand Tour.

ORNAMENTAL HARDSTONES

CHALCEDONY

Most of the hardstones familiar to us in jewellery – cameos, intaglios, Scottish pebbles, the bases of antique seals, to name but a few – are actually different coloured varieties of chalcedony. True chalcedony is greyish-white in colour and was used in Victorian brooches where the neutral tone of the material was sometimes offset by applying a spray of turquoise and gold forget-me-nots to the front. White chalcedony was also polished into teardrops and mounted in gold elongated pendant earrings and, strikingly, cut into triangular plaques and set into Maltese crosses with turquoise or ruby filigree gold decoration. The other principal varieties of chalcedony are:

Agate

This chalcedony is composed of strong, curved bands of colour and was invariably stained to display the contrasting shades. Used liberally in decorative carvings and jewellery, different names describe the various colours.

Bloodstone

Dark spinach-green chalcedony with bright red spots of iron oxide. Formerly known as 'heliotrope', the red spots represented Christ's blood. Used in desk seals, Victorian fobs and gentlemen's signet rings.

Chrysoprase

Apple-green chalcedony of uniform colour, chrysoprase was used in 18th-century jewellery in parures of gold or pinchbeck and in Arts and Crafts and Art Nouveau jewellery where the stone's charming understated colour was the perfect accompaniment for naturalistic gold settings.

Two examples of Regency moss agate: (left) a butterfly brooch mounted in gilt metal; (right) a cruciform pendant mounted in gold.

Cornelian

Apparently uniform tawny-red or orangey-red but often banded when held up to the light, cornelian was extensively used in intaglio carving, fob seals and in Regency necklaces where polished cushion-shaped plaques were mounted in 'Roman'-style seal settings.

Jasper

Mottled brown chalcedony used in Scottish pebble jewellery and often stained blue to suggest lapis lazuli, known as *Swiss Lapis*.

Moss Agate

Chalcedony with curiously realistic black or green fern-

Black and white onyx cameo ring carved with the profile of Athena, her helmet adorned with a snake and an owl, c.1800.

Imposing French gold demi-parure set with a series of oval-shaped part-faceted green chrysoprase plaques, the gold mounts of scroll and tied bow design set with rubies and half pearls, c.1830.

like structures. Used in 18th-century necklaces, pairs of bracelets and snuff boxes.

Onyx

Black and white agate, ideal for cutting as cameos or polishing into beads. Used liberally in Victorian mourning jewellery where the jet-black hardstones exhibited a contrasting band of white at the edges.

Sardonyx

Brown and white agate principally used in Victorian cameos.

FLUORSPAR

The best known variety of fluorspar is Blue John, sometimes called Derbyshire Spar. This purple to light brown material is unique to the Castleton area of Derbyshire and was mainly used in ornamental carvings such as vases and bowls as well as small-scale jewellery.

LABRADORITE

A greyish blue feldspar exhibiting rainbow-like flashes of colour and used in the 19th century for cutting into ornaments and cameos.

LAPIS LAZULI

An intense blue material containing flecks of golden colour iron pyrites, lapis lazuli has been used as an ornamental hardstone since ancient times. Lapis can vary widely in quality; the best material is a uniform royal blue colour mined in Afghanistan and Russia, whilst inferior Chilean and American lapis usually contains veins of white calcite. Lapis lazuli was used in Victorian gold jewellery in the form of beads, polished cabochons or sometimes conical-shaped drops in fringe necklaces. Early lapis was sometimes cut into cameos and Egyptian and Roman lapis intaglios were popular as seal stones.

In Art Deco jewellery, lapis lazuli was cut into geometric shapes and used in brooches, bracelets and mantel clocks favoured by the firm of Cartier and its contemporaries.

Modern gold brooch by Stephen Webster mounted with a carved labradorite 'man in the moon' between gold leaf-shaped sections embellished with sapphires, diamonds, half pearls and emeralds.

Nineteenth-century diamond tied bow earrings mounted with lapis lazuli ball drops, c.1880. The deep royal blue of the lapis suggests probable Afghan origin.

Victorian gold tubular mesh bracelet suspending below five polished malachite spheres, c.1870. The best 19th-century malachite was mined in Siberia.

Pair of fluted nephrite jade and gold cufflinks by René Boivin.

MALACHITE

A distinctive, marbled or banded green hardstone which was used in decorative ornaments such as candlesticks, desk accessories and table tops. The finest malachite originated in Russia; other deposits are found in Zaire and South Africa. Malachite jewellery includes early 19th-century cameos carved with Classical heads and scenes (see page 74) or groups and Scottish silver jewellery where malachite panels were cut into circular plaid brooches, ivy leaf necklaces and broad panel link bracelets. Modern malachite is usually fashioned into animal carvings or necklaces of graduated beads.

NEPHRITE JADE

The ornamental dark spinach-green variety of jade, nephrite was favoured by Fabergé for objects of vertu including bell pushes and cigarette cases as well as small accessories such as cufflinks. This material was extracted in Siberia although most of the nephrite jade seen today originates from New Zealand. Nephrite is usually cut into simple and fairly inexpensive souvenir jewellery – heart pendants and brooches bearing 'national symbols' such as fern leaves in gold, amuletic pendants called 'tikis' and bead necklaces on simple clasps.

Arts and Crafts silver pendant mounted with a rose quartz cabochon in a frame of pink-foiled moonstones and mother-of-pearl. The soft, understated pastel tones of rose quartz make it an ideal gem for this kind of aesthetic jewel.

ROSE QUARTZ

A pale pink variety of cloudy crystalline quartz used in objects of vertu and jewellery particularly from the late 19th century onwards. Common themes include animal carvings, necklaces of graduated beads and silver jewellery mounted with large rose quartz cabochons.

ORGANIC MATERIALS

PEARL

Arguably the most important gem material next to the diamond, pearls are surprisingly robust considering they are an entirely natural organic material. Pearls are found in many different shapes and colours and were usually worn to designate status, authority and power. In the 16th century, natural pearls from the Persian Gulf were drilled and strung as elaborate ropes or mounted on to halo-like *biliments* to be worn in the hair. At the same time, curiously shaped baroque pearls suggesting grotesque animal, bird or mythical forms were mounted in gold and worn as pendants. Pearls were even crushed and swallowed for their assumed medicinal and restorative properties curing maladies as diverse as stomach ulcers and cholera.

Pearls are an accident of nature, formed in living molluscs such as oysters and mussels. When a foreign object such as a grain of sand or grit finds its way into the shell, the mollusc secretes layer upon layer of a smooth material called *conchiolin* around the irritant which gradually builds up over time into a pearl.

There are five important factors which influence the rarity and value of pearls:

Size. Whether natural or cultured, the larger the pearl the greater its value.

Shape. A perfectly round pearl will command a higher price than another which is off-round or baroque in shape.

Colour. There are a bewildering number of different colours available in 'modern' cultured pearls, although natural pearls in antique jewellery are invariably white, grey to gunmetal, bronze, cream or yellow. Pearls with unsightly spots of brown will be correspondingly less valuable.

Purity. Since pearls are a natural organic material, they are prone to irregularities, spots, blemishes and damage. Pearls will often wear down around the drill holes in necklaces whilst cultured pearls invariably exhibit 'blisters', 'holes' and surface imperfections.

Lustre. The beautiful iridescent surface of a pearl is described as its nacre. The thicker the nacre, the higher the lustre and the greater the value. Cultured pearls are often farmed early in the pearl's development resulting in thin, lifeless nacre which sometimes peels away to reveal the artificial bead nucleus underneath.

Natural Pearls

Before the introduction of cultured pearls at the beginning of the last century, natural or *Oriental* pearls were extremely costly. In the 1920s a fairly modest necklace of graduated pearls could easily sell for several hundred pounds. Natural pearls were imported into Europe from the Arabian Gulf, Japan, the Gulf of Manaar off North West Ceylon, Australia, California and Venezuela. There are numerous different names of natural pearls dependent upon individual shape, size and colour.

(i) *Baroque pearls.* The name given to irregularly shaped pearls common in 16th- and 17th-century Continental jewellery and subsequently in 19th-century revivalist pendants and brooches. Baroque pearls were often large and imperfect, although pairs mounted in earrings are always in high demand.

(ii) *Blister pearls.* Extremely distorted baroque pearls used in naturalistic Arts and Crafts and Art Nouveau jewellery. Narrow, elongated drops were known as Mississippi pearls.

Two-row natural pearl necklace on emerald and diamond snap, c.1920.

Pair of drop-shaped Oriental pearl, platinum and diamond earrings, c.1910. This pair of earrings was sold at auction in 2012 by Woolley and Wallis at the very peak of the market for natural pearls. Perfectly matched and possessing excellent provenance they soared above their pre-sale estimate to fetch an extraordinary £1.6m.

Seed pearl parure of fruiting vine construction, c.1840. Fragile and exceptionally delicate, seed pearl jewellery is highly susceptible to damage when worn.

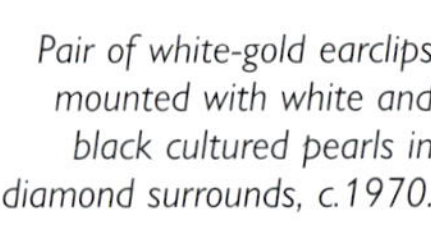

Pair of white-gold earclips mounted with white and black cultured pearls in diamond surrounds, c.1970.

(iii) *Bouton pearls.* Pearls with rounded tops and flat bases used in 19th- and 20th-century decorative diamond and gem-set jewellery.

(iv) *Seed pearls.* Very small pearls used in Victorian jewellery where the individual pearls were woven on to mother-of-pearl backplates in decorative floral clusters. Edwardian sautoirs consisted of several strands of seed pearls woven into ropes with tassel finials. Woven seed pearl jewellery is prone to deterioration and damage which reduces its value significantly.

(v) *Freshwater pearls.* Sometimes called Mussel pearls, freshwater pearls are found in rivers and inland waters. Predominantly white, freshwater pearls tend towards a dull lustre. Scottish freshwater pearls were used from the Middle Ages.

(vi) *Mother-of-pearl.* The iridescent shell of the mollusc which was cut and shaped into 'backing plates' for seed pearl clusters and Victorian lockets and portrait brooches. In the 1920s mother-of-pearl was popular in gentlemen's accessories such as cufflinks.

(vii) *Pink Pearls.* This category of natural pearl is extracted from a mollusc called the Great Conch. Pink pearls exhibit characteristic flame-like markings on their surface. Often confused with coral, pink pearls were popular in Belle Époque diamond jewellery whilst drop-shaped specimens were mounted as tiepins. Pink pearls are rare and can achieve high prices at auction, although irregular discoloured patches will reduce their value.

Cultured Pearls

Pearls created artificially by inserting a small bead of glass or mother-of-pearl into the mollusc and farming the resulting product on a commercial scale. The introduction of cultured pearls in the 1920s all but destroyed the market for natural pearls. Necklaces of cultured pearls up to 9mm (⅜in.) in diameter were extremely fashionable up to the 1960s, but their appeal has declined quite markedly so today it is only the 'new' cultured pearls from the South Seas and Australia which are commercially exploited. These pearls are farmed in sizes of 20mm (¾in.) or more and occur in many different colours, shapes and quality.

Mabé pearls. Cultured pearls often of quite large size composed of a 'skin' of cultured pearl over a bead nucleus with mother-of-pearl 'jacket.' Used in contemporary Continental jewellery and mounted into rings and earclips.

Pink conch pearl, black and white natural pearl and diamond 'Ace of Clubs', c.1885.

Faux pearl and rose diamond earrings, c.1795. Composed of hollow glass beads coated with varnish and ground fish scales, such false pearls are fragile and rarely found today.

Pair of 18th-century 'Coque de Perle' girandole earrings, c.1760. 'Coque de Perle' was an effective imitation of natural pearl. It was composed of a curved mother-of-pearl veneer filled with a composite material to provide stability and backed with a further flat section of mother-of-pearl.

Artificial Pearls

An important category of imitation gem, artificial pearls have been used in jewellery set with diamonds and costume jewellery since the Renaissance. Early imitation pearls consisted of hollow opalescent glass beads which were sprayed with ***essence d'orient,*** a solution composed primarily of fish scales. These 'pearls' were fragile and had the same composition as Christmas tree baubles. It is likely that many of the so-called pearl necklaces in early paintings were actually imitation. Most modern artificial pearls are simply sprayed glass beads.

Coq de perle. Large sections of mother-of-pearl and nautilus shell backed with cement and often set in frames of marcasite. Coq de perle or 'eggshell pearls' were fashionable in early 19th-century necklaces and earrings.

AMBER

Amber is fossilised resin which oozed from certain types of coniferous trees flourishing millions of years ago. Occasionally, the sticky sap would trap a tiny insect or leaf particle in its slow descent so producing the rare material much sought and frequently faked today.

Probably the best known variety of amber used in antique jewellery is ***Baltic*** found near Königsberg (Kaliningrad), East Prussia and on the Lithuanian coastline. Typically cloudy yellow or opaque honey yellow, Baltic amber is polished into graduated beads, cut into naturalistic brooches or fulfils many practical uses including the handles of cutlery, the stems of pipes or the shafts of parasols. Scandinavian silversmiths such as Georg Jensen found the understated colours of Baltic amber to be ideal in silver jewellery and much of the amber sold today is heavily influenced by earlier Arts and Crafts naturalistic forms. Other varieties of amber include:

Chinese – usually imported from Burma, colours range from pale yellow to rich red. Examples include bead necklaces cut into complicated patterns and scent bottles of 18th-century origin with jade stoppers.

Sicilian – deep brown or reddish with a distinctive bluish fluorescence.

Rumanian – often imperfect or cracked, this amber is deep brown or even black in colour.

Above: Georg Jensen silver brooch mounted with a brown translucent amber plaque and two smaller amber cabochons on an embossed floral frame, c.1982.

Left: Baltic amber bead necklace, c.1900. 'Butterscotch' amber has risen in value considerably in recent years. Buyers should be aware of the many amber simulants on the market such as pressed amber, copal resin and Bakelite.

Amber-like materials in common use since the end of the 19th century include:

Pressed Amber (ambroid) – small particles of Baltic amber softened by heating and pressed together into workable sections.

Copal Resin – routinely confused with amber, New Zealand copal resin is opaque russet brown and can be distinguished by applying a drop of ether which leaves a dull mark on the surface – no mark would be left on genuine amber.

Plastic, Bakelite and *Celluloid* – deceptively amber-like in appearance but will peel under a sharp knife unlike amber which splinters.

CORAL

Of all organic gem materials, coral was probably the most versatile in its use in antique gold jewellery. Coral is formed from the skeletons of millions of tiny marine animals called polyps and it is rather depressing to consider just how much of this wonderful – and irreplaceable – natural phenomenon has been extracted from the deep seas in the past few hundreds of years.

Each distinct colour of coral bears its own name. Some of these include white (Bianco), Pelle d'Angelo (Angel's skin – an off-white with pinkish overtones), Rosa Vivo (bright rose), Russo (red) and black. The very deep red coral graphically known as Ox Blood is possibly the most highly sought and is correspondingly expensive.

While the trade in antique coral jewellery is not prohibited it is certainly restricted and heavily regulated today, reflecting international conservation concerns. Permits for export and import are thus invariably required which is monitored by The Convention on International Trade in Endangered Species (CITES).

Coral never really lost popularity throughout the 19th century although designs certainly changed significantly. During the late 18th and early 19th centuries gilt-metal diadems were mounted with coral beads sometimes covered in small facets or even etched with finely milled criss-crossing lines. In this essentially romantic period, floral spray brooches with white coral flowerheads were enhanced by turquoise and ruby stamens, early Victorian coral was cut into the shape of hands, cherubs and naturalistic sprays whilst by the 1850s and 1860s Italian workers based in Naples were transforming the branch-like shapes of the natural material into all sorts of imaginative designs such as sea monsters, grotesques and skulls – the latter especially fashionable in gentlemen's cravat pins. Salmon pink and pale pink coral was an ideal medium for carving into Classical cameos and during the height of Classical revivalism coral was polished into elongated tear-shaped drops and set into

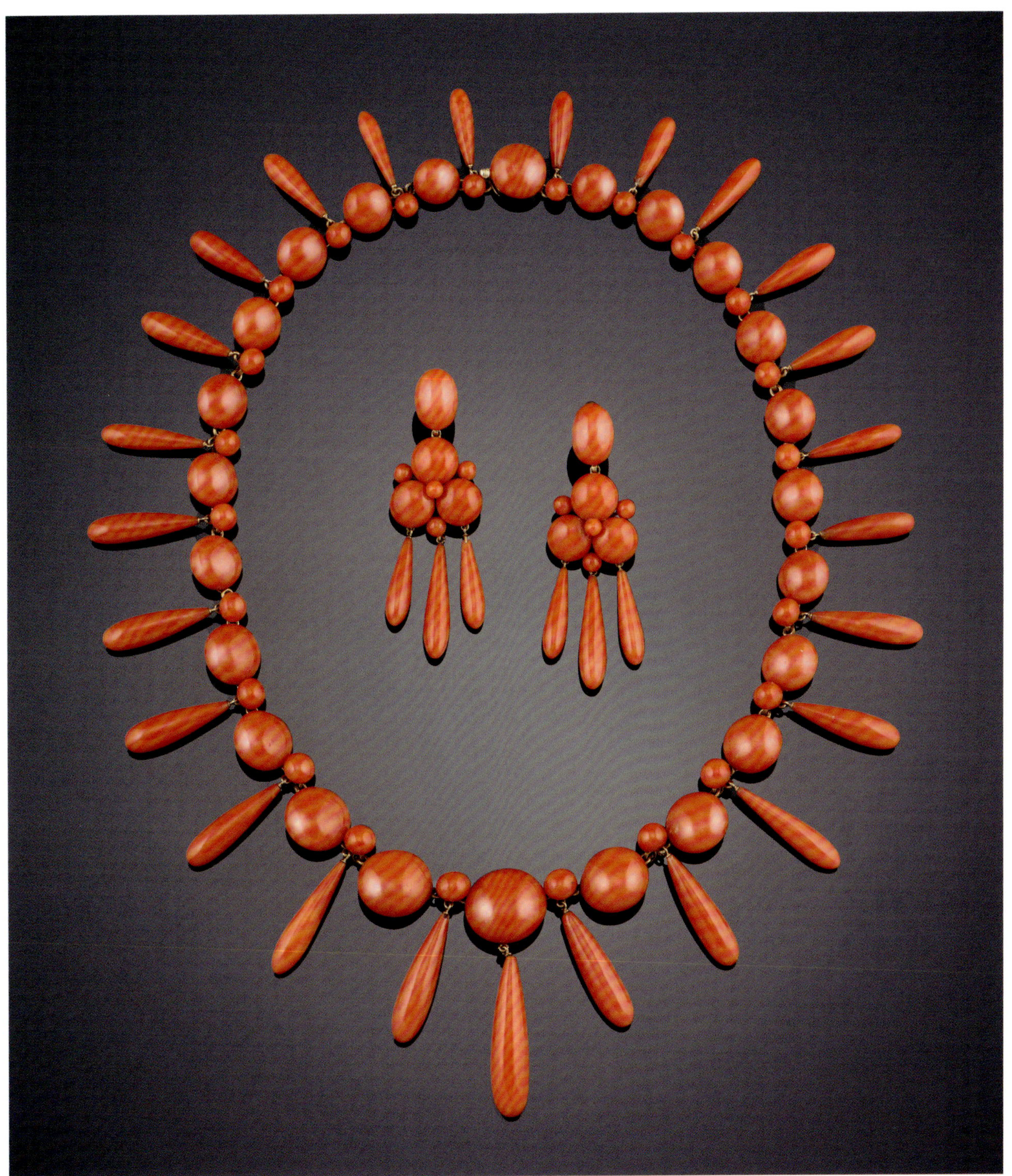

Fine-quality Continental gold mounted coral parure comprising necklace of graduated coral boutons with pipkin fringe drops together with a pair of matching earrings, c.1870.

Silver-gilt necklace suspending seven 19th-century ivory disc opera and theatre passes. The law relating to the sale of ivory means that only a very restricted number of items can legally be sold today. As a result, more 'everyday' items such as ivory beads and cameos cannot be traded.

graduated fringe necklaces in bright yellow-gold mounts. Since the colour of coral could be entirely neutral, it was ideal for either understated and modest dress rings or far more extravagant parures of several components with sky-blue enamel and diamond highlights.

During the 20th century coral was mounted in contrast with striking hardstones such as onyx, rock crystal and chalcedony. Since coral could be cut into flat plaques, pyramids or tubular batons, it was perfect for Art Deco 'architectural' brooches and bracelets favoured by Cartier in France and Theodor Fahrner in Germany. After the Second World War London jewellers such as Kutchinsky and Italian goldsmiths including Bulgari successfully adapted coral into large and visual gold and diamond-set jewels of highly individual style.

IVORY

Seen against the well-publicised backdrop of organised elephant poaching, smuggling and illegal international trade, collecting pieces made of ivory has become controversial and, in some cases, illegal.[1] As a result of the lack of demand as a decorative material, the value of ivory has dropped considerably and now reached a point where it is simply no longer commercially viable. Nevertheless, it is still important to put ivory into its historical context, if only because of its widespread use in affordable jewellery, objects and accessories since the earliest of times.

Before the 19th century the use of ivory in jewellery was limited to the backgrounds of miniatures or pretty carvings inside Regency locket rings and brooches. After the 1850s the obsession with naturalism resulted in ivory being cut and fashioned into brooches designed as floral bouquets, sprays of lily-of-the-valley and autumnal wheatsheaves. Popular from 1850 to 1880, these lifelike and imaginative carvings were somewhat let down by cheap silver or very basic gold pin fasteners at the back.

Ivory was also cut into bold cameos depicting Classical female heads in profile; a Bacchante complete with bunches of grapes in her hair was particularly favoured. In 19th-century German brooches, ivory was cut with considerable skill and finesse into the design of woodland and rustic landscapes or hunting groups of horses, stags and hounds.

In Art Nouveau jewellery ivory was cut into stylised female or animal forms accompanied by plique-à-jour enamel decoration, while in Art Deco jewellery ivory was fashioned into geometric shapes and mounted in both silver and gold.

It should be noted that ivory bears some visual similarities to bone and the two materials are routinely confused; genuine ivory exhibits characteristic wavy lines while bone is coarser, lighter in weight and contains tiny black imperfections.

1. The import and sale of ivory is illegal in the U.K. (https://www.legislation.gov.uk/ukpga/2018/30/contents) and several other countries. In the U.K., some items are eligible for an exemption certificate, see: https://www.gov.uk/guidance/dealing-in-items-containing-ivory-or-made-of-ivory.

JET

In an age when black was the outstanding colour for some forty years, jet was synonymous with a Britain plunged into mourning after the death of Prince Albert in 1861.

Real jet is a kind of fossilised wood formed under intense heat and pressure. By far the most important location of the Victorian jet industry was Whitby situated on the coast of North Yorkshire, appropriately enough the setting for Bram Stoker's *Dracula.* Whitby jet takes a high polish and is surprisingly light in weight. It was carved into any number of ornaments and objects of art although it is most closely associated with mourning jewellery. Examples range from modest crosses, oval lockets and locket back brooches to far more elaborate bracelets and necklaces with drops and festoons. Jet and its use in the context of mourning jewellery is discussed in greater detail in the chapter entitled 'The Industry of Death.'

Materials similar in appearance to jet include:

Bog-oak – dull, dark brown wood from Irish peat bogs. Popular in the 1850s, bog-oak jewellery was often well cut into flowers or brooches of national flavour such as shamrocks.

French jet – black glass. Much heavier than jet with a shiny

Irish bog-oak cross intricately carved with shamrocks with gilded wreath and pearl centre, c.1850.

Victorian carved Whitby jet knot brooch and earrings, c.1875.

French jet flower earrings, c.1880. French jet is simply polished black glass and is both colder and heavier than jet.

patina and cold to the touch, French jet was used in 18th-century brooches and hair locket rings and widely in late 19th-century costume jewellery.

Vulcanite – also known as *gutta-percha,* vulcanite was a type of treated India rubber containing sulphur.

Other materials confused with jet include plastic, black onyx and black enamel.

SHELL

See Chapter 7: Cameos and Intaglios

TORTOISESHELL

It is unlikely that the Victorians gave much thought to issues such as endangered species. Certainly, if the staggering number of beetles, butterflies, hummingbirds, turtles and tigers which were routinely exterminated in the name of Decorative Arts is anything to go by, we can only presume that they must have been supremely indifferent to the conservation of wildlife.

Tortoiseshell comes from the overlapping body plates of certain species of turtle, of which the principal contributor was the hawksbill turtle. Those plates taken from the back are dark mottled brown or reddish brown, whilst those from the underbelly are a uniform honey-brown colour, better known as blond tortoiseshell. The latter variety was used in haircomb fittings and in Art Deco vanity cases known as minaudières.

The manufacture of ivory and tortoiseshell into decorative objects and accessories can be traced back to the 17th century when French Huguenot craftsmen produced elegant and highly practical snuff boxes, patch boxes, needlework cases and étui, inlaid with precious metals and decorated with chinoiserie designs and pretty

Victorian tortoiseshell pique-work hoop bracelet with heart drop, c.1860.

patterns. Tortoiseshell becomes soft when heated, enabling the craftsman to bend and mould the material into the shape of the desired object. The surface was then polished and inlaid with mother-of-pearl, silver or gold in a technique known as 'pricking'. This gave rise to the word *piqué* and thus tortoiseshell piqué work.

Patterns of tiny stars, polka dots and bead clusters were known as 'piqué point' whilst strips of wire in floral cluster or geometric patterns were called 'piqué posé'. Both techniques were used in Victorian jewellery which originated in the 1830s and reached a peak of popularity by the 1860s. Brooches were particularly common. Fashioned as circular domed plaques or geometric in shape, they displayed bouquets of flowers or overlapping fish-scale designs. The backs of the brooches were hollowed out and the frames were mounted with simple metal or silver pins. Earrings sometimes take the form of elongated teardrops known as pipkins. Other frequently seen designs include Maltese crosses, scalloped hair combs, buttons and large belt buckles. Necklaces and finger rings are rare.

Much of the piqué seen today is damaged with the gold and silver inlay deficient or the tortoiseshell cracked and faded. A fine-quality brooch or pair of earrings will therefore sell at a considerable premium.

Further reading

Gem Testing, Basil Anderson (Newnes-Butterworths, 1971)

The Dealer's Book of Gems & Diamonds, M. Sevdermish and A. Mashiah (KAL Painting House, 1996)

Gems, Robert Webster (NAG Press, 1975)

Practical Gemmology, Robert Webster (NAG Press, 1970)

Colourful Georgian gold bracelet mounted with a collection of specimen gemstones popular in the Regency period including hessonite garnet (the largest stone in the centre), topaz, peridot, amethyst, emerald, ruby, citrine and aquamarine, c.1825.

Chapter 2

The Evolution of Jewellery from Early Times to the 18th Century

I believe there has never been a better time to collect old jewellery. True, the value of what might be described as 'primary' jewellery continues to climb as availability recedes and demand expands, but it is still perfectly possible to invest in pretty Victorian brooches, rings and bracelets at fairly modest prices, whilst numerous antique jewels and accessories such as seals, buckles, tiepins and dress studs can be purchased surprisingly cheaply simply because they are considered difficult to wear and, therefore, unfashionable. The trick is to identify which disciplines are undervalued and thus collectable before prices inevitably start to rise.

The wonderful thing about antique jewellery is that you will seldom find two pieces which match identically and so you have the added confidence of knowing that you are wearing a brooch, bracelet or buckle which nobody else will be able to imitate. A splendid £100,000 diamond necklace purchased from a leading international retailer certainly looks stunning but it can be replicated in any number of stores in a dozen different countries. An early Victorian gold cannetille work brooch set with aquamarines or pink topaz implies singular good taste, distinctive character and reinforces the suggestion that the person wearing it is breathtakingly chic. At a far more affordable price.

Ancient Gold

Surprisingly enough, it is perfectly possible to buy at auction a simple Roman gold ring or pair of ancient earrings for under £2,000. Roman, Greek and Hellenistic seal stones were produced in very large quantities and were set into bright yellow-gold or silver mounts of simple construction; earrings depicting heads of goddesses or with basic amphora (urn-shaped) drops are extremely pretty and appear in specialist auctions in London. Condition is paramount since many ancient gold artefacts were hollow and extremely soft and thus were liable to damage or crushing. The significant factor with ancient jewellery is that few people actually understand it and most dealers steer well clear of it, concentrating on more commercially mainstream periods. Unfortunately, the market is awash with fakes so it is important to buy from reliable sources where provenance is impeccable.

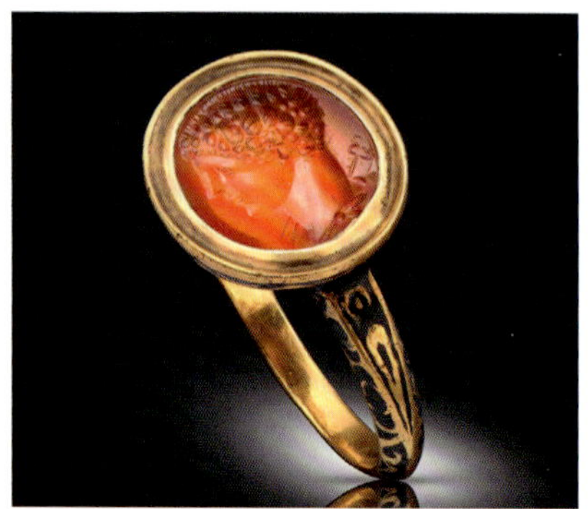

Fine cornelian intaglio depicting Mercury with caduceus attribute, probably 1st-2nd century A.D., rub-over set in a late 16th-/early 17th-century gold mount with black enamel decoration on the hoop.

Viking high-carat gold ring; 9th-11th century with plaited rope pattern front.

Rare Renaissance carved sapphire intaglio depicting Julius Caesar in a Georgian gold ring mount. When this ring appeared at auction in 2019 it generated considerable interest since it was found to have originally formed part of the famous gem collection belonging to George Spencer, 4th Duke of Marlborough. It went on to fetch £62,000.

Gold ring brooch bearing an inscription, 13th-14th century.

Saxon, Viking and Medieval Gold

The vast majority of gold rings, clasps, brooches and assorted jewels from the Dark Ages through the Viking occupation and well into the Middle Ages are invariably found by enthusiasts using metal detectors who scour the countryside, farmers' fields and the shoreline for these rare and precious artefacts. Finds such as these must, by law, be reported to the District Coroner who then decides whether the object should be declared Treasure Trove and either sold to an appropriate museum or returned to the finder.

Jewellery from this period can be extremely valuable, particularly if embellished with gems and enamel or decorated with a complicated device signifying that it originally belonged to a person of high rank. Nevertheless, more modest Saxon, Viking and later gold rings do find their way into the auction rooms and can be purchased at realistic price levels. Viking rings are especially beautiful and sophisticated, composed of entwined pale yellow-gold wires wrought together into a tapering plait. Rings of the 12th and 13th centuries are usually simple and rather austere; the bezel or top of the ring is set with an irregularly shaped polished gem – usually sapphire, ruby or garnet – which is cut *en cabochon* into a simple dome. Fourteenth-century religious gold rings known as iconographic rings are carefully engraved to depict the figures of saints, whilst 15th- and early 16th-century gold signet rings usually displayed the arms of a distinguished family in a simple shield device with accompanying inscription.

Medieval gold iconographic pendant engraved to depict Jesus walking on the water next to St. Peter in a fishing boat; the reverse bears a Roman inscription. Rope and pellet border and modern pendant fitting, c.1400-1450.

The 16th Century

Very little 'everyday' 16th-century jewellery survives today. Most pieces are displayed in museums whilst those rings or pendants offered at auction tend to be

*Renaissance gold 'gimmel' ring, probably German, c.1580, composed of two interlocking gold hoops set with an emerald and a ruby, bearing elements of white and black enamel and inscribed *Quod *Deus *Homo *Non *Conjunxit.
Separet (Whom God Has Joined Let Nobody Separate).

16th-century gold ring mounted with an irregular polished sapphire cabochon, c.1550. This unassuming little ring had a sinister alternative purpose. Behind the bezel is a hinged locket compartment which would have been used to contain a potent poison such as henbane.

English gold signet ring, the oval bezel engraved with a monogram 'W.I.' bisected by a floral spray with entwined roots in a piecrust border, c.1550-1600.

Italian freshwater pearl, white enamel and gold centaur pendant, probably 16th century. Note the way that the jewel has been imaginatively constructed to follow the contours of the pearls.

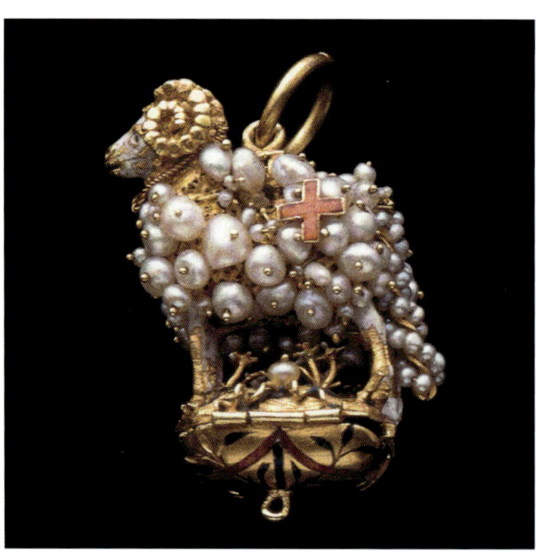

Pretty gold 'Ram' amulet jewel threaded with pearls and containing a hinged compartment at the base for a religious relic. Spanish Colonial or South Italian, c.1600-1620.

Hessonite garnet pendant carved in the form of a female head and bust, in a gold frame decorated with enamel and set with diamonds and pearls. Probably early 17th-century German.

either exceedingly expensive or so badly damaged as to render them unusable. Renaissance pendants were confined to a market made up of nobility or prosperous merchants and were fashioned from near pure gold decorated with polychrome enamel and studded with costly gems, particularly rubies, simple table-cut diamonds and (invariably) baroque-shaped pearls, known in the 16th century as *margarettes*. Religious and magical themes were important; devotional jewellery included rosaries (formerly called 'paternosters') and crosses set with emeralds and diamonds, much beloved of Spanish aristocracy. Cameos were surprisingly well carved in the 16th century depicting prominent individuals with unromanticised profiles or classical groups of figures fashioned from black and white onyx or chalcedony. Merchants' rings do occasionally appear at auction; massive and intentionally impressive, these chunky gold or silver signet rings were often engraved with a coat of arms directly on to the bezel or incised upon a transparent rock crystal plaque which was foiled in gold from behind and sometimes painted with a date signifying the year in which it was constructed. Rings during this period were often carved with baroque scrolls and brightly coloured with enamel to offset fairly simple and unsophisticated gems. By the start of the 17th century much of this ornate embellishment had given way to a far more simplified style typical of Jacobean taste.

The 17th Century

In 1912 workmen digging in the sticky clay beneath the cellar of a shop in Friday Street in the City of London stumbled upon a decayed casket containing a large quantity of gold necklaces, rings, earrings, gemstones and assorted objets d'art. How such a comprehensive range of jewels came to be buried around the corner from St Paul's is a mystery – possibly it was the stock of a jeweller fleeing the Great Fire or even the ravages of the Plague. What is certain, however, is that the Cheapside Hoard, as the treasure came to be known, offers jewellery historians an unparalleled opportunity of viewing at first hand how 17th-century jewellery was designed, constructed and decorated.

Apart from one or two 'grand' pieces such as a solid emerald crystal converted into a watch, the vast majority of items are clearly made for customers without limitless resources. Much of the jewellery is elegant, brightly coloured with enamel and set with table-cut gemstones and – worth noting – appears remarkably modern and highly wearable today. Chains are composed of enamelled floriate links while a pair of amethyst earrings are carved into the design of a bunch of grapes, appearing more Victorian than Stuart in their inspiration.

In the 17th century the dominant design in jewellery was the flower. Advances in diamond cutting resulted in the appearance of the *rose cut* and the flower in all

A group of early 17th-century enamelled gold and gem-set necklaces from the London Cheapside Hoard.

A pendant of amethyst and enamelled gold in the form of a grapevine. Seven amethysts, carved and polished to represent bunches of 'black' grapes, hang from tiered sprigs of recurving wire and a short length of chain. Part of the Cheapside Hoard.

its different forms was the ideal vehicle for showing off clusters of these little diamonds reflecting light from a series of triangular facets on the crown of each individual stone. Although gold settings were in use, the majority of gem-set jewellery was mounted in silver which extended to enclose fully the back of the jewel itself.

Enamel played an important part in the embellishment of much 17th-century jewellery providing an effective substitute for expensive gems and effectively filling the spaces both on the front and back of an object. Specific colours were favoured, especially sky-blue with white and black scrolling highlights (popular on the backs of lockets and miniatures), whilst English and Dutch necklaces and pendants often depicted charming and intricate sprays of roses and tulips in white and shades of pink. Many Stuart and later *Memento Mori* jewels were enamelled in this way, the exquisite little flowers providing a poignant counterbalance to the grim skeletons, coffins and woven hair embedded within.

From around 1620 to the middle part of the century, aristocratic ladies began to wear large and impressive jewels on the bodices of their gowns. Mounted in silver or silver gilt and set with a profusion of table-cut diamonds and coloured gems such as topaz, emerald or ruby, these splendid ornaments were further adorned with baroque-shaped pearl drops. The principal feature

Above: *Gold slide painted with a miniature under crystal of Charles II, c.1685. Memento Mori jewels usually contained a fragment of the deceased's hair.*

Above, right: *Memento Mori slide of James II, c.1701.*

Seventeenth-century gold cruciform pendant mounted with table-cut diamonds, c.1650. Probably French or Spanish.

of these incredibly imposing creations was the bow, constructed as a series of elaborate looping ribbons gathered at the centre. It was the famous French writer of letters, Madame de Sévigné, who gave her name to this particular style of jewel – the *Sévigné* bow brooch.

Flamboyant brooches worn in the hair were known as *aigrettes.* Naturalistic in inspiration, aigrettes usually took the form of a spray of flowers or a feather-like plume. Set with diamonds or lines of coloured gems, they were the perfect vehicle for showing gems off at their best, especially when displayed beneath the twinkling light of chandeliers. It is interesting to note that James I, the so-called 'wisest fool in Christendom', sold off many of the best pieces from the Royal Collection to pay for one massive aigrette brooch known as 'The Feather', which he wore customarily in his hat.

Earrings followed this opulent trend with the gradual introduction of the *girandole* in which three pear-shaped drops were suspended from a principal top stone, often with a bow or flower-shaped cluster of smaller stones in between. The fashion for wearing girandole earrings and brooches of girandole form was to continue right up to the 19th century to be gradually superseded by less flamboyant and more practical styles in the 1840s and 1850s.

Seventeenth-century Spanish jewellery was overwhelmingly devotional in design. Bright yellow-gold crosses, pendants containing boxwood scenes from the Crucifixion and religious ornaments containing

Seventeenth-century gold ring, probably English mounted with a fancy deep brownish-yellow brilliant-cut diamond weighing 3.16 carats; the carved box bezel and hoop decorated with black and white enamelling, c.1675. It is extremely rare to find fancy colour diamonds in 17th-century jewellery let alone a stone of such a complex and sophisticated brilliant cut. This suggests it was made for an individual of considerable wealth and high social status.

Seventeenth-century gold ring mounted with a flat table-cut diamond, the box-shaped bezel decorated with arched sections of black and sky-blue enamelling, c.1675. The vast majority of diamonds set in 17th-century jewellery were simple table-cut stones such as this example.

Seventeenth-century amatory gold ring, the oval gold locket bezel bearing two winged putti clasping a red enamelled heart under a faceted rock crystal cover on an enamelled gold mount, c.1675-1700.

'pieces of the True Cross' were studded with flat table-cut diamonds and the one coloured gem which took precedence over all others – the emerald. Carried along the dangerous trade routes between Europe and South America, emeralds are today strongly identified with Spanish and Portuguese jewellery although, sadly, many of these beautiful pieces are now totally unwearable and are frequently damaged.

The 18th Century

Whenever Georgian diamond jewellery comes up for auction you can be sure that competition will be fierce and prices will invariably rocket. Why should this be the case? The answer might be to take two diamond flower brooches, one made in 1775, the other in 1895. Whereas the late Victorian example will betray a rigid, machined construction with diamonds of variable colour and clarity and an altogether mass-produced finish, the Georgian flower by contrast will be fully enclosed in an elegant silver mount, the broad, uniform-sized petals will display a powerful impression of lush naturalism and, above all, the brooch will be 'pavé-set' in side-by-side formation often with fine and rare two-hundred-year-old diamonds of a singular soft white purity.

The beauty and rarity of much 18th-century jewellery reflects the growing importance of diamonds brought about by significant advances in the technique of cutting and polishing. For the first time the unrivalled sparkle of diamonds could be properly appreciated, especially when set in lines and clusters within many of the floral and naturalistic studies characteristic of the period.

By around 1720 the use of coloured enamel as the dominant feature of the complete jewel had all but disappeared and, although still a characteristic of Parisian jewellery, its application was largely confined to decoration on pretty accessories such as pomanders, étuis and chatelaines. The general trend was for settings (usually silver) to be left plain and unembellished. The influence of French ornamentation became increasingly important in jewellery and the decorative arts with the appearance of the new style of classical adornment known as *Rococo.* The so-called *Rocaille* fashion was observed in necklaces composed of scrolling sections, complicated floral embellishment and a strong lack of symmetry. By around 1750 brooches in the design of large and vibrant bouquets of flowers worn on the bodice became extremely popular, not just in England but throughout Europe. These splendid jewels could easily achieve lengths of well over 20cm (8in.) and were studded throughout with lovely 'old-mine' gemstones such as rubies, emeralds and sapphires in floral clusters faithfully replicating the genuine article. The enthusiasm for flowers in the middle part of the 18th century was ideally illustrated in rings and brooches known as *Giardinetti* or 'Little Garden' jewels. These pretty floral studies combined diamonds set in silver cut-down collets with several vari-colour gems or pastes correspondingly set in gold. Sometimes, the principal gem – possibly a ruby or an emerald – would conform to the shape of a stylised vase or flower pot.

Portuguese mid 18th-century silver naturalistic spray brooch set with foiled emeralds, rock crystal, ruby, pink topaz and amethyst.

18th-century Spanish silver-mounted vari-gem-set double-headed eagle brooch and earrings.

Eighteenth-century rings are, almost without exception, elegant and very saleable today – which is why there are so many modern copies on the market, some of which are of high quality and many downright crude. Georgian rings were worn every day and often on every finger of the hand. This meant that they easily wore out so a genuine example in top condition will fetch a considerable premium over a similar ring with tell-tale rubbed shank and scratched or damaged setting.

The classic Georgian ring was set with a cushion-shaped flat-cut diamond or precious stone in a dome-back bezel (the top of the ring) within a border of small diamonds. This bezel was made of polished silver or gold which during the 1750s might be engraved with a series of radiating fluted lines known as 'sunburst' effect. Since the bezel was fully enclosed, light could not pass through the stone and therefore it became routine to place a piece of appropriately coloured tinfoil behind the gem to strengthen its colour and improve its 'sparkle'. This did create its own set of problems. Any water which leaked into the setting would discolour the foil (diamond foil, for example, turned a nasty charcoal grey) and, if the colour of a gemstone could be 'improved' by foiling, it was a natural progression to fake, say, a sapphire by placing a piece of blue tinfoil behind a worthless rock crystal or colourless paste. Very much a case of *caveat emptor*, I am sorry to say.

Opulent diamond bouquets and jewel-encrusted brooches were all very well for those members of the aristocracy rich enough to afford them, but for those sections of society with more limited resources the next best thing was paste. Antique paste was formed by heating a compound of crushed flint, lead oxide and potash. This formula was 'invented' by a jeweller from Strasbourg called Georges Frédéric Strass (1701-1773) who discovered that the addition of lead produced glass with a soft, diamond-like brilliance eminently suitable for faceting into gem replicas. Soon paste became a versatile and socially acceptable substitute for precious gems in which the gold and silver settings were of a comparable quality to those used in 'real' jewellery but at a fraction of the price.

Cheap and practical jewels and accessories were a notable feature of the 18th century, anticipating the huge demand for inexpensive *bijouterie* which was so much a feature of jewellery in the Victorian era. Christopher Pinchbeck (1672-1732), a Fleet Street watchmaker, discovered a method of combining copper and zinc to produce an alloy which was an effective simulant of gold. A plausible way of mounting inexpensive jewellery and accessories such as buckles and chatelaines, *pinchbeck* sold in large quantities up to the 19th century when it was gradually overtaken by poorer quality gilt metal. In 1762 Matthew Boulton (1728-1809), a steam engine manufacturer, perfected a technique for faceting little

George III diamond-set six petalled flower-head brooch mounted with cushion-shaped and marquise-shaped old-mine cut stones, c.1790. 18th-century diamond jewellery was invariably fully backed in silver and to intensify their appearance the stones were backed in tinfoil.

Eighteenth-century English pavé diamond-set flower spray brooch, c.1790.

Eighteenth-century diamond sunburst cluster ring on a carved gold mount with scallop shell decoration.

A Georgian gold butterfly brooch set with citrines, c.1830.

A Georgian gold brooch designed as a spray of wild strawberries set with rubies and diamonds, c.1830.

studs of steel and setting them on to metal backplates. Comparable with diamonds in artificial light, dark grey *cut steel* was not exactly cheap but it certainly was an adaptable decoration for all manner of jewels and everyday objects in England and also in France. Another base material, not entirely dissimilar from cut steel, was *marcasite,* usually associated with 20th-century costume jewellery. Georgian marcasite proved to be a perfectly acceptable diamond simulant. Cut and faceted from brassy yellow coloured iron pyrites (fool's gold), marcasite was effective when set in the borders of royal blue glass dress rings, Wedgwood jasper cameo brooches or painted miniatures where diamonds or pearls would have been simply too expensive.

Ornate dress jewellery such as girandole brooches and earrings, much beloved of the Spanish and French aristocracy, persisted in popularity right up to the end of the century. Indeed, in Spain and Portugal the fashion for extravagantly long and ornate silver and gold earrings set with unusual gems such as hessonite garnet or pale green chrysolites had never really lost their appeal over the preceding two hundred years. Nevertheless, by the 1790s and 1800s taste and fashion were visibly changing from over-complicated 'rocaille' embellishment to a minimal 'uncluttered' look of French inspiration known as *Neo-classicism.* Rings, for example, became strongly visual where the bezel was fashioned into an elongated marquise (torpedo shape), a plain oval or a broad rectangular plaque with cut corners. Better quality examples were royal blue enamelled and studded with diamonds in cluster or floral spray formation, whilst memorial rings were painted with a miniature of a lady weeping tragically beside a tomb with an appropriate message of sentiment and a scattering of tiny pearls representing tears.

The classic English brooch of the 1780s and 1790s was the open flower, composed of six uniform-sized petals pavé set with rose-cut or 'old-mine' brilliant-cut diamonds while the Georgian collet rivière, composed of a line of graduated cushion-shaped gold and silver collets each set with a diamond, coloured gem or paste is probably one of the least complicated but most effective designs encountered in antique jewellery.

The classical influence was most powerfully portrayed in rings, brooches and necklaces mounted in 'Roman' gold seal settings. Here, a hardstone or shell cameo would be mounted in a thin rim of gold and set as a ring between broad 'trumpet'-shaped shoulders while necklaces composed of a series of cameos or colourful hardstone intaglios, some contemporary Georgian and some Roman, were joined together by three or four rows of fine link gold chain known as *en esclavage* swags. The key element was simplicity. Neo-classicism extended well into the 19th century and was clearly the dominant theme during the First Empire of Napoleonic France until it was gradually superseded by the richness and colour of the 1820s and 1830s.

Early 19th-century diamond necklace dismantling into a set of three bracelets composed of oval openwork diamond sections with single cushion-shaped diamond connections, c.1825.

Further reading

Medieval Jewellery, Marian Campbell (V&A Publications, 2009)

A History of Jewellery 1100-1970, Joan Evans (Faber & Faber, 1970)

London's Lost Jewels: The Cheapside Hoard, Hazel Forsyth (Philip Wilson Publishers, 2013)

Renaissance Jewellery, Yvonne Hackenbroch (Sotheby Park Bernet, 1979)

Jewelry from Antiquity to the Present, Clare Phillips (Thames & Hudson, 1996)

Jewels and Jewellery, Clare Phillips (Victoria and Albert Museum, 2000)

Jewellery in Britain 1066-1837, Diana Scarisbrick (Michael Russell Publishing Ltd, 1994)

Tudor and Jacobean Jewellery, Diana Scarisbrick (Tate Publishing, 1995)

Chapter 3
A 19th-Century Jewellery Panorama

An era which stretched from Napoleonic neoclassicism to late Victorian mechanisation and which encountered a breathtaking number of twists and turns along the way can be a little difficult to categorise. Nevertheless, it is possible to break the 19th century down into four distinct phases which broadly embrace the spectrum of jewellery design in a century of creative and restless change.

1800-1837 – Georgian Jewellery, William IV and the Napoleonic Legacy

There is a tendency today to pigeonhole as 'Regency' any item of English jewellery which vaguely appears to have been made during the first three decades of the 19th century. The fact is that three kings reigned during this period and jewellery design constantly evolved, particularly during the fifteen years leading up to Victoria's accession in 1837.

The years 1800 to 1810 are closely associated with neo-classicism, a style actively encouraged by Napoleon whose influence was all-consuming in the world of fashion and fine art during this time. Not that much jewellery had actually been made during the turbulent years of the French Revolution; diamond tiaras and necklaces were seen as unacceptably bourgeois and contradicted every revolutionary principle. Sadly, much of the jewellery owned by the aristocracy at the end of the 18th century was simply broken up and sold.

Napoleon's campaigns in Egypt and Italy inspired jewellery which was clearly influenced by the art and treasure of the Ancients. By the early 1800s elaborate gold tiaras, armbands and clasps were set with imposing hardstone or shell cameos, carved to depict mythological deities and classical groups. Sometimes these materials – particularly the intaglios – were genuine, excavated ancient artefacts. To reinforce the classical ideal, settings were fashioned in gold in the design of laurel wreaths, palmettes and Greek keys. Another popular 'classical' medium was the mosaic in which tiny pieces of coloured glass were carefully grouped together to form a picture such as a landscape or architectural ruin. These mosaic plaques were then mounted in thin gold frames and fashioned as necklaces and bracelets with fine-link gold chain 'swags' in between.

Naturalism – flowers, sprays, leaves and wreaths – dominated Georgian diamond jewellery with heavy closed-back silver settings gradually giving way to lighter open-back mounts in gold by the 1830s. Indeed, gold suddenly became the focal point of jewellery design with the appearance of the *cannetille* frame – elaborate gold wire decoration similar to filigree work. Cannetille was the perfect accompaniment for foil-back pastel colour gemstones such as aquamarine, pink

Gold bracelet composed of four rows of quatrefoil-shaped sections on a sapphire, diamond and gold cannetille work clasp, c.1825.

Georgian Oriental pearl bunch of grapes brooch with coloured gold finely textured vine leaves and entwined tendrils, c.1825.

Georgian long gold muff chain composed of multiple spiralled embossed links on three-colour gold barrel clasp with floral highlights, c.1825.

Gold strapwork tied bow brooch studded throughout with turquoises, the centre with rose-cut diamond accents, c.1830.

Early Victorian gold coiled serpent brooch with carved and polished garnet head and diamond eyes, suspending a garnet and gold heart-shaped drop, c.1845.

Victorian gold bracelet with folded pattern engraved front section set rubies and diamonds on a double row gold snake pattern back, c.1850.

Mid-Victorian gold demi-parure comprising brooch and earrings mounted with garnet cabochons and seed pearls with tassel fringes below, c.1855.

topaz, chrysolite and pale amethyst or subtle hardstones such as white chalcedony or pale green chrysoprase. By the 1830s complete suites of gem-set cannetille jewels known as *parures* were fashionable in both Paris and London. Comprising necklace, bracelets, earrings and a matching girandole brooch, the individual gems were usually foiled to accentuate both colour and sparkle.

The 1830s are also associated with the passion for sentimentality in which messages were conveyed in a little brooch or ring set with a line of coloured gems spelling a name or appropriate endearment such as 'Dearest' or 'Regard.' The frames of many of these sentimental jewels – padlocks, keys and hearts – or accessories such as fob seals and watch keys were richly decorated in several different colours of gold which were then embellished with floral carving and set with little gems such as ruby or turquoise. So-called 'trois couleur' or 'quatre couleur' gold was achieved by adding minute quantities of other metals such as copper (red gold), silver (green gold) or nickel (white gold).

1837-1860 – Early Victorian Romanticism

This elegant era was also the period of greatest change in jewellery development and symbolism. In the 1840s naturalism continued to influence with realistic and intricate seed pearl and gold brooches fashioned as clusters of grapes, seed pearls woven into necklaces and brooches

Archaeological Revival gold panel bracelet each section decorated with coloured enamel and set with rubies and sapphires, c.1870.

Mid-Victorian archaeological gold hinged bangle, c.1870.

on mother-of-pearl backplates and bows, tendrils, leaves and straps finely wrought in gold, chased with tiny flowers and scrolls and decorated with pretty shades of opaque enamel, particularly sky-blue and navy. Bracelets were possibly the most popular type of jewel in the 1840s and 1850s; straps of adjustable length with jewelled buckles and bangles of 'Algerian Knot' design were characteristic of the period. The 1840s also saw the development of the serpent necklace and bracelet. These cobra-like snakes were enamelled and set with diamonds, precious gems or a richly coloured stone such as a garnet in the head. A heart-shaped locket back drop was invariably suspended from the serpent's mouth concealing a plume of hair.

Mourning jewellery perfectly articulated the fashion for sentiment at this time with brooches in gilt metal and gold containing hair in chased gold mounts. The jet industry flourished, located at Whitby in North Yorkshire. Ultimately two hundred workshops prospered in Whitby alone, barely keeping pace with the country's obsession for mourning after the death of Prince Albert in 1861.

Italian mosaic jewellery persisted in popularity although the quality of much of this later material is noticeably coarser than the tiny tesserae pieces used in early 19th-century mosaic jewellery. By the 1850s and 1860s the tourist industry was in full swing and visitors to Rome, Florence, Naples and the ruins at Pompeii began to bring back souvenirs of their visits. Cameos carved from a wide

Gold ball and pedestal earrings in the classical taste, c.1875. Victorian gold earrings are always desirable. Their overall condition, elegant design and the fact this pair are in their original fitted case would ensure a high price at auction.

range of materials were fashioned locally and mounted in bright yellow-gold frames. Shell and coral from Naples proved to be the ideal media for designs which ranged from classical female deities to severe Victorian gentlemen, while volcanic lava from Mount Vesuvius was carved into cameos of prominent figures in history such as Michelangelo and Shakespeare. Coral was a particular favourite at this time, fashioned into an amazing array of imaginative shapes from simple faceted teardrops to tortured sea-serpents and grotesques. Sometimes the coral branches were wrought into brooches and tiaras, capped in gold and embellished with little coral beads with the appearance of berries. Other gems in fashion in the 1850s included turquoise, pavé-set in cluster formation, and rich, deep red pyrope garnet polished into domed cabochons and mounted in diamond and enamel naturalistic frames.

1860-1880 – Mid Victorian Confidence and Revivalism

The era of exploration, prosperity and endeavour, the 1860s to 1870s was a period dominated by jewellery of historical inspiration. During this time, the all-consuming passion for 'archaeological' gold jewels became something of a European obsession while enormous interest in the art and iconography of the Renaissance resulted in many extremely colourful designs in which enamel played just as important a role as gemstones.

The fashion for neo-classical revivalism which had been so active in the early 1800s was given new life and impetus by a group of Italian goldsmiths of which the most celebrated was Fortunato Pio Castellani. Pioneering the technique of applying minute shotwork motifs to a gold surface, Castellani managed to revive a skill which had died out with the ancient Etruscans. To reinforce the absolute integrity of their work, Castellani and his contemporaries chose to use ancient materials – Egyptian hardstone scarabs and Roman silver coins in fine yellow-gold settings crowded with academic symbolism such as acanthus leaves, fibulae, amphorae and sphinxes.

By the 1860s gemstone polishing had advanced to the extent that colourful stones such as garnet, coral and turquoise could be cut and shaped to fit the contours of a setting. Turquoises, for example, were polished into pyramids and closely set into the covers of oval gold lockets with little diamonds studded in between. Sometimes the gems themselves were chiselled and set with a diamond star or naturalistic motif such as a flower or even a jewelled insect. By the 1870s pendants and brooches were mounted with striking, deep red garnet cabochons, diamonds and pale green chrysolites in complicated multi-coloured champlevé enamel frames. Inspired by Renaissance art, these extremely pretty pieces were known as *Holbeinesque* jewels.

Interest in Neo-Renaissance jewellery became as compelling as classical revivalism in the 1870s. Goldsmiths such as Carlo Giuliano and Robert Phillips produced vibrant and highly colourful enamelled jewels mounted with compatible hardstones and simple polished semi-precious gems which reinforced the sense of 'Tudor' realism while a demand for technically superior gold jewellery wrought into designs inspired by Gothic symbolism – grotesques, masks and fierce dragons known as *broches-chimères* – became highly fashionable in France and Germany.

In Paris Alexis Falize, in collaboration with the celebrated enameller Antoine Tard, executed cloisonné enamel lockets and pendants in the 'Japanese taste' and Nature continued to fascinate the market with insect brooches – houseflies, bees and spiders – as popular as jewellery fashioned from the body plates of the hawksbill

Mid-Victorian gold brooch mounted with an oval-shaped amethyst in a diamond folate cluster frame, c.1865.

Unusual mid-Victorian pavé diamond-set curb link bracelet with matching heart-shaped padlock clasp and miniature gold key suspended below.

Nineteenth-century Renaissance Revival gold pendant mounted with a circular garnet cabochon in a champlevé enamelled gold surround set with pearls and diamonds; matching garnet drop, c.1870.

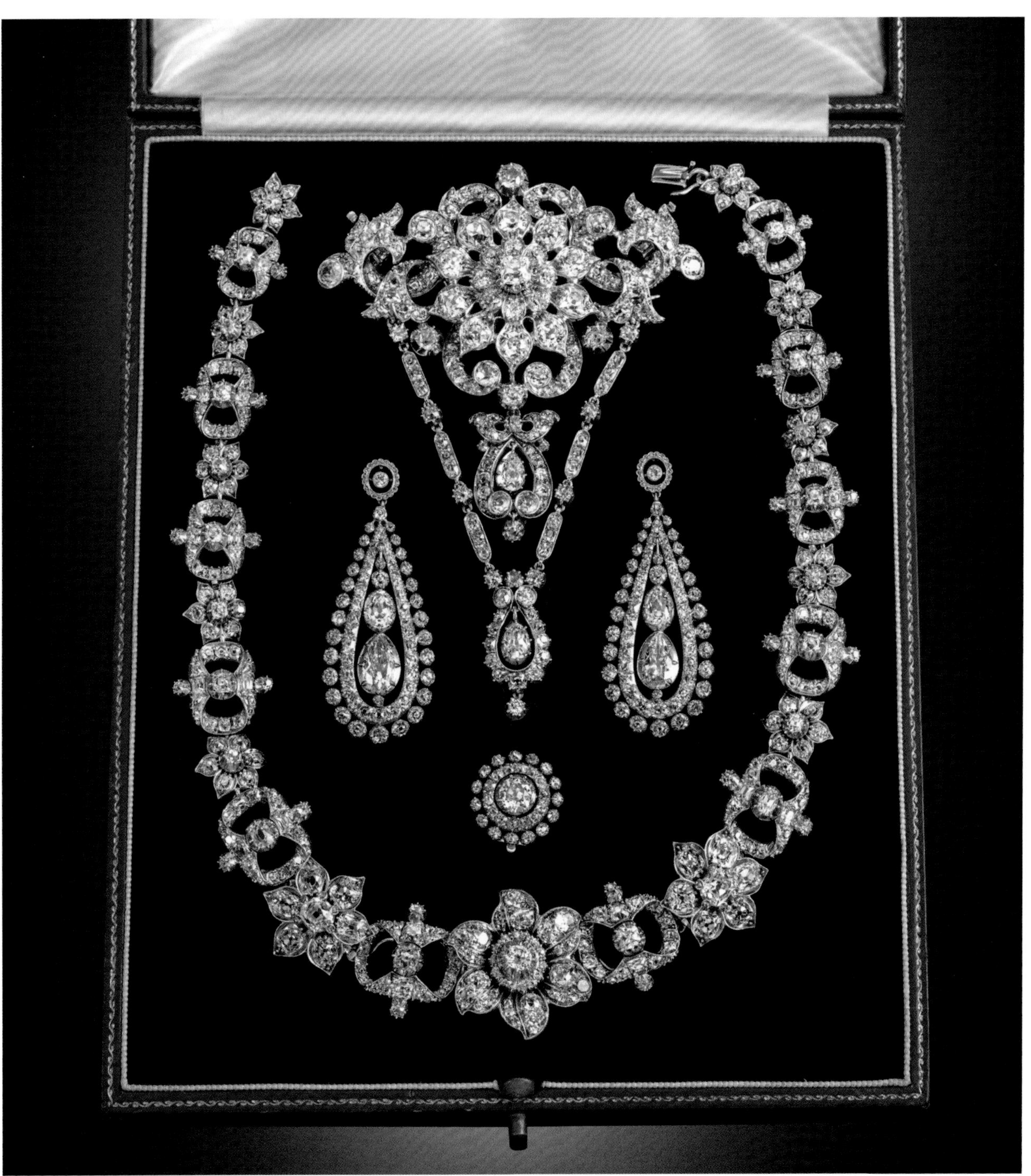

Important Victorian diamond parure comprising a devant de corsage brooch set throughout with old-mine cushion-shaped and pear-shaped diamonds, a diamond flower cluster necklace with oblong diamond spacers, a pair of pear-shaped diamond earrings and a diamond target cluster clip, c.1860. In its original fitted case. Set with approximately 70 carats of diamonds this splendid parure was made to be worn at the sort of grand state functions which were held at the height of Victorian prosperity and influence.

turtle, better known as tortoiseshell piqué work. In India tigers were shot and their claws were mounted in gold cap settings to be worn in rather hideous parures. Humming-bird heads were mounted in gold brooches, scarab beetles as necklaces and strange lid-like filters from fish known as operculum shells were grouped into livid parures. The 1870s was decidedly the decade in which wildlife – both real and artificial – played a dominant role in decorative jewellery design.

1880-1901 – Late Victorian Mass Production

It is difficult today to conceive the sheer quantity of cheap, versatile and wearable jewellery which was pumped out to sustain the demands of a near-insatiable market during the 1880s and 1890s.

For those who could afford them, diamonds were abundant and readily available, sourced from the recently discovered fields located at Kimberley in South Africa. Coloured stones – especially ruby, sapphire, turquoise and opal – were traded by international gem merchants while deposits of gold and silver were discovered and extracted from sites as far flung as Australia and North America. This was the era of prosperity, economic growth and confidence in which a burgeoning middle class possessed the disposable income to afford a diamond ring, a star brooch or even an opulent tiara readily available from a blossoming number of jewellery shops situated in most large and medium-sized towns up and down the British Isles. 'Everyday' jewellery – gold chains, sentimental brooches, curb link bracelets and a bottomless pit of simple gold rings set with small but effective precious gems – comprised the cheap but crucial 'bread and butter' sales at the bottom end of the market, sourced from a network of small jewellery workshops located in Birmingham, Sheffield and London.

Much of this output was of distinctly average quality and does not bear close scrutiny. Gems such as ruby, emerald and sapphire could be heavily flawed and inferior of colour while much of the 9-carat gold jewellery, including bangles, rings and brooches, was set with paste simulants or doublets – composition stones which looked like the real thing but which were intended to deceive.

Nine-carat gold was indeed a basic and plentiful material used in the production of jewellery for the masses. Composed of three parts gold and five parts base metal, it was inexpensive and robust and soon became the ideal medium for heavy wearing accessories such as cufflinks, pocket watches and alberts or more decorative items such as hollow locket-back brooches and guard chains. The addition of copper resulted in rose gold, a tint which was particularly favoured in curb link bracelets and watch chains. Fifteen-carat and 18-carat were reserved for better quality gem-set jewels of a decidedly superior design and finish.

(Left) Gothic Revival gold quatrefoil brooch, c.1860; (Centre) Turquoise and diamond heart locket, c.1870; (Right) John Brogden cameo pendant, c.1865.

A group of six typical Late Victorian diamond and gem-set rings of half-hoop, cluster, three stone and five stone construction.

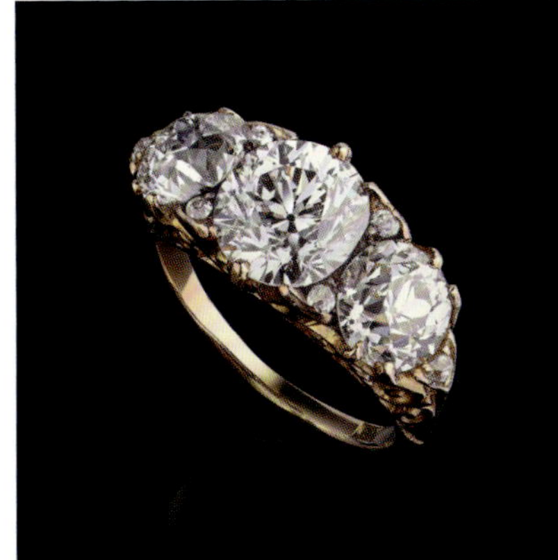

One of the most influential goldsmiths active at the end of the 19th century was Edwin Streeter, whose business established at 18 New Bond Street, London supplied a broad and varied range of diamond and gem-set jewellery and accessories (see pages 58–59). Alongside practical and conventional engagement rings and half hoop bangles, much of Streeter's stock clearly catered for a strongly sentimental public for which rings and brooches were designed as hearts, bows, lovers' knots, horseshoes and shamrocks. Sport and recreational activities were also performing an increasingly influential part in people's lives at the end of the Victorian era. Leisure pursuits such as golf, fishing, cycling, hunting and horse racing resulted in a plethora of novelty brooches and tiepins set with diamonds or decorated in enamel such as bicycles with revolving wheels, golf club bar brooches with pearl 'balls', galloping racehorse brooches with enamel jockeys and even diamond violins.

Summary of Jewellery Designs Fashionable from the 1880s to the Early 1900s

Rings

'Half hoop' gold bands with carved scrolling galleries set in silver with a line of three, five or more diamonds or coloured gems, notably sapphire, ruby, half pearl, coral, turquoise or opal.

Broad, polished gold hoops 'gipsy-set' with a single diamond or native-cut gem. Cluster rings composed of a principal centre stone in a surround of eight or twelve smaller gems.

'Crossover' rings incorporating two or more stones set in oblique formation on a waved mount. Sentimental 'heart and coronet' rings in open-back gold and silver settings.

Group of traditional and typical late Victorian diamond brooches, earrings and pendants, c.1880-1900.

Brooches

Late Victorian 'primary' brooches, i.e. those set with diamonds and coloured stones such as sapphires and rubies, were mounted in gold and set in cut down silver collets. Settings were invariably embellished with small rose-cut diamonds. Crescent brooches, for example, were set with a line of graduated cushion-shaped gems with tiny rose diamond endstones. Many standard designs such as sunbursts, stars and flower sprays were accompanied by a tortoiseshell comb which would be screwed into the back of the brooch mount once the pin had been removed.

Group of affordable Late Victorian and Edwardian gold and gem-set pendants and a gold locket.

Primary Brooch Designs
'Celestial' themes including diamond stars, sunbursts and crescent moons in open and closed formation.
Flower sprays, cascades, daisy clusters and leaves.
Tied bows and wavy ribbons.
Target clusters and diamond horseshoes.
Butterflies set with diamonds and contrasting lines of rubies, sapphires and pearls.
Dragonflies in which the wings were mounted with shaped panels of gemstones such as opal and amethyst.
Lizards which were often set with opals, emeralds or demantoid garnets.

Late Victorian gold collar suspending a bloomed gold locket applied with a spray of diamond-set ginkgo leaves, c.1885. Gold and silver collars and lockets were very popular in the late Victorian era. The lockets were invariably decorated with a gem-set floral motif or other compatible designs such as horseshoes, stars and geometric panels.

Group of silver lockets and collars, c.1885.

The £10 10s. Jewel page. 19

1026. Sapphire and Diamond Double Heart and Coronet Brooch ... £10 10 0
1027. Diamond Heart with Enamel (any color) Slipper Brooch ... 10 10 0
1028. Diamond Tie Brooch 10 10 0
1029. Diamond Fancy Heart Brooch 10 10 0
1030. Turquoise and Diamond Heart Pendant 10 10 0
1031. Cabochon Ruby and Diamond on Gold Curb Bracelet ... 10 10 0
1032. Opal and Diamond Heart Pendant... ... ... 10 10 0
1033. Opal and Diamond Fancy Pendant 10 10 0
1034. Sapphires and Diamonds on Gold Curb Bracelet 10 10 0
1035. Jade Shamrock and Diamond Heart Pendant 10 10 0
1036. Turquoise Three-Stone Ring 10 10 0
1037. All Diamond Trefoil Ring 10 10 0
1038. Cabochon Ruby and Diamond Heart Ring 10 10 0
1039. Ruby and Diamond Twisted Front Bracelet 10 10 0
1040. Opal and Diamond Double-Part Ring 10 10 0
1041 Ruby and Diamond Bangle Ring 10 10 0
1042. Opal and Diamond Cluster Bracelet 10 10 0
1043. Opal and Diamond Marquise Ring 10 10 0

THESE DESIGNS ARE DRAWN TO ACTUAL SIZE, AND PRICES ARE QUOTED NET; SMALLER ORNAMENTS OF SAME DESIGN CAN BE HAD AT PROPORTIONATE PRICES.

18, New Bond Street, W.

Three pages from *Gems* by Edwin W. Streeter, London, c.1898.

Novelty Brooch Designs

Include a wide range of sporting and recreational themes from golf and fishing to domestic pets, musical instruments, locomotives and even necrophilia in the form of enamelled 'skull' tiepins.

Secondary Brooch Designs

This category includes the vast majority of simple 9 and 15-carat gold decorative brooches which were invariably set with half pearls and a colourful gemstone such as garnet, amethyst, aquamarine or peridot. Designs ranged from basic scrolls, clusters, shamrocks and stars to rather more elaborate sprays fashioned as swallows in flight, lily-of-the-valley or wild rose set with half pearls or decorated

GEM BROOCHES. 21

1059.	Sapphire and Diamond Cluster Brooch	£100 0 0
1060.	Diamond Butterfly Brooch	110 0 0
1061.	Colored Pearl and Diamond Four Leaf Shamrock Brooch	85 0 0
1062.	Diamond Antique Pattern Brooch	60 0 0
1063.	Ruby and Diamond Double Row Crescent Brooch	45 0 0
1064.	Diamond Crescent and Comet Brooch	34 0 0
1065.	Diamond Antique Brooch	25 0 0
1066.	Pearl and Diamond Spider and Web Brooch (half size £20)	35 0 0
1067.	Pink, Black and White Pearl and Diamond Brooch	40 0 0
1068.	Pearl and Diamond Twist Knot Brooch	18 0 0
1069.	Sapphire and Diamond Half-Moon Brooch	35 0 0
1070.	Ruby and Diamond Horse Shoe Brooch	40 0 0
1071.	Opal and Diamond Heart on Bar Brooch	15 0 0
1072.	Opal and Diamond Fancy Bar Brooch	12 10 0
1073.	Opal and Diamond Fancy Bar Brooch	6 15 0

THESE DESIGNS ARE DRAWN TO ACTUAL SIZE, AND PRICES ARE QUOTED NET; SMALLER ORNAMENTS OF SAME DESIGN CAN BE HAD AT PROPORTIONATE PRICES.

18, New Bond Street, W.

22 SPORTING MODELS, mounted in Diamonds.

1074.	Diamond Pomeranian Dog Brooch	£25 0 0
1075.	Diamond Deer Brooch	22 0 0
1076.	Diamond Dachshund Brooch	22 0 0
1077.	Diamond Hackney Brooch	25 0 0
1078.	Diamond Otter Brooch	35 0 0
1079.	Diamond Woodcock Brooch	41 10 0
1080.	Diamond and Enamel Golf Player Brooch	15 0 0
1081.	Diamond Bicycle Brooch	20 0 0
1082.	Diamond Owl Brooch	23 0 0
1083.	Diamond Donkey Brooch	35 0 0
1084.	Diamond Lucky Pig Brooch	45 0 0
1085.	Diamond Running Fox Brooch	30 0 0
1086.	Diamond Polo Pony with Enamel Rider Brooch	25 0 0
1087.	Diamond and Enamel Hansom Cab Brooch	12 0 0
1088.	Diamond Collie Dog Brooch	35 0 0

THESE DESIGNS ARE DRAWN TO ACTUAL SIZE, AND PRICES ARE QUOTED NET; SMALLER ORNAMENTS OF SAME DESIGN CAN BE HAD AT PROPORTIONATE PRICES.

STREETER & Co. Ltd.

with small gems and enamel. Sentimental themes such as two hearts entwined, lovers' knots and horseshoes. Insects, especially spiders, flies and beetles, mounted on a simple gold bar. Safety bar brooches incorporating a line of matching semi-precious gems or a small single diamond.

Lockets and Pendants

Lockets were particularly popular in the 1880s and 1890s ranging from large and ornate examples in silver or gold which were worn from compatible collars to small circular, oval and heart-shaped lockets with gold 'fronts and backs' and metal linings. Many lockets were engraved with a message of sentiment such as 'regard' or were inscribed with the owner's monogram. Mid-size gold lockets were often embellished with a gem-set star or double horseshoe surmount, while expensive examples were pavé-set with half pearls, diamonds or turquoises. A classic of the time was the heart-shaped pavé diamond locket with a hinged rock crystal back cover. Inexpensive but effective materials used included jet, bog oak, ivory, gilt metal and gunmetal.

Pendants often conformed to the naturalistic scrolling designs of brooches and were set with the 'standard' gems of the day; half pearl, garnet, aquamarine and peridot being particularly common. A striking example of turn-of-the-century and Edwardian jewellery was the negligée pendant in which two gems or clusters were suspended by bars or chains of unequal length from a matching top.

Necklaces

The late 19th century was the era of the diamond rivière – a line of some thirty or forty matching graduated brilliant-cut diamonds or gemstones in simple cut-down collet settings. Diamonds were extremely plentiful and were set in somewhat repetitive designs such as the fringe necklace – a series of graduated spear, floral cluster or tear-shaped drops with knife-edge bars connecting to a diamond gallery above.

Secondary necklaces repeated this theme with fringes of drop-shaped amethyst, moonstone, garnet, peridot and citrine mounted in either silver or gold. Pearl-set 15-carat gold necklaces were both common and easy to wear and many still survive today. 9-carat gold necklaces were often 'spectacle set' with a line of cheap semi-precious gems while Indian amethyst, ruby and citrine necklaces formed a graduated tier below a gallery of woven seed pearls. Gold and silver chains were also worn at the end of the 19th century. The majority of 9-carat guard chains contained 'secret' links for strength and protection against wear, while chains were sometimes worn together with a fob watch, a locket or an embossed seal.

Typical late Victorian gold and half-pearl necklace of floral cluster and clover-leaf design. Produced in large numbers at the end of the century examples were invariably mounted in either 15-carat or 18-carat gold while cheaper versions were mounted in 9 carat.

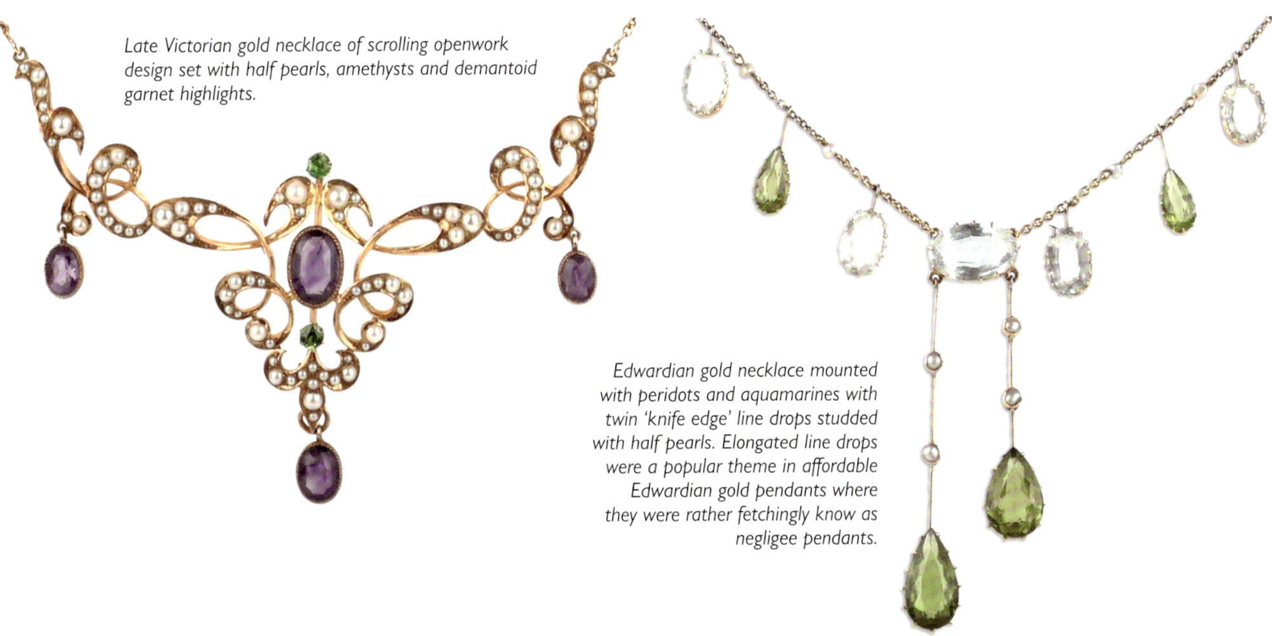

Late Victorian gold necklace of scrolling openwork design set with half pearls, amethysts and demantoid garnet highlights.

Edwardian gold necklace mounted with peridots and aquamarines with twin 'knife edge' line drops studded with half pearls. Elongated line drops were a popular theme in affordable Edwardian gold pendants where they were rather fetchingly know as negligee pendants.

Turn-of-the-century gold necklace mounted with a fringe of cushion-shaped vari-colour gems including examples in sapphire, garnet, tourmaline, citrine, zircon and amethyst.

Late Victorian/turn-of-the-century hinged gold bangle set with pearls.

Gold cartouche section bracelet mounted with oval-shaped opals, c.1905.

Group of four broad Victorian silver cuff bangles, c.1880, two with gold overlay decoration. Buckles and straps were ideal designs for this type of bracelet which remained popular well into the 20th century.

Earrings

Largely confined to the same designs used for rings such as a single diamond stud or a floral cluster of diamonds encircling a coloured gemstone or diamond to the centre.

Bangles and Bracelets

Designs were broadly similar to rings such as a line of diamonds or gems in 'half hoop' graduated formation. A plain gold hoop bangle was invariably hinged at the side and mounted to the centre with a decorative device such as a flower, a horseshoe or two entwined hearts. Inexpensive 9-carat gold models were fashionably set with cheap composition gems and rose diamond chips while broad gold and silver cuff bangles were profusely decorated with flowers, birds and scrolls or fashioned into the design of buckles and straps.

Bracelets, commonly of continuous curb link designs, were studded with gems such as turquoise, half pearl, opal and amethyst. Russian bracelets from this period were sometimes composed of a combination of 14-carat red-, white- and yellow-gold links and suspended pendants such as miniature eggs or religious charms.

Further reading

The Art of the Jeweller: A Catalogue of the Hull Grundy Gift to the British Museum (British Museum Publications Ltd, 1984)

Antique and Twentieth Century Jewellery, Vivienne Becker (NAG Press, 1980)

Understanding Jewellery, David Bennett and Daniela Mascetti (Antique Collectors' Club, 1996)

English Victorian Jewellery, Ernle Bradford (Country Life, 1959)

Jewellery in the International Era: 1789-1910, Shirley Bury (Antique Collectors' Club, 1997)

Victorian Jewellery, Margaret Flower (Cassell, 1951)

Jewellery in the Age of Queen Victoria, Charlotte Gere and Judy Rudoe (British Museum Press, 2010)

Chapter 4
Enamels

Enamel is a combination of glass silicate and powdered metallic oxide fused on to a metallic surface by heating at high intensity in a furnace. Versatile, decorative and visually enriching, enamel can be just as effective when used exclusively as when accompanied by diamonds or gems. Indeed, during the 16th and 17th centuries, enamel invariably took the place of gemstones which were hard to obtain, expensive and difficult to cut and polish.

Enamel was widely used in 19th-century jewellery, either exclusively as a decorative embellishment to mid-Victorian naturalistic gold pendants, bracelets and brooches or as a further decoration to gem-set pieces such as snake necklaces and bangles, where blue enamel was the ideal accompaniment for diamonds, rubies and half pearls. Coral jewellery was often lifted by a splash of green or blue enamel and black enamel is so closely associated with mourning jewellery that it is nearly impossible to associate the colour with anything else.

From a purely technical point of view the medium probably reached its zenith during the early part of the last century when Fabergé, Cartier and Art Nouveau goldsmiths such as Lalique took their own enamelling techniques to levels of excellence never seen before.

Sixteenth-century enamel gem-set figurative gold ring, c.1550-1600. The technique of enamelling figures 'in the round' was known as encrusted enamelling or émail en ronde bosse.

There are several methods of enamelling which were fairly common in the Middle Ages but which are so rarely seen today as to render them academic. The more common varieties encountered in antique jewellery are as follows:

Cloisonné Enamelling

Thin strips of wire – gold, silver or metal – are soldered to the surface of a metal object and are shaped into individual

Early 17th-century enamelled brooch of the Annunciation in a later gold frame. A fine example of basse-taille enamelling in which brilliant translucent colours are applied to a gold or silver ground in low relief.

George and the Dragon brooch, c.1630. Opaque white enamel was usually termed émail en blanc. Another example is illustrated on page 42.

Fine royal blue painted enamel and diamond commemorative jewel celebrating George IV's coronation in 1820.

decorative 'cells' known as cloisons. Each cell is filled with powdered enamel which is then fired and polished when cool. Cloisonné enamel was used in China and Japan on large-scale objects such as vases whilst the technique was revived by the French goldsmith Alexis Falize (1811-1898) and his son Lucien (1839-1897) in colourful gold pendants, lockets and bracelets depicting animals, birds and flowers in the Oriental taste.

Champlevé Enamelling

The opposite of cloisonné; the metal surface of an object was hollowed out into cells forming individual patterns which were then filled with coloured enamel, fired and smoothed flat. A technique known since ancient times, champlevé was used to striking effect in 19th-century Neo-Renaissance jewellery known as *Holbeinesque* in which colourful gemstones such as garnets and chrysolites were mounted in polychrome enamel frames.

Pair of gold buttons by the jewellers Falize decorated with cloisonné enamel birds in the Japanese taste, c.1870.

Charming French gold sentimental ring designed as a pair of doves nestling upon flowering branches decorated with black, white, green and blue enamel and set with rubies and rose-cut diamonds. The reverse bearing an indistinct French inscription, c.1765.

Victorian gold articulated snake bangle en plein *enamelled in royal blue and set with a flame cluster of diamonds and pearls with demantoid garnet eyes, c.1865.*

Nineteenth-century Renaissance Revival gold brooch of Holbeinesque design mounted with an emerald and diamond cluster in a champlevé polychrome enamelled frame set with rubies, c.1870.

Fabergé two-colour 14-carat gold and silver-gilt cigarette case en plein enamelled on a wavy engraved guilloché ground in light blue with seed pearl edging to the hinged lid. Workmaster Feodor Afanassiev, c.1910.

Mid-17th-century gold locket elaborately painted to depict a vase of flowers including peonies, tulips and daffodils within a scrolling border.

Gold, polychrome enamel and cabochon water sapphire pendant by H.G. Murphy, c.1928. Harry Murphy trained with Henry Wilson, one of England's most important artist craftsmen active in the early part of the 20th century. Working from his studio in London's Marylebone, Murphy produced a range of exquisite enamelled jewels with designs which extended from Arts and Crafts naturalism to the colourful vibrance of Art Deco.

Nineteenth-century gold bracelet mounted with a series of colourful Swiss enamel scenes in twisted rope pattern surrounds, c.1850.

En Plein Enamelling

Coating a relatively large area such as a cigarette case or photograph frame with several layers of enamel which have been individually fired and allowed to cool. Technically difficult, poor *en plein* enamelling exhibits an uneven surface and tiny air bubbles.

Guilloché Enamelling

Coats of transparent enamel covering a metal surface which has been finely engraved with a geometric pattern such as a 'sunburst' or 'watered silk'. This technique was mastered by Fabergé whose ability to create objects as small as a pair of cufflinks or as large as an Imperial Easter egg decorated with guilloché enamel was simply incomparable.

Painted Enamel

An early method, usually executed on copper. Layers of colour were individually built up and separately fired; designs were sometimes enhanced by metal foiling.

Counter Enamelling

Coating the back of an object with a layer of strengthening enamel. Seventeenth-century Dutch or English lockets were often counter enamelled in sky-blue.

Swiss Enamel

Popular in 18th- and 19th-century brooches and bracelets, 'Geneva' enamel depicted Alpine landscapes or girls wearing the costume of their national Swiss canton. These portraits were highly proficient but care should be taken

A group of translucent shaded blue enamel and silver-gilt butterfly brooches by Child & Child, c.1905.

to ensure that examples are free of chips which reveal the copper background. Damaged Swiss enamel is impossible to restore.

Plique-à-jour Enamelling

An important technique which is closely associated with Art Nouveau jewellery. The individual cells do not have a metal backing so the light shines through when the object is held up to the light. The enamel therefore acts in much the same way as a stained glass window and was ideal for naturalistic pendants depicting colourful flowers or dragonfly brooches where shades of coloured plique-à-jour enamel filled the individual cells in the insect's wing.

Further reading

The Art of the Jeweller: A Catalogue of the Hull Grundy Gift to the British Museum (British Museum Publications Ltd, 1984)
Jewellery. The International Era: 1789-1910, Shirley Bury (Antique Collectors' Club, 1997)
Enamelling. Development of the Art, Lewis F. Day (B.T. Batsford, 1907)
Silverwork and Jewellery, Henry Wilson (Sir Isaac Pitman, 1948)
Jewelry & Metalwork in the Arts and Crafts Tradition, Elyse Zorn Karlin (Schiffer Publishing Ltd, 1993)

Chapter 5
'False Diamonds': Paste Jewellery from the 1750s to the 1930s

Antique paste – particularly the 19th-century material – was one of those commodities which quite literally could be bought for next to nothing. Then, in the 1970s, M.D.S. Lewis' superb book on the subject brought paste to a wider audience and suddenly collectors were clamouring for pretty Georgian buttons, flower spray brooches and classical diadems which could previously be bought for well under £100. Today a 'Queen Anne' necklace of faceted paste collets foiled a desirable colour such as aquamarine blue or emerald green can easily sell for £5,000 at auction. Therein lies the great strength of fine old paste jewellery. Instead of mere copies of real diamonds and gems, it should be embraced for what it truly is: elegant, beautifully constructed jewels, marvellous to handle, versatile and enriching to wear and a perfect expression of the period in which it was constructed.

Glass had been extensively used in decorative ornamentation since ancient times. Roman rings, for example, were sometimes set with little coloured glass plaques while brooch pins of Saxon origin were decorated with sections of glass or further embellished with enamel. Such glass was soft and fragile and wore down easily, often resulting in an abraded and unattractive lustre. It was not until the 17th century that an Englishman, George Ravenscroft, began experimenting with new compounds of flint, potash and lead oxide producing 'glass of lead', a lustrous material which proved sufficiently hard to cut and polish like a gemstone. However, it was the pioneering endeavours of Georges Frédéric Strass (1701-1773), a jeweller working in Paris, which fundamentally influenced the manner in which everyday jewellery was worn in the 18th century.

Like Ravenscroft, Strass experimented with lead crystal which could be faceted to imitate diamonds and which was mounted in silver settings to simulate genuine and costly alternatives. The key to Strass' success was to market his so-called 'false diamonds' to the French King and the Bourbon Court. Soon this new product became both fashionable and essential in a society fraught with crime where display of real jewellery could be positively dangerous. The paste Strass produced was soft enough to cut into any number of shapes which could then be set to follow the contours of the mount. In this way cushion, round and drop-shaped pastes were snugly set in gilt metal, silver or silver gilt which fully

Georgian mid-18th-century gilt-metal double-row foil back purple 'amethyst' paste necklace with large faceted drop, c.1750. Confusingly known as 'Queen Anne' paste and found in a range of colours, necklaces, bracelets and earrings of this mid 18th-century period are rare today and in high demand. Buyers should beware of high-quality modern copies on the market which often exhibit minimal wear.

Georgian colourless paste cluster earrings, c.1775. Earrings such as these were invariably mounted in silver and foiled behind the paste to enhance their appearance.

Georgian colourless paste butterfly brooch, c.1800. Note the tiny faceted black glass eyes. This charming brooch featured its original fitted case - something of a rarity where antique paste is concerned.

Group of four Georgian colourless paste flowerhead brooches, c.1790.

enclosed the back of the setting. In common with much 18th-century jewellery, the individual pastes were backed with tinfoil to intensify brilliance and sometimes the front of the piece was decorated with strips of gold or little gold beads to add a touch of glitter.

French paste conformed to the same patterns fashionable in diamond jewellery such as sévigné bows, girandole drops, feathers, flower sprays and butterflies. English paste, however, veered towards the simple and altogether less elaborate. A common 18th-century theme for brooches in diamonds or paste was the six-petal flower cluster, while Maltese crosses, curling plumes and uncomplicated leaf shapes are often encountered today. Late 18th-century rings of both French and English origin followed the classical ideal such as large octagonal or marquise-shaped plaques enamelled in royal blue within paste borders while earrings were somewhat curiously set with two large but unmatched pastes in plain mounts with rather thick hook fittings on the back. Possibly the most wearable design for English mid- to late 18th-century paste jewellery was the collet necklace, in which a series of graduated cushion-shaped sections mounted in dome-back gilt metal were each set with a fully faceted foiled paste. These were usually in standard colours meant to imitate real gems such as 'emerald' green or 'ruby' red but one particular variety stood out. Known as 'opaline', this pinkish-blue material was used extensively in necklaces, earrings, buttons and brooches where its soft rose colour foil was the ideal accompaniment for sparkling colourless paste.

Generally speaking, 19th-century paste lacks the beauty, finish and 'density' of the 18th-century variety. Necklaces, brooches and pendants could often appear rather cheap and flashy, unsurprising when one considers that the paste was uniform in shape, size and cut where a large number were set together to look like diamonds. The biggest development was the setting – or rather lack of it, since 19th-century paste was left exposed at the back for all the available light to pass through. This did away with the need for foiling and – another development – gold began to be used rather more liberally.

Nineteenth-century paste brooches, diadems, tiaras and necklaces copied their diamond counterparts faithfully. Heavier collet settings gradually gave way to lighter, thinner 'millegrain' settings and after 1840 the individual pastes were often 'silvered' to achieve a permanent glitter. As the century progressed, paste jewellery became increasingly versatile and plentiful with large numbers of cheap and pretty pendants manufactured in silver, brooches in an enormous range of designs including flowers, birds, animals, insects and reptiles and cluster necklaces and hair combs described generally as 'French paste'. Much of this kind of jewellery is, frankly, extremely cheap and cheerful and can easily deteriorate with careless handling.

Early 20th-century paste was elegant and pretty, particularly pendants and brooches of 'Belle Époque' design which could sometimes mimic diamonds extremely well. By the 1930s paste double clips in highly polished

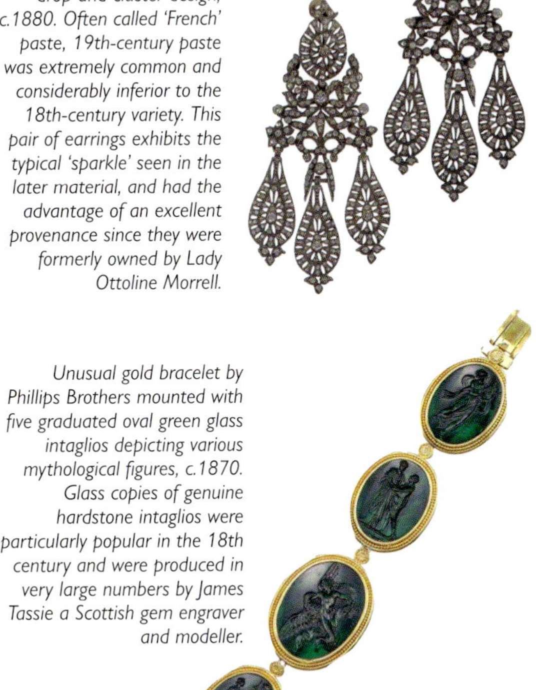

Nineteenth century colourless paste earrings of elaborate triple chandelier drop and cluster design, c.1880. Often called 'French' paste, 19th-century paste was extremely common and considerably inferior to the 18th-century variety. This pair of earrings exhibits the typical 'sparkle' seen in the later material, and had the advantage of an excellent provenance since they were formerly owned by Lady Ottoline Morrell.

Unusual gold bracelet by Phillips Brothers mounted with five graduated oval green glass intaglios depicting various mythological figures, c.1870. Glass copies of genuine hardstone intaglios were particularly popular in the 18th century and were produced in very large numbers by James Tassie a Scottish gem engraver and modeller.

Regency foil-back green paste and silver-gilt parure, c.1825, in its original morocco red leather case.

'chrome-like' mounts or geometric bracelets and necklaces copied expensive gems and exhibited the best of costume jewellery design, particularly pieces of French manufacture set with well-cut 'ruby-red' or 'sapphire-blue' paste which combined visually bold materials with effortless style.

Vauxhall Glass

Known as 'mirror-back paste', this was a striking variety of paste fashionable in the 18th and early to mid-19th century. It originated at the Vauxhall Glass Works in London and usually took the form of highly reflective panels of glass set in floral clusters, stars or naturalistic designs which were invariably mounted in base metal as pendants, earrings, rings and diadems.

Further reading

Anne Clifford's Antique Jewellery: The Story of a Collection, Derek Clifford (Nottingham Court Press, 1985)

Antique Paste Jewellery, M.D.S. Lewis (Boston Book and Art Publisher, U.S.A., 1970)

Georgian Jewellery 1714-1830, Ginny Redington Dawes and Olivia Collings (Antique Collectors' Club, 2007)

Old Paste, A. Beresford Ryley (Methuen, 1913)

Chapter 6
The Industry of Death: Memento Mori and Mourning Jewellery

One of the more common varieties of antique jewellery one is likely to come across is a Victorian gilt-metal and black enamel brooch inscribed 'In Memory Of.' In the centre a locket compartment will contain a plume of hair and the back of the mount will be engraved with the name of the deceased – long gone and sadly forgotten.

Today, the idea of placing the hair of a loved one into a brooch or ring would be seen as morbid, if not a little eccentric. Yet for over 350 years the fashion for wearing such jewellery remained consistently popular in a Britain which was both highly sentimental and religiously devout. Milestone events such as the execution of Charles I, the death of Nelson and the premature loss of the Prince Consort – a catastrophe which plunged Queen Victoria into forty years of mourning – all played their part in fuelling public fascination in the 'Industry of Death.'

The 17th Century

During a period when disease, plague, war, infant mortality and malnutrition meant that life after forty was a comparative rarity, it was the custom for several identical gold rings to be bequeathed to principal mourners as a keepsake of the deceased. The more influential or celebrated the individual, the greater the number of rings which would be made and distributed. Thus when Charles I was executed in 1649 there was a massive demand amongst Royalist sympathisers for a memento and literally hundreds of gold and silver slides, pendants and rings were produced containing a portrait of the King, usually set under a cover of rock crystal.

The inevitability of death was summed up in the grim expression 'Remember that you must die', better known in its Latin translation, *Memento mori*. Seventeenth-century memento mori jewels can be macabre and rather gruesome. A typical gold slide – worn on a black velvet ribbon – would contain a bed of human hair upon which rested a miniature coffin or a recumbent skeleton enamelled in white and black together with various symbols of mortality such as an hourglass or gravedigger's shovel. The back of these slides might be engraved with a simple monogram or date of death. It was not unknown to insert a piece of human

Gold and rock crystal slide containing an enamelled skeleton on bed of woven hair, c.1683. A rather gruesome relic but clearly resonant with the grim mortality of the time.

Rare Charles I gold double-sided swivel memento mori seal ring, c.1640, depicting on one side an engraved coat of arms and on the other a skull and crossbones in black enamel with coloured enamel floral border and matching enamelled gallery.

A mid-17th-century diamond-set enamelled gold skull ring.

White enamel and gold memorial band ring, c.1740. The skeleton extends around the entire hoop. White enamel meant that the deceased was unmarried.

Late 18th-century diamond, royal blue enamel and pearl mourning brooch.

skin into these extraordinary little lockets; clearly these are jewels for the purist. Stuart mourning rings also conformed to this stark ideal with enamelled death's head bezels set with diamonds in the eyes with crossed bones behind on a hoop fashioned in the design of an elongated skeleton.

The 18th Century

As time wore on, the stark symbolism of early memento mori jewels was gradually superseded by a gentler, altogether prettier range of mourning jewellery culminating at the end of the century in hopeless sentimentality.

Early 18th-century rings were still enamelled in black and white with little crystal bezels, but pendants and slides began to be set with diamonds or gems such as garnets or rubies in heart-shaped frames. The use of white enamel after the 1750s inferred that the deceased was unmarried whilst the appearance of a coiled serpent with its tail gripped in its jaws suggested eternal love. Mid- to late 18th-century mourning rings were typically designed as a scrollwork band in which the name, date of birth and date of death of the individual would be highlighted in gold capitals on an enamelled field.

Group of three fine late 18th-century mourning rings, c.1790. The birdcage in the locket ring on the extreme right represents the soul trapped in the earthly realm after death awaiting release while 'weeping' willow trees convey serenity and acceptance.

Late 18th-century neo-classical funerary urn ring with characteristic 'weeping willow' decoration. English, c.1785.

Georgian gold mourning brooch dedicated to 'Samuel Chettle · Died 15 Nov. 1789 · Aged 27'. Note the finely plaited hair of the deceased behind the funerary urn.

Collection of Victorian woven hair work jewellery, c.1850.

By the end of the century, mourning jewels – particularly brooches and pendants – became strongly romanticised. The frames were of simple, plain form and neo-classical in shape, usually octagonal, navette (pointed at both finials) or oval. Sorrowful rather than savage, these lockets contained little pictures under glass painted to depict distraught ladies prostrate by a plinth with a funerary urn and bearing the message 'Not Lost But Gone Before' or 'Asleep With Jesus'. A weeping willow tree picked out in hair would form the background and the miniature might be decorated with tiny seed glass pearls suggesting tears. Superior examples were bordered by enamel, sometimes with diamond highlights, whilst fine-quality rings contained a classical urn studded with numerous diamonds on a bed of hair.

Another curious manifestation of the time was the 'Tear' jewel in which a small gold slide or brooch would be painted on ivory with the miniature of a single eye weeping a solitary tear; charming and highly collectible (see illustration on page 102).

The 19th Century

By the early 1800s mourning rings took the form of a broad gold band with hoops of black or white enamel bearing an inscription, while the romantic influence led to the appearance of gold locket rings set with clusters of half pearls symbolising tears, jet or French jet (faceted black glass). The enormous popularity of mourning jewellery in the 19th century led to the manufacture of literally hundreds of thousands of items so any example with the hair (and rock-solid provenance) of a prominent figure would be considered highly collectable today. Monarchs (such as George III or George IV), war heroes (particularly Nelson, Wellington or Napoleon), politicians, actors and authors will fetch a considerable premium in price, although condition is usually a critical factor.

Much of the mourning jewellery made during Queen Victoria's reign was so romanticised as to barely hint at its true meaning. Gone were the morbid icons of death to be replaced by pretty plumes of hair tied with gold wire in borders of half pearls and frames of rococo gold. More recognisable brooches were poorly constructed from gilt metal and enamelled in jet black. Easy to damage and uncommercial, most Victorian mourning brooches are both cheap and easily available today.

In the 1840s and 1850s a fashion developed in which hair was finely woven into plaited ropes and delicate openwork 'balls' suitable for earrings or 'tubes' for brooches. Hair is surprisingly robust and it is still possible to come across perfect jewellery composed entirely of hair mounted in gold fittings. Unfortunately, unscrupulous jewellers resorted to the use of horsehair which was both plentiful and easy to work. Horsehair jewellery is a decorative material distinct from the human variety and is occasionally found today in elaborate necklaces and bracelets dyed off-white or coral red.

A pair of enamelled gold bands dedicated to Spencer Perceval, assassinated on 11 May, 1812.

A coloured engraving by George Cruikshank describing the heinous deed. Spencer Perceval was Prime Minister at the time of his murder. The combination of political memorabilia, a violent end and the fine condition of the rings (left) indicate a value of several thousand pounds today.

Group of typical Victorian gold, black enamel and half pearl-set mourning jewellery, 1850-1900.

The prime material which we most closely associate with mourning jewellery is, of course, jet. After the death of the Prince Consort in 1861, the jet industry located at Whitby on the North Yorkshire coast produced thousands of carved brooches, necklaces, bracelets and crosses supplied by scores of little shops which sprang up to cater for the public demand. The range of products was extra-ordinarily diverse and on the whole highly proficient. Today there are still excellent specialist jet shops in Whitby. Prices, however, reflect the quality and skill of the craftsmen, so early original pieces can fetch several hundred pounds for a good necklace or cameo brooch.

After the death of Victoria there was a conscious desire to embrace a lighter, more frivolous lifestyle so clearly absent for forty years and the very British passion for mourning jewellery evaporated almost overnight. It is difficult to imagine it ever being revived.

Rare 18-carat gold and enamel mourning ring for Lord Byron, 1824. The central cushion-shaped plaque inscribed 'BYRON' in gold reserve with enamelled baronial coronet above on a black enamelled field, the band inscribed 'In Memory Of' between carved scrolling sides, the interior with locket compartment containing a lock of Byron's hair. Bearing hallmarks for 1824 and engraved within the hoop 'Died 19 April at. 36'.

Further reading

Antique and Twentieth Century Jewellery, Vivienne Becker (NAG Press, 1980)

Victorian Sentimental Jewellery, Diana Cooper and Norman Battershill (David and Charles, 1972)

Jet Jewellery and Ornaments, Helen Muller (Shire Publications Ltd, 2003)

Jewellery in Britain 1066-1837, Diana Scarisbrick (Michael Russell Publishing Ltd, 1994)

Impressive early 19th-century neoclassical two-colour gold and Russian malachite cameo parure comprising necklace, tiara, brooch, ring and earrings.

Chapter 7
Cameos and Intaglios

I must say that I feel a particularly close affinity with this subject since I started my career at an antique jewellery shop near the British Museum in Bloomsbury, London called Cameo Corner. First, a definition of the two media:

A cameo is a carving in which the design stands out in relief from its background and an intaglio is a gem in which the design has been carved into the surface.

This is a technical description, but there is another important difference between cameos and intaglios: the former are visually striking and thus extremely wearable, whereas the latter are subtle, understated miniature works of art usually more of interest to the academic collector.

CAMEOS

The vast majority of cameos which appear on the market today are 19th century or later. Roman cameo rings are rare and occasionally turn up in specialised auctions of antiquities and Renaissance cameos are exceedingly scarce, tricky to identify and often imperfect. Eighteenth-century cameos are more common but are easy to date incorrectly. Their settings can assist in making an accurate judgment.

Condition is all when valuing cameos. They were meant to be worn and shell, the most common material we see today, is a soft organic material which routinely fractures, breaks or simply wears smooth with regular use so the surface features become indistinct. A fine unworn cameo with a lovely female head in profile in an undamaged gold frame will thus command a considerable premium, whilst a tired, split old cameo in a frame smothered in lead repairs can be bought very cheaply.

Shell Cameos

Although shell cameo carving is found in 16th-century jewellery, nearly all shell cameos mounted in jewellery are 19th century or later. The industry was first developed in Sicily, then Naples, and Italian craftsmen worked in France and England in the 1850s and 1860s. Most shell cameos are caramel brown and white and are cut from a large helmet-shaped natural seashell called *Cassis tuberosa*. Pink shell cameos were taken from the queen conch shell and tend to be confused with coral. Sometimes these large and imposing seashells were themselves carved to display a mythological scene or classical group and were placed in shop windows for display purposes.

Hardstone Cameos

The great advantage of hardstone is that it can be carved in far greater detail than shell (which is much softer) and, furthermore, the contrasting background colour will take a near mirror-like polish. Hardstone cameos are somewhat

Early 19th-century gold necklace mounted with ten oval graduated shell cameos carved to depict mythological deities in cannetille work gold frames. Care should be taken when buying cameos to ensure they are in fine condition. The cameo three down from the clasp on the left exhibits a hairline crack which will inevitably impact upon its value.

Left: Italian 19th-century shell cameo and gold brooch, c.1865. The subject matter is finely carved and very commercial.

Right: Late 19th-century sardonyx cameo brooch of a female head in profile in a gold beadwork and scrolling frame, c.1885.

heavy, creating a tendency for brooches to fall forward when pinned on an outfit. They are almost always more expensive than shell. The principal varieties are:

Sardonyx: rust-brown or pinkish-brown background with white or cream carving.
Onyx: jet black background (sometimes stained) with white carving.
Agate: usually a dove-grey background with white carving.
Malachite and Lapis Lazuli: used in late 18th- and early 19th-century parures and often carved with neo-classical scenes.

Precious and Semi-Precious Gem Cameos

Rare and very expensive, rubies, sapphires and emeralds have been fashioned into cameos since ancient times. Usually small and of simple design due to their ungiving hardness, one is most likely to find a rare, precious gem

Italian finely carved coral cameo of Bacchante in a gold frame with vine leaf decoration, c.1865.

Classical pink and white agate brooch in a gold cannetille frame, c.1835-45.

Fine bejewelled black and white onyx cameo habillé of a Nubian princess in matching ruby and diamond frame, c.1880.

Superb mid-19th-century Italian gold architectural necklace mounted with various onyx and sardonyx classical cameos.

cameo in a Roman ring and very occasionally in a simple 18th-century gold setting. Two less valuable but colourful gems which appear in late 19th-century brooches are golden citrine and purple amethyst. The greater size of these stones meant that carvings were usually intricate in detail with profiles including classical heads and ladies in Tudor costume. Another gem which is sometimes found in turn-of-the-century rings and brooches is opal, carved with a range of unusual subjects such as Native Americans and exotic animals in which the natural colours and contours of the stone added to the effectiveness of the carving.

Italian gold brooch mounted with a pale brown lava cameo of a Greek philosopher, c.1865.

Interesting 'Grand Tour' gold bracelet, c.1800, mounted with a colourful range of assorted hardstone and gem cameos including agate, jasper, lapis lazuli, amethyst and onyx.

Renaissance Revival gold pendant, c.1880, mounted with an opal cameo attributed to Wilhelm Schmidt, the cushion-shaped black opal carved to depict Arion and Delphinius in a polychrome enamelled gold frame set diamonds, emerald and pearls.

Lava Cameos

Popular with travellers on the Grand Tour, volcanic lava from Mount Vesuvius ranged in colour from chalk-white through beige, terracotta, pale grey to dark grey and black. Subjects included famous ancient Greek philosophers, statesmen and historical figures such as Leonardo da Vinci and Shakespeare. Usually simply set in low-grade gold mounts as brooches, bracelets or complete parures.

Other Organic Materials

These included coral, extensively used in the 18th and 19th centuries, ivory, where quite large brooches were set in very basic frames, and jet, a very English phenomenon in which flower studies were just as popular as the standard classical head in profile.

Imitation Materials

An imitation cameo usually suggests a cheap copy. Certainly, some of the plastic and composition cameos produced in the 1930s-1950s are pretty basic, but 19th-century glass cameos can be very effective. These were usually deep purple or blue, imposing in size and portrayed the head of Bacchante in profile. The frames, as expected, are in base metal.

Josiah Wedgwood produced blue and white jasper stoneware in the 18th century which can be mistaken for cameos. Most subjects were neo-classical and the frames were usually metal or cut steel.

Finally, some early 20th-century costume cameos are composition doublets, in which the bust has been glued to the background.

Subjects and Their Settings

Considering their age, many medieval and later cameos are remarkably accomplished although extremely scarce today. Sixteenth- and 17th-century cameos do appear occasionally at auctions of early rings and antiquities. The carvings are shallow and sometimes irregular in shape while fine-quality examples may be set in bright yellow-gold frames embellished with colourful enamel, diamonds and pearls.

The two guiding themes of 18th- and 19th-century cameo cutting were classicism and romanticism. From the mid-18th century to the early 19th century, neo-classical cameos represented the very finest execution of detail and realism. Subjects were noble and powerful including mythological deities, Greek and Roman philosophers and emperors, prominent statesmen and figures from the Church, nobility and military. The frames were usually simple rims of gold known as 'Roman' seal settings. Sometimes these individual cameos were joined together as necklaces or bracelets by three or four tiers of fine gold chains called *en esclavage*.

Early 19th-century cameos often depicted complete groups of mythological figures and animals with little cherubs known as *putti* in attendance. Carved in hardstone, shell or occasionally malachite, the settings gradually became more elaborate so by the 1830s and 1840s many cameos were framed in intricate gold filigree surrounds known as *cannetille* work.

The early Victorian era heralded an age of Romanticism. Cool classicism gave way to a softer, less austere definition of cameo carving in which the female form predominated. (Subjects such as Bacchante, Minerva and Medusa were hugely popular.) This diversification led to all sorts of subjects appearing on cameo brooches; naturalism and realism competed with scenes from the Bible, ladies in Tudor costumes, figures standing in a rustic landscape and profiles of Victorian gentlemen on the Grand Tour immortalised by Italian carvers such as Tommaso and Luigi Saulini.

From the 1860s to the 1880s Italian craftsmen mounted bold hardstone cameos in fine yellow-gold frames decorated with twisted wirework and shotwork motifs. Subject matter was again strongly classical, verging on the heroic. Popular mythological deities – Apollo, Mars, Diana and Mercury – were carved in high relief from onyx, sardonyx and pale grey agate.

Charming late 18th-century cameo ring of two lovebirds in a diamond frame signed in Greek characters by Giovanni Pichler (1734-1791).

Nineteenth-century oval unmounted turquoise cameo depicting four dancing classical maidens.

1970s Continental gold textured oblong plaque bracelet mounted with a series of eight assorted hardstone, coral and shell cameos. Modern cameo carving is invariably far inferior to the antique; note the similarity between each of the profiles and their lack of subtle detail.

Five examples of hardstone and gem intaglio carving. Above, left to right: Small Romano-British oval red jasper 2nd-3rd century AD of a gryllus – the head of a ram and two heads of deities conjoined; Carnelian depicting the head of Roma in profile; 18th-century garnet intaglio depicting Hercules beneath Eros with allegorical reference to love conquering strength. Below, left to right: 19th-century hexagonal amethyst of a seated owl; Small early 19th-century carnelian of a seated owl.

By the end of the century the fashion and passion for cameos dwindled. Twentieth-century cameos, sometimes set in 9-carat gold or silver with marcasite highlights, lack the subtlety and detail of earlier examples and mass-production in the modern era has resulted in some very crude, repetitive and charmless carvings being sold by high street jewellers.

INTAGLIOS

These perfect little works of art represent some of the very oldest examples of stone cutting and gem embellishment existing today. They are difficult to wear individually although in the 18th century it was fashionable to mount fine examples by prominent gem engravers as finger rings in gold 'Roman style' seal settings. Regency necklaces composed of twenty or more genuine Roman intaglios in several different colours of hardstone were invariably seal set in gold, whilst classical revival goldsmiths such as Castellani used ancient intaglios in some of his architectural jewels.

There were several important gem engravers active in the 18th century whose work is highly collectable today. Nathaniel Marchant (1739-1816) worked in Rome as a portrait engraver. Edward Burch (1730-1814) exhibited at the Royal Academy and specialised in historical profiles, while Giovanni Pichler (1734-1791) and his half-brother Luigi (1773-1854) specialised in superb engravings of classical heads and groups in a range of different hardstones. Prince Stanislaw Poniatowski (1754-1833) amassed a large collection of cornelian intaglios with faked signatures while James Tassie (1735-1799), a Scotsman, produced large numbers of imitation gems in glass which regularly appear in sizeable numbers on the market today.

Details of the three central hardstone intaglios on the bracelet below.

Fine and rare early 19th-century gold bracelet mounted with nine oval 18th- and 19th-century graduated hardstone intaglios comprising from left to right: (i) sardonyx – a man standing before a tree holding a wreath; (ii) sardonyx – a seated philosopher; (iii) carnelian – Athena Lemnia in profile; (iv) sardonyx – Heracles Farnese leaning on his club draped with the Nemean lion; (v) sardonyx – signed by Carlo Costanzi: a young man with tied flowing hair; (vi) sardonyx – signed by Luigi or Giovanni Pichler: a young man's head in profile; (vii) sardonyx – signed by Luigi Pichler: a robed maenad holding a thyrsus and a cup; (viii) carnelian – a traditional Dionysiac procession; (ix) onyx – a bearded man kneeling before a krater.

Further reading

Multum in Parvo. A collection of engraved gems. Exh. Cat. (Wartski, 2019)

The Art of the Jeweller: A Catalogue of the Hull Grundy Gift to the British Museum (British Museum Publications Ltd, 1984)

Engraved Gems, John Boardman (Thames & Hudson, 1968)

Antique Gems: Their Origins, Uses and Value, Rev. C.W. King (John Murray, 1866)

The Guy Ladrière Collection of Gems and Rings, D. Scarisbrick, C. Wagner and J. Boardman (Philip Wilson Publishers 2016)

Chapter 8
Mosaics

Colourful, evocative and intricate, mosaics provided some of the most expressive and proficient examples of the craftsman's skill in which the smallest possible materials were amalgamated to create a work of art in miniature.

Inspired by the frescoes, ceilings and floors of ancient Roman interiors, mosaics used in jewellery depicted the sort of subjects which the expanding numbers of visitors to Italy most admired: historic buildings like the Colosseum and Pantheon, architectural sites such as St Peter's, Rome, as well as a wide variety of classical and romantic symbols – cherubs, domestic and wild animals, evocative ruins, colourful flower studies and swooping birds.

Mosaics were not only confined to small-scale plaques set into brooches or necklaces. Some of the most virtuosi examples of the craft were reserved for large scale objets d'art such as wall plaques and table tops in which the sheer quantity of tiny individual pieces of coloured glass used to fill such a large surface area is, frankly, extremely difficult to comprehend.

There were two principal varieties of mosaics differentiated by the name of the city from which they originated.

Fine rectangular micromosaic plaque signed 'L.M.' for Luigi Cavaliere Moglia (c.1813-1878) depicting a spaniel standing in a grassy landscape with distant hills beyond, mounted on copper with metal frame. A good example of the sheer number of individual tesserae which were painstakingly set into these miniature works of art. Dogs, particularly spaniels, were extremely popular subjects resulting in large numbers of faithful hounds being immortalised by remarkable craftsmen such as Moglia.

Roman Mosaics

In recent years, the term 'Roman mosaic' has been superseded by the rather less inspiring description 'micromosaic' to avoid any possible 'historic' confusion. Roman mosaic can trace its roots back to the Renaissance when a Vatican workshop was established in the late 16th century. By the 18th century large numbers of tourists visiting Rome on the Grand Tour triggered widespread popular interest in the medium leading to inevitable commercial exploitation.

Roman mosaics are decorative plaques, usually oval or rectangular, in which thousands of tiny pieces of coloured glass or stone were carefully selected, positioned and cemented together to create a recognisable picture. These fragments were known as *tesserae* and were usually made by cutting up rods of glass which had been stretched in order that hundreds of subtle shades of colour could be introduced into the material itself. The technique was not entirely dissimilar from *millefiore* in which clusters of coloured glass were grouped like so many sticks of rock, sliced up and mounted together in bead necklaces and paperweights. The sheer range of colour means that tesserae which fall out of antique mosaic jewels are almost impossible to replicate – one very good reason why perfect pieces are significantly more expensive than damaged ones.

Early Roman mosaics – those dating from the 18th and early 19th-century – are superior (and dearer) than 19th-century examples because the size of the individual fragments of tesserae are that much smaller. Early mosaics are much more subtle and better defined, often appearing like miniature oil paintings, smooth to the touch and so cleverly set that the cement between each fragment is barely visible. Nineteenth-century mosaics, on the other hand, are coarser, cruder, uneven to the touch and somewhat two-dimensional in appearance.

Early mosaics were strongly neo-classical in theme. Landscapes with rivers and waterfalls, pastoral and hunting scenes and domestic animals (particularly dogs)

Late 18th-century octagonal micromosaic and gold ring by Giacomo Raffaelli (1753-1836) depicting a dove seated on a branch, the copper backplate signed to the reverse 'Raffaelli fece 1793'. Signed mosaic jewellery is rare. This example is in exceptionally good condition and is by one of the most accomplished mosaicists of his day. As a general rule, the greater the age of the mosaic the tinier the individual tesserae and the finer the finish.

Raffaelli double-sided micromosaic and gold ring, c.1795, displaying a butterfly on one side and a goldfinch on the other.

Superb archaeological gold and micromosaic bracelet by Castellani, c.1860.

were typical of the period, along with romantic doves, cherubs and assorted symbols of sentiment. These mosaics were simply set in plain gold rims or joined together by tiers of fine gold chains as necklaces or pairs of bracelets. In the 1830s and 1840s mosaics were set in elaborate gold cannetille frames combining neo-classical and romantic themes. The colour of the background tesserae was usually white and it was popular to encircle the individual designs within borders and backs of blue or red glass. Sometimes bright gold tesserae were introduced to reinforce the 'classical' impression.

By the 1860s and 1870s Egyptian Revivalism resulted in bright and colourful mosaics depicting standard symbols with which tourists could easily identify – scarab beetles, the heads of Pharaohs, cobras and vultures. In yellow-gold frames decorated with wire loops, twisted rope and soldered beads called shotwork, the word 'subtle' is less than appropriate; such Revivalist jewels would occasionally bear raised lettering with the words 'pax' or 'Roma' just in case one forgot from where the piece had originated.

Three 19th-century Italian micromosaic and gold bangles, c.1865-1870.
Left: Broad stylised 'star' design, the domed circular centre inset with a mosaic cross above 'PAX' with bouquets of flowers and enamel strap work frame.
Below: Three circular plaques inset with colourful mosaic scarab beetles.
Bottom, left: Archaeological, with central cartouche-shaped panel inset with early Christian 'Chi-Rho' symbol between doves on a blue mosaic ground.

Set of Italian micromosaic pendant and earrings depicting doves on a terracotta red mosaic ground in elaborate scrolling gold frames with blue and white mosaic highlights, c.1865.

Group of 19th-century gold-mounted Florentine mosaic 'pietra dura' bracelet, earrings and brooch, c.1870. Flower studies were by far the most popular subjects where Florentine mosaics were concerned.

Florentine Mosaics

Whilst Roman mosaics were invariably set with glass tesserae, the individual petals and leaves which formed the floral studies in Florentine mosaics were almost always colourful hardstones such as white chalcedony, red sard, sky-blue turquoise, royal blue lapis lazuli, pink marble and mottled green malachite. The background used was dull black Belgian slate which was cut out and carefully filled with the appropriate piece of shaped hardstone in much the same way as a jigsaw puzzle. The effect of white and pastel colours against a jet black background was incredibly effective; lilies of the valley and sprays of forget-me-nots were powerfully portrayed in bright yellow-gold frames enhanced, like Roman mosaic, with rope pattern decoration. The technique of inlaying colourful hardstones into a contrasting background is known as *pietra dura* (literally 'hardstone').

Fine-quality oval-shaped Florentine mosaic and gold brooch, c.1870.

Florentine mosaic pendant, c.1870-80. This example is certainly colourful and effective but rather lacks the subtlety of the flower studies on the preceding page.

Micromosaic stickpin, c.1880. By the end of the 19th century, mass production of mosaics resulted in a visible loss of quality. The subject, an iridescent beetle, is attractive but note the crude white tesserae

Late 19th-century Florentine mosaic stickpin. Note how badly cut the individual hardstone pieces are compared with earlier pietra dura examples.

Late 19th-century micromosaic necklace and matching ring, c.1900. While this necklace is certainly pretty and wearable the mosaics lack definition and detail and consequently appear rather crude and repetitive. Ring not to scale.

Decorative Mosaics

Towards the end of the 19th century and the start of the 20th century, small and cheap pieces of souvenir jewellery and miniature accessories were set with colourful – and coarse – mosaic in low-grade silver-gilt or gilt-metal mounts. These were surprisingly common but are still fairly effective, fashioned in designs ranging from novelty objects such as 'guitars' and 'bicycles' to prosaic button brooches and pretty little picture frames. A rather crude variety of Florentine mosaic made of shiny glass was also used in late 19th-century costume jewellery, but this is difficult to confuse with the genuine material.

Further reading

The Gilbert Collection: Micromosaics (Philip Wilson Publishers Ltd, 2000)

Antique and Twentieth Century Jewellery, Vivienne Becker (NAG Press, 1980)

Chapter 9
Jewellery in Scotland

Whenever we think of 'Scottish jewellery', we automatically associate the term with those distinctive Victorian gold and silver brooches and bracelets mounted with citrines, rock crystals and a variety of colourful hardstone sections which fall under the catch-all definition of 'pebble jewels.'

As popular and collectable as this type of jewellery has become in recent years, it is also important to recognise the significance of Scotland in the history of decorative metalwork over the past five hundred years. Mary, Queen of Scots was enormously influential in the manner in which ladies of nobility wore their jewellery, favouring pearls above all gems, mounted within gold pendants which were further embellished with colourful enamel, set with hardstone cameos or decorated with simple table-cut diamonds and polished gems. Rings – worn extensively throughout Scotland and England – took on a new significance after the execution of Charles I in 1649 when large numbers of Royalist mementoes were produced containing an enamelled portrait of the unfortunate king. In Scotland sympathisers of the Jacobite cause wore similar miniatures depicting Prince Charles Edward Stuart, better known as Bonnie Prince Charlie. Simple ring brooches of flattened form made from gold, silver and base metal – as functional as they were decorative – were used to fasten the material of coarse plaid worn by women during the 17th and 18th centuries. Ring brooches can still be picked up quite cheaply and sometimes exhibit beautiful engraving, complex in its intricacy. Another popular Scottish brooch, the luckenbooth, was worn as a good luck token offering protection against the 'evil eye'. Usually made from silver or brass, designs were based on the heart and could be

Victorian hardstone and gold Celtic cross mounted with bloodstone and jasper sections, c.1870.

Good quality Scottish vari-colour agate brooch with crown surmount and Queen Mary monogram to the centre. Note the combined French and Scottish fleur-de-lis and thistle motifs.

Scottish group including a fine silver plaid brooch at bottom left mounted with foil-back amethyst and 'Cairngorm' citrine. Note the discoloration caused by water damage.

extremely simple or highly elaborate. Some luckenbooths contained a monogram of two entwined hearts shaped like the letter 'M' which were known as Queen Mary brooches.

Queen Victoria's tremendous affection for Scotland is well known. In 1848 she purchased Balmoral Castle and in those happier days before the untimely death of Prince Albert in 1861 the Royal children customarily wore tartan dress, whilst at the Great Exhibition Ball of 1851 all the guests were expected to wear Scottish dress

Scottish jewellery in gold and silver mounts. Condition is a critical issue since missing hardstones are extremely difficult and costly to replace. Novelties such as keys and axes or accessories such as the vinaigrette at lower right are rare and desirable today.

adorned with jewelled accessories such as brooches, dirks and buckles. This highly romanticised idealism was further reinforced by Sir Walter Scott who wrote passionately about the sweeping grandeur of the hills and valleys, so articulating an emotional fascination with Scotland which, even today, has barely diminished.

By the 1850s Scotland's soaring popularity resulted in large numbers of people visiting the country, all clamouring for a souvenir of their holiday. A pretty hardstone brooch, curio or accessory served this purpose

Unusual vari-colour agate coiled serpent bangle, c.1860.

Top: Victorian cylindrical baton bracelet with faceted gold cap finials and red jasper floral padlock clasp together with a gold-mounted grey-banded agate. Above: Jasper bracelet with citrine and agate centrepiece, c.1850.

admirably. Scottish hardstone or 'pebble' jewellery was largely inspired by the established designs of centuries old Celtic and folk jewellery. Probably the best example was the silver plaid brooch which was used to secure the tartan at the shoulder. These large ring-shaped brooches were often set to the centre with an imposing golden-brown citrine called, appropriately enough, a cairngorm. In other examples the cairngorm would be substituted by a very pale lemon-yellow citrine, a colourless rock crystal or even golden glass. It was also common to leave the centre aperture entirely vacant. The broad silver frames would then be mounted with a series of vari-coloured hardstone panels, individually cut and shaped to fit the contours of the hoop-shaped surround. The colours of these hardstones were, in themselves, highly suggestive of the wild cragginess of the Scottish countryside, blending the rich browns, yellows, greys and russet shades of heath and heather, mountain and stream. Thus, a typical Scottish silver brooch would be composed of a combination of orangey-brown cornelian, subtle grey banded agate, deep green bloodstone with its characteristic flecks of red, mottled jasper with curious marbling of red, mustard and black, and onyx with distinctive bands of black and white.

Cutting these stones was often difficult and many were sent to Idar-Oberstein in Germany for finishing and polishing. These thin stone slices would then be set into plain or engraved silver mounts, often with a black tar-like shellac material behind to strengthen the colours when seen from the front. Apart from citrine and rock crystal, the other crystalline material in frequent use was amethyst, a particularly appropriate gemstone when carved into the shape of thistles.

William IV Scottish gold bracelet composed of a series of square agate plaques with smaller agate spacers, the clasp mounted with a portrait miniature of a Scottish fusilier. Engraved on the reverse 'Mary Field, Edinburgh, 6th August 1833'.

Gold and gilt-metal stickpin mounted with a miniature portrait of Robbie Burns. Signed on the reverse 'W.B.Ford 1886'.

Victorian gold-mounted citrine, agate, bloodstone and jasper circular brooch engraved 'Mrs Francis J W Sutton – Falkirk', c.1850.

Victorian circular Scottish gold brooch with Maltese cross centre in a hoop frame decorated with black line enamel and set with five Scottish freshwater pearls, c.1850.

Plaid brooches and thistles were just two examples of a broad range of Scottish themes, including miniature dirks with tiny removable daggers slotted in the front, rapiers with polished hardstone shafts, hearts, knots, buckles, straps, shields and anchors. The use of hardstones was not purely confined to jewellery; indeed a whole spectrum of practical small accessories was also produced including vesta boxes, vinaigrettes and sovereign cases.

By 1870 over one thousand people were directly or indirectly employed in Edinburgh alone in the pebble industry and smaller communities thrived in Aberdeen, Glasgow and even as far south as Birmingham. The Aberdeen firm of Rettie & Co. was particularly associated with a locally extracted pink and grey granite which proved an effective combination when set in geometric brooches and bracelets. Not all the hardstones were indigenous to Scotland, however. Malachite, frequently carved into the shape of ivy leaves, was actually imported from the frozen wastes of Siberia, via Germany.

Although the majority of Scottish pebble jewellery was mounted in silver, some extremely fine pieces were also fashioned in gold. Bracelets, for example, were either composed of hinged sections decorated with flat polished hardstone panels in 'marquetry' formation or in three-dimensional 'barrels' with engraved gold cap fittings.

Scotland was also an important location for the Arts and Crafts movement at the end of the 19th century, standing out for the incredible wealth of creative talent which seemed to gravitate to the Glasgow School of Art. Here innovative craftsmen and women formed close working (and personal) relationships producing a wonderful range of decorative arts both rich in symbolism and proficient in technical application. Probably the best known of all these exponents was Charles Rennie Mackintosh (1868-1928) who pioneered ground-breaking organic forms in furniture and interiors.

Among many designer jewellers, three women made a particular impact: Jessie M. King (1875-1949) was a somewhat eccentric illustrator who also made silk fabrics for Liberty & Co. and designed naturalistic gold jewellery for the London store; Mary Thew (1876-1953) was a metalworker who used abalone shell in interesting Celtic brooches whilst Phoebe Anna Traquair (1852-1936) was probably the most versatile and celebrated of all the Glasgow School goldsmiths producing beautiful, glowing enamelled gold necklaces and pendants heavily influenced by the work of the Pre-Raphaelite movement.

Further reading

Victorian Jewelry: Unexplored Treasures, Ginny Redington Dawes and Corinne Davidov (Abbeville Press Publishers, 1991)

The Art of Jewellery in Scotland, edited by R.K. Marshall and G.R. Dalgleish (Scottish National Portrait Gallery, 1991)

Chapter 10

Jewelled Flora and Fauna

Flowers, from the basic trefoil of three petals to massive bouquets worn as corsage ornaments by the aristocracy, have underpinned jewellery design since the 17th century. Early floral sprays were usually enamelled in several colours since gemstone cutting, particularly diamond, was still fairly rudimentary.

As time progressed designs became increasingly lavish, especially when gold replaced silver as the standard metal. Eighteenth-century diamond brooches and aigrette sprays could be extremely flamboyant, setting hundreds of diamonds in pavé formation with superb coloured gems such as Burmese rubies and Indian emeralds highly prized for their exquisite colour and rarity. Many jewelled bouquets were embellished with tied bows around the stems allowing individual craftsmen to show off their skill by deftly weaving trails of ribbon within their framework. English late 18th-century diamond brooches often conformed to a simple and highly effective design in which six uniform size petals were fully enclosed in silver and pavé-set with clusters of 'old-mine' diamonds of pure quality surrounding a larger stone to the centre. Tasteful, practical and perfectly wearable today, Georgian diamond flowers attract strong competition when they appear at auction.

Impressive Victorian fully articulated diamond corsage brooch, c.1880, designed as a trailing spray of wild rose, the principal flowerhead mounted en tremblant*; at the apex of the brooch rests an exotic butterfly, its outstretched wings set with diamonds, emeralds, sapphires, golden topaz and ruby cabochon eyes. Something of a tour de force of the manufacturing jeweller's prowess, this splendid brooch exhibits all the confidence and technical virtuosity of English diamond jewellery at the height of the Victorian era.*

A particularly charming example of 18th-century naturalistic jewellery was the *giardinetti* ring or brooch. These 'little gardens' were set with a cluster of rose diamonds, emeralds, rubies and occasionally sapphires in floral compositions in which the principal gem sometimes formed a stylised vase. Care should be taken since many cheap and inferior modern copies regularly turn up on the market; the later examples are often badly set with modern-cut stones.

Floral jewellery of the early 19th century was delicate and feminine in inspiration. Brooches, earrings and necklaces placed great emphasis on gold work in which the settings were finely textured, realistically engraved to represent leaves, embellished with wirework tendrils or complicated granulation and cannetille scrolls. There was far greater use of colourful semi-precious stones such as amethyst, aquamarine, topaz and turquoise which were ideal companions for naturalistic and floral designs. Turquoise in particular was liberally used in flower jewellery of the 1830s and 1840s because of its direct association with forget-me-not. The bright blue gem was thus the perfect vehicle for expressing affection and sentiment captured in charming dove brooches bearing messages of love in their beaks, ears of corn and woodland sprays.

Another gem which was ideally suited to the naturalistic passion was coral. A speciality of Italy and particularly associated in England with Robert Phillips, the celebrated London jeweller, coral was of sufficient hardness to carve into all manner of highly elaborate designs such as sprays of flowers with accompanying

Regency diamond brooch fashioned as a spray of dog rose, c.1825, the principal flowerhead mounted en tremblant *and set with a large old-mine cushion-shaped diamond collet in a diamond encrusted frame with similarly set leaves and buds.*

Pretty late-Victorian gold-mounted and silver-set diamond flower brooch designed as a posy of gingko leaves and foliate spray, c.1880.

Late 18th-century oval gold and blue glass plaque locket-back brooch/pendant applied with a rose-cut diamond floral spray, the principal flowerhead mounted en tremblant*; rose diamond border.*

Elegant Art Nouveau gold brooch/pendant, c.1900, designed as a bouquet of anemones, their petals matte enamelled in merging shades of pastel pink and lilac with tiny rose diamond stamens and pearl suspension drop; matching neck chain.

Unusual diamond and gem-set giardinetto ('little garden') brooch, c.1910, the vase composed of a single fancy-cut light yellowish-brown diamond and containing a spray of colourful flowers set with rubies, fancy colour diamonds and a demantoid garnet.

Nineteenth-century realism; French gold brooch attributed to Fonseque et Olive mounted with frosted green glass berries with diamond stems and gold leaves, c.1890.

Early 19th-century gold two-row necklace, c.1815, the centrepiece designed as a cannetille work butterfly set with a colourful combination of gems including amethyst, garnet and chrysolite, the back chain of later manufacture interspaced with matching coloured gem collets and drops.

Colourful turn-of-the-century gold grasshopper brooch, c.1905, mounted with a blue opal abdomen, enamelled wings and diamond-set thorax.

Insect brooch by Giuliano with polished amethyst cabochon body and half pearl-set wings with enamel veins, c.1890.

Highly realistic gold brooch modelled as a red admiral butterfly with painted enamel wings, diamond body and ruby cabochon eyes, c.1880.

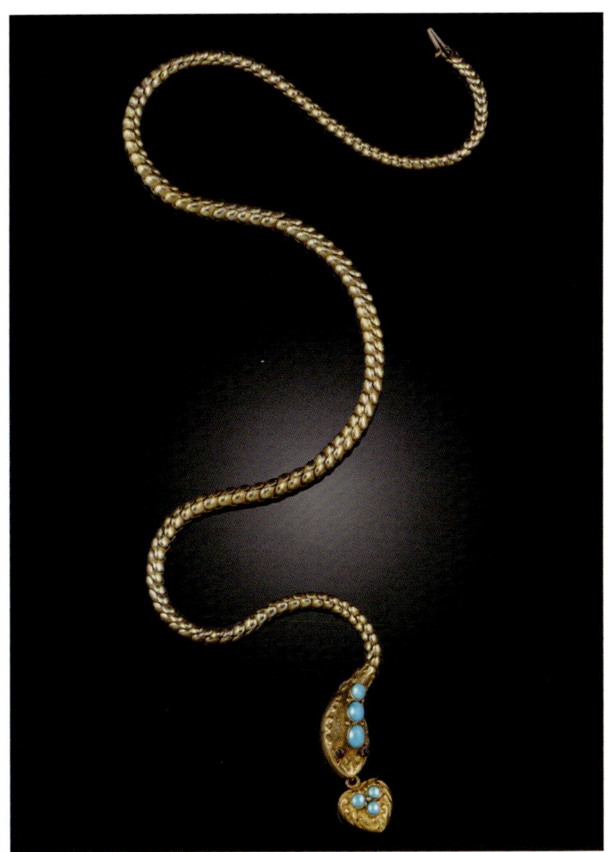

Early Victorian sentimental gold coiled serpent ring, c.1845, with a large diamond set in its head and ruby cabochon eyes. Note the discreet gold locket compartment set in the hoop.

Early Victorian gold serpent necklace, c.1845, the head and heart-shaped locket back drop set with turquoises.

Jewelled reptiles and amphibians: a group of Victorian gold snake necklaces, bracelets, brooches and rings, c.1840-1850, including examples decorated with turquoise, pyrope garnet, diamond, ruby, opal, royal blue enamel and sky-blue enamel together with a late Victorian demantoid garnet and diamond frog brooch.

leaves and buds or 'woodland' themes such as trees and branches. Coral also takes a satisfyingly high polish and larger pieces were reserved for rather extraordinary and imaginative forms such as grotesques, satyrs, sea serpents and monsters which ingeniously conformed to the shape of the original material. Much of this type of coral was a characteristic salmon pink colour, but white coral was also suitable for pretty flower brooches and necklaces carved into sprays of orange blossom or convolvulus with little rubies studded in their engraved gold mounts.

The 19th-century fixation with nature extended to animals, birds, reptiles and insects. The snake was especially popular in the 1840s and 1850s and considerable numbers of necklaces, bracelets and rings were produced in bright yellow gold, fully articulated to suggest the sinuous flow of the serpent's body with cobra-like heads set with diamonds and gems enamelled in royal blue, sky-blue or even studded all the way round with scores of little cabochons of turquoise. Usually a heart-shaped pendant containing a lock of hair was suspended from the reptile's mouth and the eyes were set with ruby or garnet cabochons. Snakes represented 'love eternal' in Victorian England and were thus a potent symbol of sentiment as well as a highly effective design for fashion jewellery.

Another mid-Victorian curiosity was the *reverse crystal* where a domed piece of colourless rock crystal was carved from behind and painted with the image of an animal, bird, insect or flower. Designs were limitless and examples ranged from favourite domestic pets such as pug dogs, cats and even goldfish to wild animals of which lions, tigers and foxes were especially popular. The little paintings were often colourful and highly accomplished; bumble bees were so realistic that many people assume today that the insect is genuine, perpetually trapped beneath a magnifying dome of crystal. Mounted in gold with backplates of mother-of-pearl, reverse crystal is extremely collectable either in large-scale brooches or small-scale stickpins and cufflinks.

Jewelled insects: a flight of late Victorian and turn-of-the-century diamond and gem-set dragonfly and bumble bee brooches.

Victorian reverse crystal jewels, c.1860-1880. Painted miniatures depicting animal, insect and bird subjects captured beneath a dome of rock crystal. Many of these painted miniatures were not only highly proficient in their execution, but examples such as the bumble bee and hen harrier were anatomically remarkably accurate to life. Hugely popular, these intricate painted miniatures encompassed a vast range of subjects from domestic pets to exotic Bengal tigers and decorative birds. Clockwise, from top left: Reverse crystal and gold bumble bee pendant, c.1870; Hen harrier; Robin; Swan; Red squirrels; White domestic cat.

By the end of the 19th century 'scatter bugs' fashioned in gold and silver and set with diamonds and appropriately colourful gems were produced in an enormous range of designs from spiders, flies, bees and butterflies to reptiles, in particular frogs and salamanders.

These cleverly fashioned lizards were often set with diamonds and demantoids, the lovely and valuable green variety of commonplace red garnet in which the striking green colour aptly suggested the skin tone of the living creature.

Many of these insects and flowers were mounted on coiled gold springs so that even the gentlest of movements resulted in a fluttering or scintillating effect. Known as *en tremblant*, the delicate trembling both allowed the gems to twinkle with little flashes of light and reinforced the realism of nature elegantly displayed in a man-made jewel.

Further reading

Jewellery in the Age of Queen Victoria, Charlotte Gere and Judy Rudoe (British Museum Press, 2010)

Chapter 11
Jewels of Sentiment and Love

Jewellery, of all man-made objects, must surely represent the most tangible and enduring method of conveying long-term commitment and undying affection between friends and lovers. In its simplest form – a simple band of gold or metal – the tradition can be traced back to the Romans when a ring would be presented as a solemn pledge symbolising a formal contract or agreement between families. Hardly sentimental, but this practice ultimately led to the concept of giving an engagement ring representing a formal intention of betrothal before the wedding ceremony took place. The fashion for wearing wedding rings on the fourth finger of the left hand also has its origins in Roman times since it was believed that a nerve ran directly from there to the heart itself.

Above: An early 19th-century gold fede or friendship ring in its closed position.

Above, right: The ring opened to reveal its construction of three flat gold bands pinned together at the back. The raised motif at the top of the centre hoop is a tiny gold heart.

Throughout the Middle Ages and well into the 18th century, rings were made bearing a sentimental inscription or an affectionate message either within or engraved upon the surface of the hoop itself. These rings were collectively known as *posies* and appear on the market fairly regularly. Superficially, they look rather like plain gold wedding rings and thus can avoid detection unless examined carefully with a loupe. The inscriptions were usually in English, occasionally in French, and took the form of a simple verse such as 'God Above Increase Our Love' or 'In Thee A Flame – In Me The Same' or an intimate message on the lines of 'Joie Sans Fyn' (Joy Without End). The introduction of the Wedding Ring Act made hallmarks a compulsory feature in gold wedding bands and the fashion for posy rings quickly lapsed.

A form of betrothal ring popular in the 16th and 17th centuries was the *gimmel* named after Gemellus – a twin. Gimmel rings were composed of two identical hoops, usually enamelled and inscribed, which fitted together snugly but could be disconnected and worn separately by each partner. Two halves forming a whole was thus highly symbolic and it is perhaps surprising that the fashion for

Group of three late 17th-/early 18th-century gold posy rings engraved with the following inscriptions, from left to right: 'Feare God'; 'Let our accord bee blest O Lord'; 'Love for ever'.

Heart-shaped diamond, ruby and enamel heart and coronet ring – an extremely desirable example of early 18th-century sentimentality.

Gold bracelet mounted with a group of early 19th-century gem-set gold lockets and locket back pendants. These pretty jewelled appendages were often decorated with three- or four-colour gold foliage.

gimmels has been dormant for so long. Another romantic love token of the 18th and early 19th centuries was the *fede* or 'hand-in-hand' ring. Fede rings were generally made out of three separate hoops, either gold or silver, which were joined at the back by a tiny connecting rod which allowed the hoops to swivel. When fully closed, the top of a fede ring shows two hands clasped together in friendship but when parted the hands reveal a miniature heart. This idea became particularly widespread in Ireland with the claddagh ring fashioned in the design of a heart flanked by two hands but in a single rigid construction.

The combination of 'two hearts entwined' has been an enduringly popular design for rings and small brooches from the early 18th century to the present day. Superficially, their appearance has barely altered over the years; however, Georgian examples are decidedly prettier than their later counterparts, invariably set with cushion-shaped 'old-mine' diamonds and gems in fully enclosed backs which may exhibit engraved sunburst fluting. The shoulders of these earlier rings are often carved with

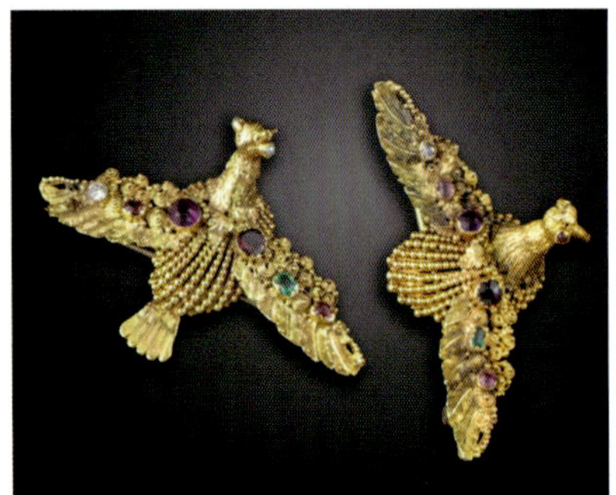

Two Regency gold acrostic cannetille work dove brooches, c.1825, each set with Ruby, Emerald, Garnet, Amethyst, Ruby and Diamond, spelling the motto 'Regard.'.

Regency gold acrostic quiver of arrows brooch, c.1825, set with coloured gems spelling 'regard'.

George III gold double heart ring, c.1780, set with a pear-shaped garnet and rock crystal in a border of rubies and emeralds with gem-set coronet above.

rococo scrolls whilst the hearts themselves are further decorated with a bow or miniature coronet above. Victorian and later examples are altogether more flashy and 'harder' looking with tell-tale open backs, machined gold hoops and – needless to say – modern-cut gems.

The heart is unquestionably the most potent symbol of love used in all aspects of Victorian jewellery from brooches to lockets and bracelets to cufflinks.

Hearts were ideal for decorating in enamel – frequently sky-blue or navy – and later examples were sometimes pavé-set with half pearls or rose diamonds. A most charming idea was particularly fashionable in the 1830s and 1840s where a heart-shaped locket was set with a line of coloured stones on a mount richly embellished with *trois couleur* or *quatre couleur* gold floral decoration. The initial letter of each stone spelled a message of intimacy such as REGARD (Ruby, Emerald, Garnet, Amethyst, Ruby, Diamond) or DEAREST. A miniature key attached to the suspension ring locked or unlocked the heart itself which might contain a woven plume of hair.

This idea of conveying intimacy was an important feature of early Victorian romantic jewellery with a wide range of sentimental subjects – cupids, arrows, keys, padlocks, anchors and bows – set with pretty gems (especially turquoise, pearl, ruby and diamond) in finely engraved gold settings decorated with twisted wire, beading and cannetille scrollwork. Flowers suggested their own particular mood or sentiment; roses for happiness and love; ivy for friendship; broom for humility; turquoise

Gold meshwork bracelet, c.1830. This ravishing example is embellished with rubies and diamonds to the cuff, the hand and the hoop.

Fine Regency trois couleur *gold acrostic heart-shaped locket with gem-set motto spelling 'regard', pearl cluster centre, foliate decoration and glazed locket-back compartment.*

Regency gold acrostic gem-set purse-locket suspended from a finely textured gold hand with ruby 'finger ring' and coloured gold cuff.

Regency gold cannetille-work sentimental padlock pendant/brooch studded with turquoises with similarly set heart and key suspension drops, c.1825. The colour of forget-me-nots, turquoise conveyed true love and adoration in the era of 'the language of flowers'.

William IV gold sentimental bracelet, c.1835, composed of a series of six rhomboid glazed sections, the four central sections each containing two painted miniatures depicting the children of the Suffolk Nottidge family, the two end sections each with two painted eye miniatures; the reverse of the bracelet engraved with the individual children's names. Quatrefoil link connections.

Victorian gold hinged bangle with entwined twin natural white pearl and diamond heart and bow cluster centre between diamond scroll shoulders, c.1880.

Victorian entwined double diamond heart brooch with diamond bow surmount, c.1880.

Late Victorian ruby, diamond and sapphire twin heart, coronet and hoop brooch in patriotic colours which coincided with the Diamond Jubilee of 1897.

for remembrance and pansy for dwelling in my thoughts. Late 18th- and early 19th-century French rings, brooches and seals were almost cloying with this sentimental ideal; cameos and intaglios depicted fat little putti, doves and lovebirds in tiny cages and lions harnessed to miniature chariots symbolising 'love tamed' or 'love trapped'.

Unswerving devotion was also the key feature of late 18th- and early 19th-century memorial jewellery in which classically shaped brooches and rings contained under glass covers vignettes of ladies weeping tragically beside a plinth with urn surmount apparently containing the remains of the dear departed. Decorated with blue and white enamel, they were set with tiny rose diamonds or seed pearls symbolising tears and touchingly engraved with a suitable inscription on the back of the mounts.

Late Victorian Britain was deluged with a tidal wave of cheap and cheerful sentimental jewellery from silver 'name' brooches to little gold pins decorated with gem-set and half pearl flowers, horseshoes and birds – particularly swallows. Inexpensive engraved heart-shaped lockets fashioned in metal with gold 'fronts and backs' were made to contain a photograph or a lock of hair, while circular glass lockets in rims of gold or gilt might display the photograph of a brave young soldier off to fight in the Boer Wars. Needless to say, the number of these evocative mementoes rose steeply during the early years of the First World War, as did Regimental bar brooches and patriotic 'emblem' pins such as bog-oak shamrock brooches and 'Good Luck' horseshoe pendants, stickpins and bangles.

Further reading

A History of Jewellery 1100-1870, Joan Evans (Faber & Faber, 1970)

Victorian Jewellery, Margaret Flower (Cassell, 1951)

The Triumph of Love: Jewellery 1530-1950, Geoffrey C. Munn (Thames & Hudson, 1993)

Jewellery in Britain 1066-1837, Diana Scarisbrick (Michael Russell Publishing Ltd, 1994)

English Posies and Posy Rings, Andrew Schuller (facsimile edition Wartski and ACC Editions, 2012)

Chapter 12

Reviving History in the 19th Century

The Great Exhibition of 1851

For those successful, privileged and wealthy Victorians living in Britain in the middle part of the 19th century, cultural life must surely have been a grand and exciting experience. A burgeoning tourist industry meant that people who had the means to do so were travelling to European cities such as Paris, Rome, Venice and Florence and further afield to Athens and exotic Cairo to wonder at the astonishing architecture and treasures of the Ancients. At the same time intrepid explorers were bringing back from their travels the art and merchandise of Africa, Asia and the Orient. In 1851 a vast accumulation of artefacts were assembled for 'The Great Exhibition of the Works of Industry of All Nations'. Here, in an area covering nineteen acres in what was subsequently known as the Crystal Palace, the wealth and cultural diversity of the British Empire and beyond was put on

Carrying in the Peacock *by John Dawson Watson exhibiting a range of Gothic necklaces which would have been fashionable in 1869, the year in which this painting was completed.*

display for the benefit of well over six million visitors. Unsurprisingly, the Great Exhibition also gave scores of international jewellers a unique platform to show off their artistic creations inspired by themes as diverse as nature, archaeology, the Church, the Renaissance, the Middle Ages and ancient Rome.

Classical Revivalism

Looking back 150 years, it is today a little difficult to comprehend the overwhelming fascination bordering on obsession felt by the Victorians for the rich treasures of the ancient world. Intrepid exploration had led to some amazing discoveries from the long forgotten civilisations of Assyria, Etruria, Mesopotamia and Greece, many of which were still in superb condition and extremely sophisticated in both design and execution. Soon the public were clamouring for jewellery which matched the breathtaking beauty of two-thousand-year-old Greek gold torcs, Roman collars and bracelets, Assyrian armlets and Etruscan earrings. The so-called *archaeological* jewellery of the 1860s and 1870s represented an extremely important development in the way gold was both fashioned and worn and also saw the success of a number of Italian, French and English goldsmiths who were key to the evolution of jewellery design in the 19th century.

Without doubt, the most celebrated of goldsmiths working in the archaeological style was Fortunato Pio Castellani (1794-1865). As early as the 1830s Castellani and his son Alessandro (1823-1883) had studied the lost art of the granulation mastered by the ancient Etruscan civilisation.

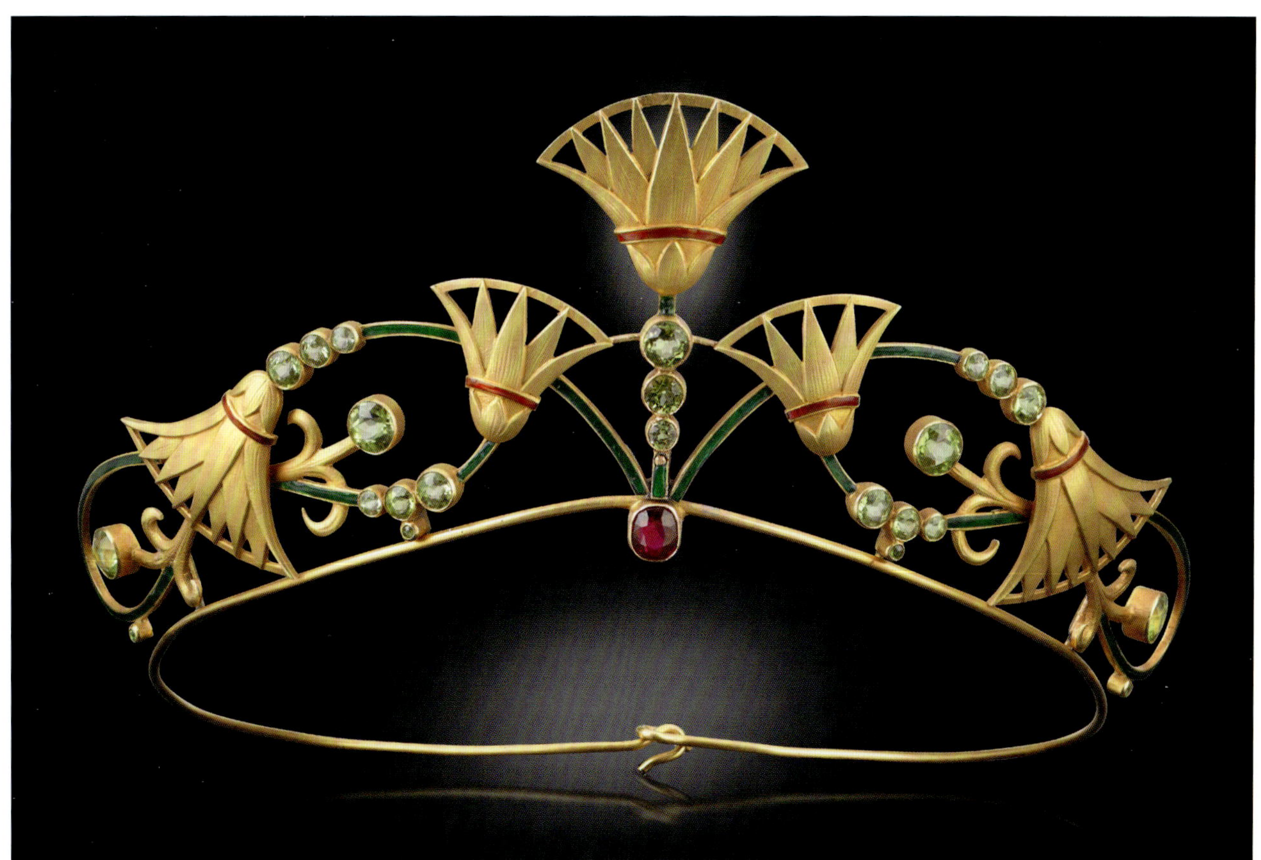

Superb Egyptian Revival gold hair ornament, c.1900, convertible to a choker necklace designed as entwining lotus flowers of finely textured gold with translucent red and green enamel decoration, a central ruby collet and circular graduated peridots to the gold stems.

This technique involved the application of thousands of tiny beads of gold on to a smooth surface which was further embellished with filigree wires soldered into coils and scrolls. Although Castellani never quite achieved the prowess of the ancient craftsmen, he certainly did manage to produce a superb range of bright yellow-gold jewellery which, to reinforce the classical ideal, was often mounted with Roman or Greek coins, gem cameos or intaglios and Egyptian scarabs carved from hardstones such as cornelian and lapis lazuli. After F.P. Castellani died, the business was continued by Alessandro and his brother Augusto (1829-1914), selling an extensive output primarily from Naples as well as branches located in Paris and London. Considering the sheer quantity of pieces which were produced well into the 20th century, it is surprising that such a limited number appear on the market today; fine examples can easily fetch well into five figures although condition is an important consideration. The Castellani mark is a monogram of two entwined 'Cs' in back-to-back formation.

The classical ideal was embraced in motifs which brought to mind symbols easily associated with the

Italian classical revival gold brooch in the style of Castellani, c.1860, with ram's head centre amidst clusters of millefiori flowers, arched surround with twin ram's head finials and gold amphora drops and circular pendant below with a grotesque mask.

Classical revival gold brooch by Castellani of quatrefoil-shape with deep green and turquoise cloisonné enamel decoration and set with emeralds and ruby cabochons with four pearls extending from the edge of the frame, c.1865.

Fine-quality 19th-century Italian Etruscan revival gold ram's head bangle, c.1860, the tapering cylindrical hoop profusely decorated with scrolling rope pattern wirework, the ram's head finely engraved to suggest the fleece.

Late 19th-century Egyptian revival pendant designed as a spray of lotus flowers decorated throughout with polychrome enamel, set to the centre with two small lapis lazuli beads and five larger lapis lazuli ball drops, c.1890.

Austrian Egyptian revival gold pendant by Carl Bacher fashioned as a vulture mounted with a diamond-set sapphire cabochon suggesting a scarab beetle, its outstretched wings decorated with white and blue enamel; ruby-set claws and pearl chain, c.1880.

ancients. Popular designs included the *amphora,* a vessel for holding wine which lent itself perfectly to drops on a necklace or pairs of earrings. The *bulla,* a type of round, hollow container, often depicted Latin words such as 'pax' or 'Roma', the *fibula* was a simple 'Roman' gold cloak fastener while Egyptian symbols such as lotus flowers, scarabs, pharaohs and the Sphinx were effortlessly adapted for use on pendants and brooches by means of colourful and exotic micromosaic panels.

Leading contemporaries of Castellani are also celebrated for their accomplished gold work. Giacinto Melillo (1846-1915) initially studied as Castellani's pupil in the Naples workshop before setting up his own business specialising in intricate granulation on classical motifs such as the cornucopia and the putto. Ernesto Pierret (1824-1898) and Eugène Fontenay (1823-1887) both produced outstanding gold necklaces and pendants decorated with mosaic and enamel while John Brogden (active 1842-1855) was a London goldsmith who produced technically fine pieces, strongly Assyrian in influence, which incorporated fine cameos in gold frames decorated with colourful enamel or sturdy bangles and brooches mounted with eye-catching coral, turquoise and cabochons of almandine and pyrope garnet.

Gothic Revivalism

In exactly the same way as 19th-century craftsmen revived the lost techniques and designs of ancient goldsmiths, so jewellers in England and France became fascinated with the art, culture and associated symbolism of the Middle Ages. Classical revivalist jewellery is nearly always set in bright yellow

Bangle wrought to depict medieval rustics in bacchanalian revelry, a tour de force of French 19th-century revivalist goldwork c.1870.

Nineteenth-century neo-Gothic gold necklace and pendant by Louis Wiese, c.1890. Of medieval inspiration, designed as a young woman in a Gothic scrollwork frame, the accompanying chain is interspaced with heads and grotesque masks.

Nineteenth-century neo-Gothic gold pendant, c.1890, with enamelled portrait of a young woman in French medieval costume in an enamelled scrolling frame. Many similar French pendants and brooches were mounted with colourful Limoges enamel plaques of Joan of Arc, undoubtedly the best-known character from the medieval period.

gold frames but, in keeping with the near-primitive output of the 13th and 14th centuries, many of the 19th-century 'medieval' jewels are fashioned in silver set with extremely basic cabochon-cut gemstones or panels of coloured glass.

Gothic revivalism extended from the 1830s to the late 1890s. Much Berlin ironwork jewellery was strongly medieval in design and the black shiny metal lent itself admirably to themes which were clearly inspired by church architecture, angels and deities. François-Désiré Froment-Meurice (1802-1855) was a Parisian craftsman well known for ornate, three-dimensional bracelets and brooches fashioned in a combination of gold and oxidised silver which became known as the *style cathédrale*. Chivalry, the romance of the Arthurian legend, knights in shining armour and monstrous grotesques all strongly influenced craftsmen working in the Gothic taste; probably the two best known English designers were A.W.N. Pugin (1812-1852) and the architect William Burges (1827-1881) who both produced wonderfully evocative jewels in silver and gold which were plainly inspired by religious symbolism. Jules Wiese (1818-1890) and his son Louis (1852-1923) used simple gem cabochons such as ruby and sapphire in curiously distinctive hammered gold jewellery which was almost crude in its 'medieval' simplicity. This distinctive aspect of Wiese gold work is highly collectable today and correspondingly expensive. Towards the end of the century brightly coloured enamel, silver and gem-set pendants and necklaces became fashionable throughout Europe. So-called 'Austro-Hungarian' jewellery combines both Gothic and Renaissance themes using traditional

Nineteenth-century neo-Gothic gold bracelet by Castellani composed of six sections each embossed with the profile of a medieval scholar, philosopher or artist with a further embossed section of an owl representing wisdom all within black enamel borders, c.1860.

Nineteenth-century neo-Gothic silver and green enamel brooch by François-Désiré Froment-Meurice designed as the figure of 'Harmonie' playing a cello flanked by cherubs in a frame of ivy leaves and winged dragons with pearl drops and finials, c.1850.

Nineteenth-century neo-Gothic silver cruciform brooch attributed to John Hardman & Co., the design in the manner of William Burges, c.1875. The crosspiece finials enamelled in cream and white with Tudor rose motifs and set with tourmaline cabochons.

and legendary subjects such as a 'Pelican in Piety' or 'St George slaying the Dragon'. Frequently crude, garish and extremely common, these Continental jewels – brooches, crosses and pendants – can often be bought at auction for as little as £250.

Renaissance Revivalism

From around 1860 to 1880 several versatile jewellers began to work in a combination of two styles – neo-classical and neo-Renaissance. The highly colourful and imaginative designs of the 16th and early 17th centuries inspired 19th-century goldsmiths to create polychrome enamel and gold pendants, necklaces, brooches and earrings which were frequently set with hardstone cameos and a variety of semi-precious and precious gems in a range of styles which included galleons (called nefs), mythical beasts, classical deities, animals and birds.

Pearls were particularly important in 19th-century neo-Renaissance jewellery. Just like their earlier counter-parts, pendants were mounted with unusually shaped

Nineteenth-century neo-Gothic silver bracelet by Froment Meurice, c.1850, the oval centre plaque embossed with a figure of a maiden playing a lute flanked by two silver angelic figures holding either a hawk or a mirror, the silver-gilt bracelet profusely decorated with scrolls, birds and the heads of cherubim.

Late 19th-century neo-Renaissance pendant fashioned as an enamelled swan with diamond and pearl-set enamelled gold mount, c.1880. Many 16th-century jewels are virtually indistinguishable from 19th-century copies. Fortunately, advances in the scientific testing of enamel are paving the way towards conclusively verifying the age of jewellery such as this pendant.

Late 19th-century neo-Renaissance polychrome enamel and baroque pearl pendant depicting Porphyrion, king of the Greek Gigantes with the arrow of Apollo in his hand and wearing the laurels of Delphi, c.1880.

baroque pearls which could be cleverly set with little stones or embellished in gold to suggest, say, the body of an animal, a sea-serpent or a mermaid. These 19th-century copies were sometimes so well crafted that they are extremely difficult to tell apart from earlier 'genuine' examples, a factor which has led to several well-documented – and quite acrimonious – disputes.

A popular variety of neo-Renaissance gold work is the aptly named *Holbeinesque* jewel. Richly enamelled in several different colours and set with a combination of gems such as cabochon garnet and pale green chrysolite, these polychrome pendants and necklaces were made in the 1870s and are notable for their fine tracing of flowers and scrolls on the back of the frames. Neo-Renaissance jewellery was largely inspired by the Romantic movement which spread through Europe in the first half of the century. The goldsmith most closely associated with the fashion – and one of the most important figures in the world of antique jewellery – was Carlo Giuliano (1831-1895), a Neapolitan who trained under Castellani and subsequently settled in London where he opened a shop at 115 Piccadilly specialising in both classical and Renaissance art jewels. Giuliano excelled in the application of enamel in beautifully wrought gold settings.

Austro-Hungarian late 19th-century neo-Renaissance silver necklace composed of a series of circular domed clusters set with garnet and turquoise and decorated with coloured enamel, c.1880. Jewellery such as this is often fairly crudely made and easy to identify. Mounted in silver, the backs are frequently pierced with elaborate scrolling decoration.

Austro-Hungarian neo-Renaissance silver cruciform pendant set with pale cloudy emeralds, baroque pearls and pink gems, c.1880.

The enamel itself was sometimes further decorated with little spots of a contrasting colour and the mounts were sympathetically matched with bouton pearls and gems notable for their reticence and character rather than their opulence and value. After Giuliano's death the aesthetic ideal was continued by his two sons, Carlo and Arthur, who produced wonderfully understated jewellery primarily enamelled in black and white. Carlo Giuliano's signature is the monogram 'CG' in an oval cartouche while later pieces are signed 'C & AG'. Care should be taken since signatures

'Holbeinesque' neo-Renaissance emerald, diamond and enamel pendant, c.1870.

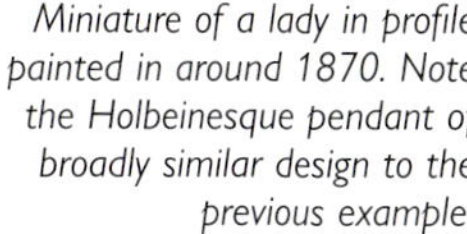

Miniature of a lady in profile painted in around 1870. Note the Holbeinesque pendant of broadly similar design to the previous example.

Carlo Giuliano at his most accomplished. A set of gold necklace and earrings mounted with pyrope garnet and green enamel flowerheads with pearl and enamel fringe drops in between. Registered in November 1867.

Opposite page: Elegant gold necklace by C. & A. Giuliano composed of six rows of natural pearls with diamond-set black and white enamelled arabesque panel sections extending to scrolling enamelled openwork finials and suspending a matching diamond-set enamelled pendant with pearl drop, c.1895. The Giuliano workshop specialised in this kind of intricate gold work featuring monochrome enamelling, often set with subtle understated coloured gems such as zircon and chrysoberyl.

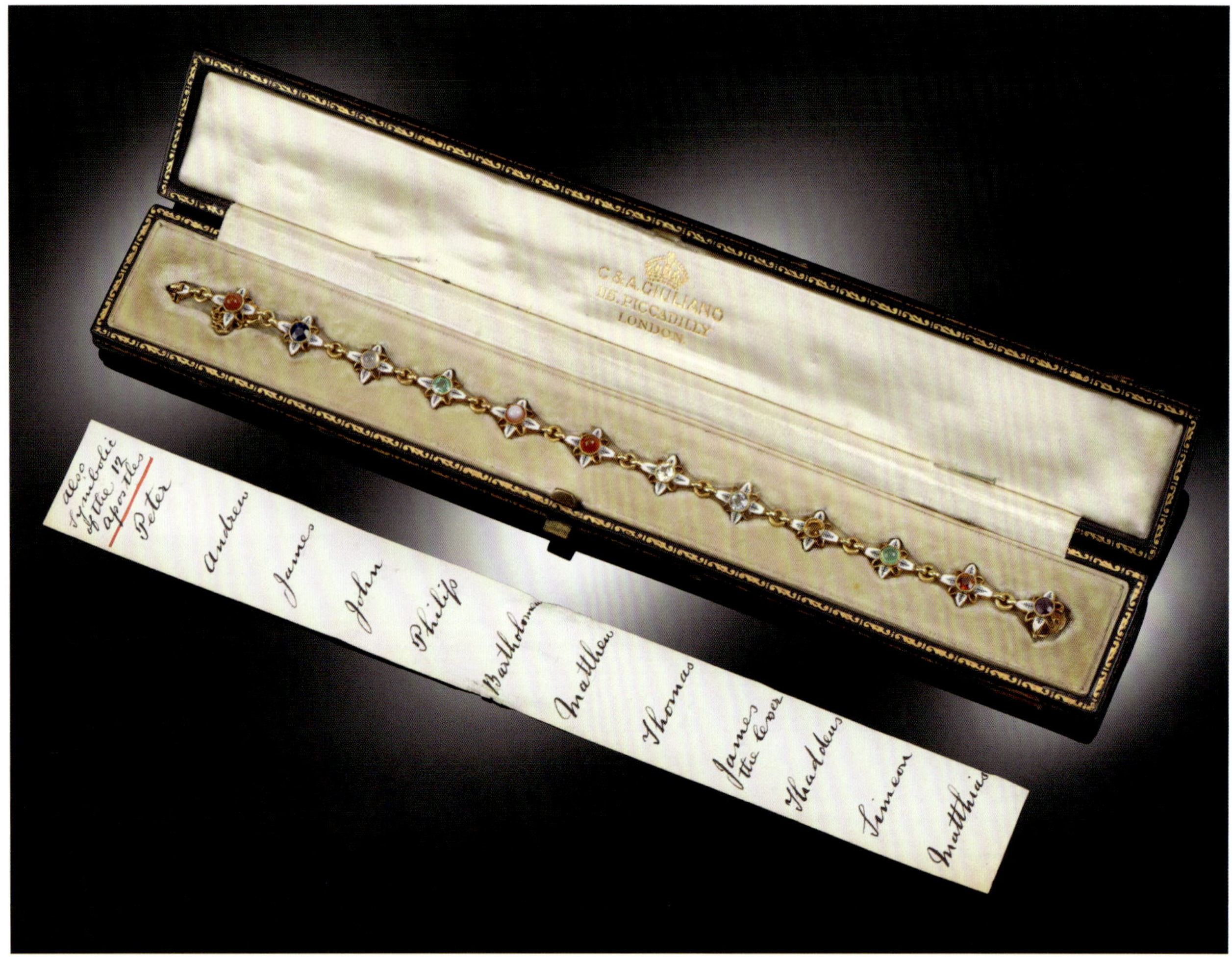

Giuliano gold bracelet, c.1896, featuring a series of twelve uniform sections each set with a coloured gemstone collet in a black and white enamelled quatrefoil frame, together with a handwritten key stating that each of the twelve stones is mentioned in the Bible and is symbolic of the Twelve Apostles.

are easy to fake and are relatively common.

Robert Phillips (1810-1881) was another jeweller equally accomplished in neo-classical and neo-Renaissance themes. 'Phillips of Cockspur Street', as he is generally known, produced fine archaeological gold work and is particularly associated with the use of coral which he adapted into fringe necklaces. He subsequently produced a series of 'Tudor' style gold cruciform pendants which, although similar to the work of Giuliano, are distinctive for their use of bold hardstones such as onyx. Robert Phillips signed his pieces with a stylised Prince of Wales feather motif in a shield or the monogram 'RP'. After his death in 1881 the business was taken over by his son, Alfred, who specialised in naturalistic gold scrolling pendants and brooches translucent enamelled in several vibrant colours and set with gems fashionable at the time such as opal, demantoid garnet and diamond.

Further reading

Castellani and Giuliano – Revivalist Jewellers of the 19th Century, Geoffrey C. Munn (Trefoil, 1984)

Pre-Raphaelite to Arts and Crafts Jewellery, Charlotte Gere and Geoffrey C. Munn (Antique Collectors' Club, 1996)

Castellani & Italian Archaeological Jewellery, Edited by S. Soros and S. Walker (Bard Graduate Centre, 2005)

Chapter 13
Base Metal Jewellery and Materials

Cut Steel

Cut steel was an extremely effective variety of base metal jewellery, popular throughout the 18th and 19th centuries. Unlike paste, it was, on close inspection, difficult to confuse with diamonds. Nevertheless, it makes a significant impact when worn in artificial light and some of the superior examples of 18th-century origin can be just as elegant and carefully constructed as expensive gem-set alternatives.

Cut steel can be traced as far back as the 16th century, although it was only in the mid-18th century that large quantities were produced commercially in England and France. The English cut steel industry was primarily located at Woodstock in Oxfordshire. Here many useful everyday accessories were made including chatelaines, buckles, buttons and watch chains with seals. Chatelaines were particularly compatible with steel: the shiny grey metal links looked business-like and they were strong and hard wearing, perfect for suspending below a variety of domestic appendages such as scissors, thimble, pencil and keys.

From the 1760s the vast majority of cut steel was manufactured at Soho near Birmingham. The leading producer was Matthew Boulton (1728-1809), an entrepreneurial industrialist better known for steam traction than dainty buttons and bows. Early cut steel was composed of clusters of small faceted and polished individual studs riveted on to a base plate. Eighteenth-century examples were sometimes composed of steel mesh with polished steel flowers and fancy quatrefoil-shaped plaques attached whilst, ever faithful to the neo-classical ideal, the studs were threaded in lines and mounted on broad clasps which were further enhanced by the addition of imitation pearls or jasperware plaques depicting mythological deities.

The tiny facets on each stud supplied the necessary glitter effect. Eighteenth-century steel exhibits up to 15 facets on each stud whereas the mass-produced 19th-century variety contains as few as five facets. Victorian cut steel is visibly coarser and cruder than its earlier counterpart and, needless to say, it is a lot less expensive. The two periods can be further differentiated by looking at the back of the object; whilst early steel exhibits individual hand-made rivets, the later machine-made variety does not. Indeed, many later pieces are made from punched out metal strips betraying their 'factory' origin.

Necklaces and tiaras are particularly sought today. Necklaces often conformed to a popular design of star or flowerhead clusters (which sometimes revolved). Occasionally, long thin drops known as *pampilles* were suspended below. Bangles are quite common composed of four or five lines of studs in side-by-side formation. These were fastened by pressing a ball-shaped finial into a hole at the opposing end. Brooches were fashioned as circular clusters, stars or flowers. More interesting or novel designs such as butterflies, peacocks, fish, insects

French cut-steel, blue glass and silver brooch, c.1800. Note the number of facets on each individual stud, an indicator of early steel jewellery. Later steel may only exhibit as few as five facets on each stud and is thus far cruder.

or Halley's comet will inevitably encourage higher prices. Earrings are rare and accordingly expensive.

The one great disadvantage of cut steel is its tendency towards rusting when left in a damp atmosphere. Rust is unsightly, invasive and difficult to remove without damaging the object itself.

Berlin Ironwork

The idea of a necklace composed of sections of black iron sounds, on the face of it, to be fairly uninspiring yet Berlin ironwork jewellery – particularly the elegant neo-classical pieces – offers the collector some of the prettiest and most intricate examples of the jeweller's art.

Precise origins of ironwork jewellery are unclear. In the late 18th century a foundry at Gleiwitz in the Prussian province of Silesia specialised in the manufacture of a grey colour woven iron mesh of gossamer-like consistency. In 1804 a factory was established in Berlin for the production of iron objects, both functional and decorative, known as the Royal Berlin Factory. Jewellery represented only a fraction of total production which included small-scale practical objects such as buckles, keys, tinder boxes and purses to massive-scale industrial output encompassing gates, grilles, balustrades and bridges.

The development of ironwork jewellery as a distinct commodity really began to take off between the years 1813 to 1815 as a response to a general plea by the Prussian authorities for members of the aristocracy to

Two 18th-century steel mesh bracelets with flower and quatrefoil-shaped polished steel pailettes together with a pair of earrings.

Late 18th-/early 19th-century cut-steel and red glass parure comprising necklace, brooch and earrings.

Typical mid-19th-century cut-steel group of necklace, bracelet, bangles and hair comb. Compare the rather crude, machine-like faceting exhibited on the individual studs against the superior multi-faceted studs seen in the example on the preceding page.

'donate' their gold and jewels for the war effort against Napoleon. Appealing to patriotism tapped perfectly into the psychology of the people, since in exchange for gold jewellery they were given ironwork necklaces, crosses, brooches and bracelets, sometimes bearing the emotive inscription 'Gold gab ich für Eisen' (I gave gold for iron) or 'eingetauscht zum Wohle des Vaterlandes' (exchanged for the welfare of the Fatherland). To get some idea of the scale of production, over 41,000 items of jewellery were made in 1814 alone.

Berlin iron jewellery was produced by shaping wax moulds into the desired design and enclosing them in iron boxes packed with sand. Once the mould had been removed, molten iron was poured into the remaining cavity. After it had cooled down, the object was removed from its sand impression for cleaning and hand finishing.

The application of a varnish made of linseed oil and white pitch protected against rusting; a coat of black lacquer gave further protection and provided an attractive patina.

Jewellery passed through several strongly contrasting and recognisable styles. From about 1800 to 1820 neo-classicism predominated; thus a typical necklace would be composed of a series of oval plaques delicately wrought to depict mythological deities, nymphs, putti and songbirds connected together by several tiers of fine link chains or gauze-like mesh. Occasionally the plaques were set in thin rims of gold or the mesh was embellished with steel stars or sequins known as *paillettes.*

Right: Berlin ironwork necklace designed as a series of graduated openwork leaf motifs with detached centrepiece, c.1815.

Below: Berlin ironwork bracelet of Gothic revival design composed of a series of vari-sized openwork sections, c.1825.

A fine Berlin ironwork panel bracelet by Geiss of ornate Gothic design, c.1840.

Late 19th-century Japanese shakudo-work bracelet composed of six roundels decorated with birds and foliage in gold frames, c.1880.

From about 1815 to 1830 neo-classicism gave way to naturalism in which flowers, leaves and butterflies were the guiding theme. A popular design for bracelets and necklaces was a scallop or ivy-shaped leaf delicately pierced to suggest the leaf's veins and stem. From the 1830s onwards a heavier Gothic style entered general use characterised by sections of ornate tracery and complicated cartouche or quatrefoil patterns more associated with church architecture than dainty jewels. Gothic ironwork might be designed as elaborate pillars with ornate scrolls and figures of saints.

After around 1850 the popularity of Berlin ironwork

Fine-quality late 18th-/early 19th-century sky-blue glass and marcasite parure of necklace, brooch and earrings, c.1800.

Early 19th-century long pinchbeck chain of floral embossed sections with stippled hoop links between, c.1825.

rapidly receded although it was also sold as mourning jewellery in France from the 1820s. There are several prominent manufacturers whose work is particularly sought; probably the best known are Johann Conrad Geiss, who was active in the 1830s, and Devaranne, who showed iron jewellery at the 1851 Great Exhibition.

Marcasite

Although marcasite is well known today for its abundant use in affordable and decorative 20th-century jewellery, its origins can actually be traced back as far as the 18th century when it was set in inexpensive accessories such as buttons and buckles as well as cheap but pretty items of silver jewellery.

Marcasite is iron pyrites – sometimes called 'fool's gold' – which has been faceted to give it its characteristic yellowish-grey glitter. This means that it is routinely confused with cut steel, a problem compounded by the fact that it was frequently used in late 18th- or early 19th-century neo-classical jewellery as a border to jasperware plaques, 'coq de perle' necklaces or cobalt blue glass copying much more expensive blue enamel.

Three early Victorian gilt-metal and hardstone bracelets, c.1825.

Silver whistle with cross-hatched black niello-work surface decoration, c.1900. Niello was extensively used in small scale accessories such as snuff boxes and was particularly popular in Russia in the 19th century. It is an alloy of sulphur, silver, copper and lead.

Art Nouveau gunmetal cigarette case with silver highlights.

Aluminium

Summed up by the expression 'light and white', aluminium was a rare and expensive commodity during the 19th century and much of the jewellery was heavily influenced by Gothic revivalism. The surface of the metal was invariably chased with elaborate scrolls and the hard white colour of the material was also always offset by yellow gilt-metal backing plates and mounts. Modern aluminium jewellery is sometimes given a delicate tinted surface by a procedure known as anodising.

Gunmetal

Gunmetal was extensively used in late 19th-century accessories such as mesh purses, chatelaines, cigarette cases and vesta boxes as well as assorted jewellery, chains and the cases of fob watches. The material exhibits a characteristic blue-black colour and satin-like sheen which could be an ideal contrast to gemstones or even small diamonds. It was popular in Russia, Germany and Austria, but its tendency towards rusting and general deterioration considerably affects its value.

Pinchbeck

An alloy of zinc and copper invented by Christopher Pinchbeck (1672-1732), a clock- and watchmaker of Fleet Street, it appeared to all intents and purposes exactly like gold and was used in its own right in the manufacture of robust belcher link muff chains, pairs of mesh bracelets and long decorative earrings, as well as an accompaniment to bold coloured agates and hardstones in brooches and necklaces.

In the 19th century it was fashionable to remove the pinchbeck 'watchcocks' from the movements of pocket watches and mount them together into rather effective necklaces in which no two watchcocks are identical.

Pinchbeck should not be confused with later, inferior gilt metal which usually discolours after prolonged use.

Further reading

Cut-Steel and Berlin Iron Jewellery, Anne Clifford (Adams & Dart, 1971)

Victorian Jewelry: Unexplored Treasures, Ginny Redington Dawes and Corinne Davidov (Abbeville Press Publishers, 1991)

Georgian Jewellery 1714-1830, Ginnie Redington Dawes and Olivia Collings (Antique Collectors' Club, 2007)

A colourful collection of inexpensive English butterfly brooches enamelled on silver and metal, first half of the 20th century.

Chapter 14
Period Accessories and Functional Jewellery

Shoe Buckles

If you are thinking of starting a collection of antique jewellery, you could do far worse than begin with a few Georgian buckles. Reasonably common and surprisingly cheap, buckles were an obligatory accessory for both men's and women's footwear throughout the 18th century. By the 1760s there were as many as 8,000 people employed in the buckle-making industry in the Midlands with returns of £300,000 per annum, mainly from exports.

The frames of Georgian buckles were usually oval or rectangular in shape and were curved to fit over the instep. The central section, known as the chape and composed of the pin and tongue, was invariably made of steel. Matthew Boulton, famous for his pioneering work in cut steel, was also a prominent buckle-maker.

Buckles made during the 1720s-1750s were often composed of engraved silver frames while examples made between 1750 and 1800 were generally set with paste. Colourless paste buckles are extremely common and coloured paste is considerably rarer, while unusual materials, such as earthenware, tin and French jet (black glass), can still be found in 'box lots' at auction.

Pair of fine small Georgian silver buckles each set with faceted blue paste, c.1790.

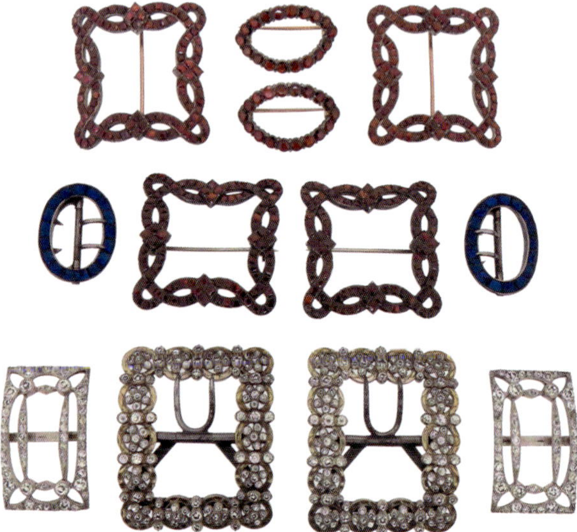

Two pairs of Georgian buckles set with garnets, two pairs in colourless paste and a small pair set with blue pastes.

The major problem with buckles is that they are impractical for wearing nowadays. Some have been converted into brooches but this reduces the value. Another problem is the difficulty in finding matched pairs, as you might expect with an accessory subjected to robust everyday use 275 years ago. Identical pairs are, therefore, very collectable especially if lodged in their original fitted boxes.

Buttons

Buttons are keenly sought today and fine-quality 18th-century sets of six or twelve can fetch several hundreds or even thousands of pounds. Buttons were manufactured from a large and varied number of materials, usually of a fairly modest value, while gold and gem-set buttons can be traced from the 17th century through to the 1920s and 1930s when firms such as Cartier produced elegant platinum, gold, diamond and jewelled buttons to match pairs of cufflinks and dress studs.

A complete set is absolutely vital since the loss of a solitary component will reduce the value quite significantly – a fitted box containing eleven buttons and one gap is extremely vexing and near-impossible to remedy.

Among the many designs used for antique buttons, some of the more common examples include early 18th-century dome-backed silver 'ball' designs set with colourless paste imitating diamond; clusters of cut steel (produced in very large numbers during the 18th and 19th centuries);

Set of six Georgian colourless paste buttons of flowerhead form.

Pair of early Victorian gold sprung lorgnettes, c.1845, with coloured gold decoration.

gilt-metal rococo plaques decorated with colourful enamel 'romantic' landscapes and novelty subjects which were mass-produced from the 1890s onwards.

Perhaps the prettiest and most desirable period for collectors today is Art Nouveau in which the individual buttons were decorated with flowers or perhaps embossed with a female head which was further embellished in green and blue enamel. Signed sets by Liberty, Charles Horner or Murrle Bennett are especially prized. Condition, as always, is crucial.

Lorgnettes

The French word *lorgnette* broadly embraces a group of functional accessories including miniature spy glasses fashionable at the opera and the theatre in the 18th century and lorgnettes used for reading. Quizzing glasses were composed of a single lens and were worn at the end of a long chain or ribbon. Lorgnettes enjoyed widespread use in the 19th century; inexpensive examples were made of silver, gilt metal, gunmetal and tortoiseshell, while superior models were fashioned in three- or four-colour gold embellished with gems such as ruby, turquoise and pearl. Fabergé produced a range of lorgnettes with enamelled stems, while Cartier and French jewellers before the First World War made elegant lorgnettes in platinum set with clusters of small diamonds. The vast majority of lorgnettes were opened by retraction of a small cylinder or compression of a lever causing the lens to spring open. Progressive use weakens the mechanism and can affect value.

Nineteenth-century Continental gold lorgnette decorated with white enamel flowers and scrolls on a black enamel field with a retractable eyepiece, c.1880.

Fine neo-classical gold chatelaine, c.1800, set with blue glass plaques and suspending a watch with accompanying key and seal.

Chatelaines

The most practical of all 'everyday' accessories, chatelaines were popular from the early 18th century through to the end of the 19th century when their use became purely functional rather than decorative.

Chatelaines were composed of a gold, silver, steel or gilt-metal shield-shaped hook inserted into the belt from which was suspended a series of matching chains, each with a useful appendage such as étui, scissors, fob watch, pomander or miniature purse. Fine examples made in the 18th century were mounted in three- or four-colour gold chased with repoussé decoration and studded with gems. Fine French chatelaines were enamelled with pretty scenes and landscapes while the fob watch was accompanied by a matching watch key and seal. Eighteenth-century pinchbeck chatelaines often suspended several needlework appendages, but finding complete sets with the contents fully intact is extremely unusual.

Seals

Seals can be divided into two principal categories: fob seals – small and practical accessories worn on a watch chain or as an appendage to a chatelaine – and desk seals which were, as you might expect, larger, more imposing and kept for sealing documents, usually of a legal or formal nature.

Seals are among the earliest artefacts which can be traced back in civilised history composed of materials such as faience and basalt and fashioned into cylindrical shapes suitable for rolling on wax. Simple and fairly crude medieval seals, often mistaken for later examples, were made from silver or metal while mid-18th-century 'Jacobite' fob seals in steel, the base engraved with a head or coat of arms, are fairly common. Occasionally the 'business-end' of the seal could be made to swivel – a feature of some Victorian seals where a semi-precious stone, usually citrine, was engraved on three faces with a coat of arms, a family crest and the owner's monogram.

Mid- to late 18th-century seals are characteristic for their classical austerity. The pedestal, or handle, was usually of a stylised bell-shape and typical of the prevailing taste; the base took the form of a foil-backed amethyst, citrine or rock crystal or a hardstone such as cornelian, onyx or chalcedony, carved with a head in profile. In keeping with the fashion for sentiment at the start of the 19th century, seals were smaller, prettier and elaborately embossed in

Group of three heavily embossed Georgian gold fob seals mounted with amethyst, carnelian and citrine bases each engraved with full armorials, all suspended from a Georgian gold split ring, c.1800.

Three embossed Georgian gold seals, c.1800, including two good examples illustrating the complexity of their engraved armorials in citrine and amethyst.

several different colours of gold. The hardstone stamp was engraved with a suitably feminine device such as doves in flight and a simple expression of affection such as 'amitie' or 'pour vous.' These seals were often further embellished with little gems, particularly rubies, turquoises and half pearls, and it was not unknown to place a locket compartment in the base for containing hair.

Victorian seals are extremely common and variable in quality. Many were strengthened for everyday use by adding a core of metal and care should be taken to ensure that a seal called 'gold' is indeed as described. Many seals made from the 1840s to 1860s were simply gilt metal with glass bases and are, quite frankly, extremely crude, whilst late 19th-century seals were invariably 9-carat gold mounted with two predictable hardstones – cornelian and bloodstone. Seals such as these were worn on the end of a gold watch chain and are realistically priced today.

As pocket watches gave way to wristwatches, the fashion for wearing fob seals on the end of alberts also faded so that by around 1910 production more or less evaporated. Today, 9-carat gold 'Victorian-style' seals are produced to be worn on charm bracelets or as decorative pendants. Modern seals usually exhibit identifying hallmarks.

A musical seal might contain a hidden compartment often with an erotic scene within which, to put it delicately, the figures moved in time to the music.

Early 19th-century gold musical seal with enamelled erotic study concealed within the base. Clearly an amusing conversation piece for a dilettante gentleman. French, c.1800.

Cufflinks

Demand for traditional Victorian and Edwardian cufflinks has somewhat plateaued in recent years, no doubt because the era of formal shirts has largely become a thing of the past; men tend to prefer wearing shirts with button cuffs and collectors have become considerably more selective with their choice, tending to favour unusual

Art Deco and Post-War examples particularly if made out of platinum, set with striking colourful gems and diamonds and signed by a leading jewel house such as Cartier or Tiffany. Nevertheless, cufflinks do offer collectors one of the few areas of jewellery readily available (and socially acceptable) for men. Today most high street menswear shops sell a wide range of silver, gilt and enamel cufflinks contributing to a greater awareness and appreciation of the discipline and intensifying demand for good quality pairs which appear in the salerooms or which are sold in specialist shops.

The two important aspects which must be borne in mind when buying period cufflinks are *design* and *condition*. A pair of Edwardian 9-carat gold oval plaque cufflinks will certainly do the job for which they were intended but are stylistically repetitive, while a pair with, say, chipped enamel, worn settings and connections falling apart are frankly more of a liability than an asset.

The fashion for wearing cufflinks can be traced back to the early 18th century when pairs of rock crystal mounted 'Memento Mori' buttons were joined together in silver; in Scotland polished agate or hardstone plaques were similarly constructed in extremely simple settings. Victorian and Edwardian gold cufflinks, usually 15 or 18 carat, were made in a wide range of designs. It is, however, those subjects which are described as 'novelty' or inspired by a specific theme such as sport, hunting or nature which are most desirable today. Thus, diamond studded foxheads, enamelled gamebirds or freshwater fish will predictably appeal to sporting enthusiasts while amusing designs such as enamelled skulls and crossbones or 'ruination' cufflinks, enamelled to depict the four gentlemen's vices of drink, cards, racehorses and easy women, are enduringly popular.

The vintage era for cufflink production was the first thirty years of the 20th century when jewellers such as Cartier and Tiffany produced elegant and highly original examples in a range of materials set in gold and the versatile new metal which was revolutionising jewellery construction – platinum. Using platinum as well as gold could provide craftsmen with limitless opportunities of creating intricate and innovative designs in all sorts of fancy patterns set with gemstones and hardstones cut into suitably compatible shapes. Van Cleef & Arpels and Cartier, for example, produced distinctive square 'chequerboard' cufflinks with matching dress studs invisibly set with diamonds, rubies and sapphires, while Fabergé sold diamond, gem-set and enamel cufflinks in tasteful neo-classical shapes from his shops in St Petersburg, Moscow and London.

It was a natural progression for complete sets of accessories comprising cufflinks, buttons and dress studs to be made for gentlemen wearing formal attire; less expensive examples common from the 1920s to the war years were composed of mother-of-pearl discs or plaques bordered by onyx or enamel and set in 9-carat white and yellow gold or silver. These sets were nearly always sold in neat fitted boxes, an aspect which certainly increases value, although the loss of a single component reduces appeal.

Cufflinks have always been both functional and, at the lower end of the market, cheap; mass-produced examples in 9-carat gold, silver or gilt metal are extremely common. The majority of gold cufflinks made from the 1890s to the 1920s were usually fashioned in oval, circular or torpedo shapes, were elaborately engraved and bore a full set of hallmarks.

Do inspect cheaper cufflinks with great care for indications of later repair and dents. Damage to enamel is often concealed by 'cold painting' but it is near impossible to match the original patina. Some cufflinks are quite simply four buttons which have been recently 'joined up', so check that the connecting chains are original. Finally, examine any makers' marks extremely carefully. A Russian '56' stamp, a French gold 'eagle head' control mark or an individual series of numbers on the edge of the setting can increase value substantially.

Pair of Fabergé blue chalcedony and enamel cufflinks, c.1900.

Right: Dress set of translucent lilac guilloché enamel cufflinks and matching buttons.

Below: Dress set of enamel 'All the Aces' cufflinks and matching buttons.

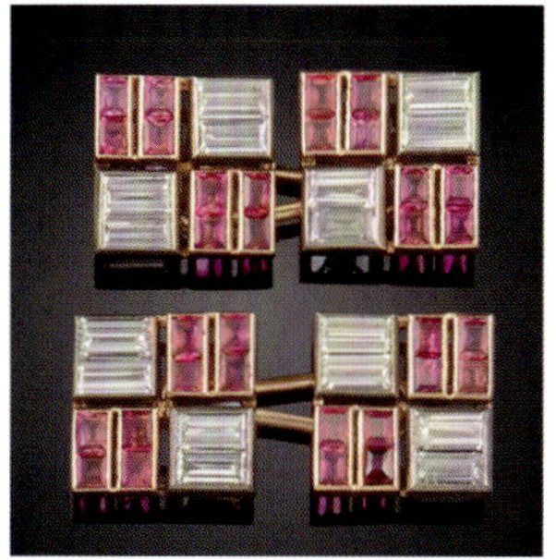

Four pairs of Edwardian and Art Deco cufflinks (from left to right): Green-stone cabochon, black enamel and diamond discs, French emerald chequerboard plaques, ruby and baguette diamond squares and rock crystal and sapphire chequerboard plaques.

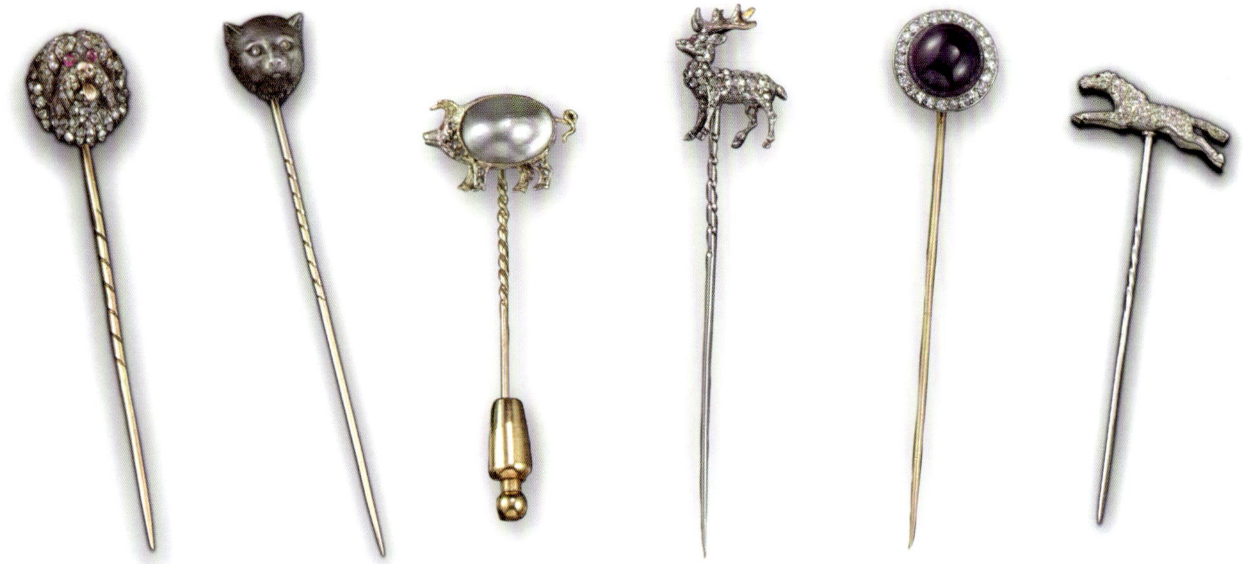

Turn-of-the-century novelty gold tiepins (from left to right): Diamond-set Pomeranian dog with ruby eyes; silver cat's head with diamond eyes; mabé pearl and diamond piglet; diamond stag; Cartier amethyst and diamond cluster; diamond galloping racehorse.

Tiepins

Unlike cufflinks, tiepins (also known as scarf pins or stickpins) are seldom worn today and tend to be bought by collectors for their novelty or rarity value. Tiepins were very much a 19th- and early 20th-century feature. Indeed, during the last quarter of the 19th century, an enormous number were produced to be worn on ties or cravats of which the vast majority are, to put it bluntly, extremely dull with uninspiring designs ranging from simple crescents, horseshoes and flowerheads set with little pearls or cheap gems to embellished gold plaques sometimes set with a small diamond. It is only when the subject matter or the gemstones featured start to be interesting that prices for tiepins rise sharply. The evidence of a signature – particularly Fabergé or Cartier – will certainly heighten demand.

Eighteenth-century tiepins were altogether smaller and daintier than later examples. The pin itself was generally twisted in the centre to form one of several interesting shapes such as a zig-zag or a coil. The head of these Georgian pins was usually pretty basic, nothing more than a cushion-shaped paste, a coloured gem such as a ruby or garnet or a rose diamond in a gold collet setting. Late 18th-century tiepins were rather similar to the rings fashionable at that time – a floral cluster of gems, a hardstone in a border of garnets or a sentimental 'In Memoriam' subject such as a sepia painted weeping lady in a border of seed pearls or enamel.

Nineteenth-century tiepins were extraordinarily diverse utilising a wide and varied range of materials. The themes largely paralleled whatever was fashionable at the time – thus when neo-classicism was the dominant style tiepins faithfully conformed with hardstone, shell and coral cameos carved with the heads of deities in profile. Nature and naturalism, always key to Victorian jewellery, was observed in coiled snakes enamelled in blue surrounding a diamond or a pearl, while birds of prey such as eagles or falcons were carved from gold or set with turquoises. A recurring theme from the 1860s to the 1880s was the reverse crystal intaglio in which a domed plaque of rock

Pencils offer collectors an almost limitless resource of designs, ranging from functional Victorian combinations of pens with pencils to novelty subjects such as the champagne bottle and spinning top illustrated above. The best known maker was Sampson Mordan & Co. and most examples were constructed with a 'telescopic' mechanism, extending their length to twice or three times their normal size.

crystal was engraved at the back and painted with the design of an animal or a bird – domestic pets such as tabby cats and pug dogs particularly appealed to Victorian sentiment. Insects, especially jewelled house flies, beetles and spiders, were keenly collected along with all manner of sporting and recreational subjects which, by the 1890s, played such an important role in people's everyday lives.

Just like cufflinks, the prime factor affecting the value of tiepins is novelty and originality so, whereas a diamond foxhead, diamond pheasant or enamel flag will certainly be collectable, a rare or amusing subject such as a diamond bicycle, a fully articulated enamel clown or a pin with a political message will achieve a far higher price.

By the early 20th-century, tiepins were fashioned in platinum as well as gold and motifs were usually gem set, from the single drop-shaped Oriental pearl to interesting fancy-cut diamond and gem-set novelties by Cartier and Boucheron, such as a miniature yacht set with triangular diamond 'sails'. These tiepins are highly sought and can easily fetch well into the thousands, especially if the diamonds are in a combination of fancy colours underlining the 'novelty' factor so important to tiepin buyers.

Pocket Watches and Fob Watches

Pocket watches with their accompanying chains, commonly known as alberts, turn up at auction with relentless frequency. The vast majority of gold and silver pocket watches fetch prices commensurate with their smelt value so, in spite of the remorseless rise in the price of gold, when we consider the price of many modern sport or fashion wristwatches on the market today, a fine old Victorian timepiece really can represent a solid and reassuring investment at a reasonably affordable outlay. Gentlemen's pocket watches were invariably worn in the waistcoat pocket at the end of a chunky gold or silver chain while smaller, daintier ladies' fob watches were clipped to the end of a long guard chain or were suspended from a matching brooch, usually of tied bow design and worn on the blouse or jacket.

Rolex 9-carat gold open face pocket watch with Roman numerals and subsidiary seconds dial; Birmingham 1946.

The majority of pocket watches at the end of the 19th century contained keyless lever movements in hunter or half-hunter cases. These outer covers were often engraved with a monogram or flowers; better quality gold examples repeated the quarters or the minutes. The dials were invariably enamelled white with black Roman or Arabic numerals. Many old dials betray fine hairline cracks so close inspection is recommended since damage reduces value considerably. American manufacturers such as Waltham and Elgin produced large numbers of gold-plated pocket watches which are often mistaken for gold. A signature will make a significant difference to the potential value of any timepiece. Prominent makers' names include Patek Philippe, Cartier, Rolex and Vacheron Constantin.

Generally speaking, fob watches from the early part of the 20th century are more interesting and valuable

Frodsham 18-carat gold demi-hunter with Arabic numerals and subsidiary seconds dial; Glasgow 1925.

Thos. Russell & Sons 18-carat gold demi-hunter with Roman numerals and subsidiary seconds dial; Chester 1920.

J.B. Bankes 18-carat gold full hunter with Roman numerals and subsidiary seconds dial; London 1877.

Amusing asymmetric silver and enamel minaudière featuring a caricature of Enrico Caruso, c.1925. Minaudières were multi-purpose vanity cases popular from the 1930s to the 1950s. Containing compartments for mirror, lipstick, comb, cigarettes, money and even a watch, they quickly became an indispensable accessory for women in society.

Fine Art Deco diamond, black and red enamel and gem-set fob watch by Vacheron and Constantin, c.1930; the rectangular watch with pearl winding button suspended from a matching fob brooch top section set with a buff-top emerald, black onyx and sapphires with marquise and circular-cut diamond connection and matching back cover.

Gold purse watch by Van Cleef & Arpels of rectangular form, the sliding cover engraved with diamond-set flowerhead opening to reveal the manual wind watch movement by Jaeger-LeCoultre, c.1960.

than the standard gold models in production during the Victorian era. Edwardian and Belle Époque fob watches are frequently enamelled in pretty translucent colours and are sometimes decorated with a geometric cluster of small diamonds or a line of half pearls to the bezels. These small but extremely elegant timepieces were occasionally accompanied by matching chains interspaced with 'batons' – or a series of cylinders enamelled in compatible colours to the watch itself. Probably the best known manufacturer of fob watches was the French firm Le Roy et Fils who invariably signed their products upon the inner gold cover.

Further reading

Chatelaines – Utility to Glorious Extravagance by Genevieve E. Cummins and Nerylla D. Taunton (Antique Collectors' Club, 1994)

Understanding Jewellery by David Bennett and Daniela Mascetti (Antique Collectors' Club, 2003)

Georgian Shoe Buckles, Bernard and Therle Hughes (Greater London Council, 1972)

Chapter 15

Arts and Crafts and Art Nouveau

ARTS AND CRAFTS

To attempt to put into perspective the mood which captured Britain at the end of the 19th century for hand-made, artistically decorated gold and silverware, it may be helpful to inspect a reasonable jewellery auction taking place today. Together with the usual assortment of contemporary manufactured jewels, wristwatches and accessories will no doubt feature a cross-section of late Victorian and Edwardian rings, brooches, pendants and chains – certainly pretty and wearable, but often repetitive in design and lacking in artistic inspiration. To put it another way, one diamond half hoop ring or crescent brooch can look very much like another, while mass-produced silver bangles, engraved lockets, safety bar fasteners and gem pendants can be disappointingly unimaginative.

The Arts and Crafts Movement evolved as a direct backlash to the tidal wave of mechanical, industrialised output which engulfed Britain in the 1880s and 1890s. The problem was not only confined to the cheap end of the market since the discovery of the South African diamond fields served to flood jewellery shops with unexceptional and over duplicated designs for a wealthier clientele. It soon became apparent that much of this produce was ill-conceived, lacked artistic integrity and had 'lost its way' in the drive for commercial gain and profit.

Arts and Crafts inspired silver and enamel brooch by Ramsden & Carr depicting a galleon in full sail; engraved on the reverse 'Good luck 2nd September 1924 with all Wynn's love, Omar Ramsden me fecit'.

Artistic jewellery had existed on the market since the 1850s, largely inspired by influential commentators such as John Ruskin and William Morris who, for example, deplored the sort of over-decorated and seemingly insensitive designs on show at the Great Exhibition of 1851. By the late 1880s several Guilds and Art Schools were founded upon socialist principles to promote a better understanding of decorative arts and to teach the theory and practical application of techniques such as enamelling, engraving, silversmithing and metalworking. In 1890 the Birmingham Guild of Handicraft was established and very soon numerous groups of artisans and students began to set up small workshops all over the country in which individual skills could be encouraged and perfected in an atmosphere of creative artistic harmony.

Adhering closely to idealistic principles, the sort of materials commonly used in Arts and Crafts jewellery were simple, understated, invariably inexpensive and lacked the flashy 'shallowness' of many precious gems. This was also a case of financial necessity, since many workers quite simply could not afford to use diamonds and gold in their designs. The primary metal was silver, sometimes decorated with strips of gold wire, while preferred gemstones included pearl, garnet, moonstone, turquoise, rock crystal, opal and amethyst. Hardstones were extensively used in all manner of buckles, necklaces and pendants, invariably polished *en cabochon*. Among many varieties and colours, the most popular included royal blue lapis lazuli, bright green chrysoprase, onyx and sardonyx, cornelian and chalcedony. Enamel was the perfect substitute for gems and much Arts and Crafts jewellery is beautifully enhanced with translucent polychrome enamel decoration, sometimes in subtle merging shades and tones of which blues and greens were particularly favoured.

Examples of Arts and Crafts necklaces, brooch and pendants. Clockwise, from top left: Silver pendant, c.1900 with enamel plaque of a maiden seated at the shoreline, the frame set with moonstones; Gold Artificers Guild naturalistic gold pendant, c.1905, set with an opal in a naturalistic gold frame further set with pearls, emeralds and garnets; Silver brooch by the Gaskins, c.1900, set with moonstones and pearls in a naturalistic frame; Silver necklace, c.1900, attributed to Arthur and Georgina Gaskin (1862-1928) and (1866-1934) of rectangular naturalistic form set with blister pearls and chrysoprase.

Arts and Crafts silver and part silver-gilt pendant of medieval inspiration by Omar Ramsden (1873-1939) designed as a female minstrel kneeling on a musical score and playing a stringed instrument against a naturalistic backdrop. Engraved on the reverse 'I was wrought by Command of John de Seyfried for Alma his Wife A.D. MMXXVIII'.

Arts and Crafts silver and polychrome enamelled tabernacle pendant by Omar Ramsden (1873-1939), c.1905, the pendant with double door front opening to reveal a polychrome enamelled image of three kneeling saints; the frame set with peridots, mounted on a fancy link silver chain

Arts and Crafts silver and translucent blue enamel flower brooch attributed to Charles Robert Ashbee (1863-1942), c.1905, with turquoise cabochon centre and three matching drops suspended below.

Undoubtedly, the most celebrated and influential coalescence of artists and artisans was the Guild of Handicraft, established in 1888 by Charles Robert Ashbee (1863-1942). Idealist, teacher and mentor to scores of artisans and designers, Ashbee never compromised his artistic principles – a factor which ultimately led to a serious falling out with 'commercial' entities, most notably Liberty & Co. Initially situated in London's East End, the Guild subsequently located in 1902 to Chipping Campden in Gloucestershire – a move which ultimately led to its decline and closure in 1908. As popular and appreciated as Arts and Crafts jewellery may be today, it also needs to be seen in the context of the time when much of the output was seen to be crude, primitive and artistically naïve.

Several designers certainly enjoyed a measure of success in their own lifetimes. Henry Wilson (1864-1934) trained as an architect before setting up a workshop in Kent. Inspired by medieval, Renaissance and Church symbolism, he produced important gold and silver jewellery and objects incorporating hardstones and gems decorated with powerful polychrome enamelling. Wilson employed a team of young assistants who were encouraged to learn the essential techniques of metalwork, enamelling, engraving and the setting of stones.

John Paul Cooper (1869-1933) and Henry George Murphy (1884-1939) eventually progressed to launch their own businesses in which the influence of their apprenticeship served under Wilson was clearly apparent. Both men designed highly proficient gold and silver jewellery set with colourful gems such as star ruby, sapphire and moonstone. Murphy in particular specialised in champlevé enamelling in settings which extended effortlessly in their range from the Gothic to the Renaissance and even the Orient.

Phoebe Traquair (1852-1936) was an Edinburgh artist who specialised in iridescent enamels embellished with highlights of gold in naturalistic gold frames which were sometimes suspended below iridescent 'gemstones'

Gold necklace, c.1905, possibly designed by Carl Otto Czechka (1878-1960) at the Austrian Wiener Werkstätte of naturalistic inspiration set with vari-shaped opals in the asymmetric pendant front and oval-shaped opals in the openwork necklace back.

Arts and Crafts gold pendant, c.1908, attributed to John Paul Cooper (1869-1933), designed as a cluster of enamelled flower heads and a cluster of gem cabochons suspending a turquoise matrix drop.

Scottish gold and dappled blue and white iridescent enamel pendant by James Cromar Watt (1862-1940), c.1905, set with an amethyst cabochon on a fancy link gold chain.

of foil-backed glass. The technique of using metallic foil to accentuate a design was first pioneered by Alexander Fisher (1864-1936), formerly a partner of Henry Wilson. Fisher was a highly influential teacher of the art of medieval and later enamelling and his work exhibits a strong influence of early designs from Limoges in France.

Arthur and Georgina Gaskin (1862-1928 and 1866-1934) met while students at the Birmingham School of Art. After marrying, they began to design jewellery distinctive for its extraordinary detail of densely clustered leaves, flowers and naturalistic motifs enamelled in bright pastel colours such as pink, blue and green and embellished with pearls and mother-of-pearl plaques.

Those designers willing to allow their jewellery and silverware to be exposed in the commercial sector found the ideal venue for their talents at the London premises established by Arthur Lasenby Liberty (1843-1917). Liberty & Co. initially specialised in selling Oriental textiles and works of art before its founder turned to commissioning contemporary metalwork from a group of influential Arts and Crafts designers such as Christopher Dresser, Bernard Cuzner, the Gaskins and Jessie M. King, a student of the Glasgow School of Art celebrated for enamelled jewels, accessories and fabrics.

Probably the best known of all Liberty's craftsmen was Archibald Knox (1864-1933), an extraordinarily versatile goldsmith, silversmith and metalworker equally adept in the production of small-scale gem-set pendants or massive bowls decorated with enamel. Knox was chief designer of Liberty's 'Cymric' range of silver goods based upon Celtic themes. Jewellery such as brooches, buckles and pendants were strongly organic in inspiration, often exhibiting Knox's characteristic 'whiplash' motifs, while enamels in subtle shades of blue and green were particularly favoured.

Omar Ramsden (1873-1939) and Alwyn Carr (1872-1940) met while students at the Sheffield School of Art and subsequently formed a partnership based in London

Arts and Crafts necklace and matching pendant, c.1905, by Henry Wilson (1864-1934); the necklace composed of a series of stippled silver bobbin-shaped beads alternating with enamelled silver beads; suspending below an enamelled silver locket depicting flowering branches in a gem-set frame.

Gold necklace designed by Archibald Knox (1864-1933) for Liberty & Co., c.1905, composed of three polished gold sections studded with turquoise matrix collets interspaced with blister pearls extending to the back chain.

Fine and highly colourful silver 'carpet of gems' bracelet by Sibyl Dunlop (1889-1968), c.1935, mounted with six large water opals in frames of black enamel and set with integrally cut-and-shaped coloured hardstones including amethyst, yellow, green and blue chalcedony.

Opposite page: Examples of turn-of-the-century jewels and accessories by the English firm Child & Child, c.1900-1905. Child & Child specialised in simple naturalistic gold and silver jewels such as butterflies and birds which were frequently translucent enamelled in green and blue. The amethyst, demantoid garnet and white sapphire pendant (top right) was probably made for a supporter of the suffragettes while the green stained ivory heart-shaped cufflinks (bottom left) were after a design by the Pre-Raphaelite artist and jewellery designer Sir Edward Burne-Jones. See also the group of butterfly brooches on page 66.

from 1898 to 1919 where they produced a wide range of jewellery, silverware and ceremonial pieces of medieval inspiration.

Murrle Bennett & Co. was a competitor to Liberty founded in 1884 and owned by Ernest Murrle, a German who settled in London. Much of the firm's output was similar to the Liberty 'Cymric' range; indeed, Murrle Bennett even sold goods to their rivals. Jewellery designs included gold pendants, brooches and bracelets which were often mounted with blister pearls and turquoises polished *en cabochon* or left in their native matrix.

Child & Child, a London shop owned by Walter and Harold Child, specialised in Arts and Crafts silver jewellery such as buckles and hatpins which were enamelled in striking shades of metallic blue and green on a guilloché field. The firm also experimented with plique-à-jour enamel; much of their output was sold in their characteristic bright green leather boxes.

Charles Horner was a Halifax firm which produced very large quantities of silver accessories such as hatpins as well as inexpensive brooches and pendants containing enamel, small pearls and gems.

Finally, Sibyl Dunlop (1889-1968), while not strictly speaking a competitor of Liberty, established a retail shop in Kensington Church Street with a team of craftsmen specialising in bold silver jewels set with clusters of multi-colour hard stones and polished gem cabochons in distinctive integral patterns known as 'Carpet of Gems'.

Gold brooch by Murrle Bennett mounted with a turquoise matrix pebble, c.1900.

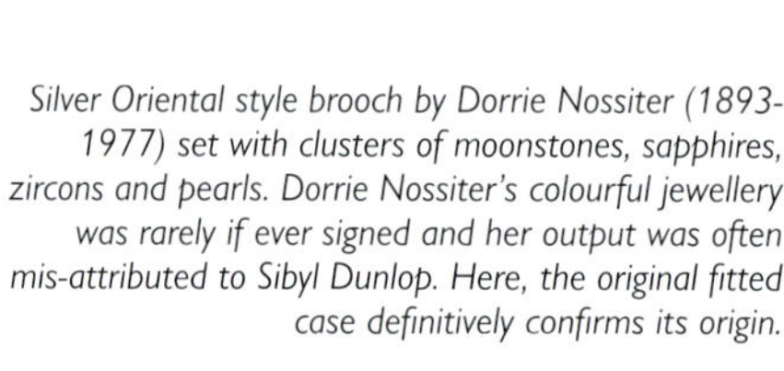

Silver Oriental style brooch by Dorrie Nossiter (1893-1977) set with clusters of moonstones, sapphires, zircons and pearls. Dorrie Nossiter's colourful jewellery was rarely if ever signed and her output was often mis-attributed to Sibyl Dunlop. Here, the original fitted case definitively confirms its origin.

Arts and Crafts in Europe

The impact of the Arts and Crafts movement was felt throughout Europe and Scandinavia, even extending to America where firms such as Tiffany & Co. produced exotic jewellery using a range of new and innovative materials. Art Nouveau in Germany was known as 'Jugendstil' ('Youth Style') and drew heavily on both the rich symbolism of nature fundamental to the Arts and Crafts movement and the strong linear forms of 1930s Art Deco.

Theodor Fahrner (1859-1919) was a German manufacturer of 'affordable art jewellery' who initially collaborated with Murrle Bennett in the manufacture of elegant, naturalistic silver and enamel brooches and pendants and then switched production towards functional, architectural themes set with marcasite and bold hardstone combinations such as coral and onyx. The Darmstadt Colony was a community of artists and designers located at Pforzheim while in Austria the Wiener Werkstätte (Vienna Workshop) largely drew inspiration from the English Guild of Handicraft.

The Danish silversmith Georg Jensen (1866-1935) founded a workshop in Copenhagen in association with Mogens Ballin (1871-1914). Adopting a range of themes including flowers, birds and leaves, Jensen specialised in the use of polished hardstone cabochons – moonstone, lapis lazuli, coral and garnet – in bold silver figurative settings which make as great an impact today as they did in the early 1900s.

ART NOUVEAU

Chronologically Arts and Crafts and Art Nouveau ran side by side and stylistically there are several clear comparisons to be drawn: the overwhelming influence of nature; organic imagery in which the cold, mechanical forms of late 19th-century mass-produced adornment were totally shunned; the abundant use of enamel and particular gems selected for their aesthetic beauty such as pearl, opal, moonstone and turquoise.

Of the differences, the most obvious was the overwhelming impression of sensuousness and nature running riot, where enamel flowers or jewelled insects and serpents were woven into exotic armlets or stunning

A range of silver brooches and pendants by the leading Danish Silversmith and Designer Craftsman Georg Jensen (1866-1935). The majority of these examples date from around 1910 to 1925 and are set with opal, coral, garnet green agate and mother-of-pearl.

Elegant French blond-tortoiseshell Art Nouveau hair comb 'Goa' by Falize Brothers, c.1902, the upper gallery applied with a realistically observed sprig of gold mistletoe mounted with seven opal berries.

Fine and rare French gold brooch by Lalique, c.1900, designed as a cicada with diamond-set eyes, the insect's body composed of pâte-de-verre glass, its folded wings decorated with plique-à-jour enamel with diamond highlights to the extremities. Signed 'Lalique' on the underside.

hair combs. As well as the modest, understated hardstone cabochons of the standard Arts and Crafts ornament, the Art Nouveau equivalent was frequently mounted in gold and set with valuable precious stones such as emerald, ruby, sapphire and, notably, diamond – as a decorative embellishment or even the focal point of the complete jewel. Innovative and breathtaking 'new' materials typified the Art Nouveau period and ground-breaking designer goldsmiths such as René Lalique pioneered the application of daring organic media such as horn or artificial materials like moulded glass to reinforce the naturalistic ideal or accentuate fantastic, dream-like symbolism.

The term 'Art Nouveau' was taken from a Parisian shop called 'Maison de L'Art Nouveau' which was owned by an influential entrepreneur, Samuel Bing. The period in which the movement flourished was the last decade of the 19th century until the outbreak of the First World War. During these twenty-five years, Art Nouveau gained enormous influence in France, Belgium, Italy, Spain and America, the latter in no small part due to the great commercial success of Tiffany & Co.

Whilst nature and naturalism were the driving forces behind nearly all the decorative output, there was an altogether darker side to many of the jewellery designs. A sensuous female form would bear the torso of an insect such as a moth or dragonfly with folded enamel wings. A bouquet of flowers would, on closer inspection, be in a transitional state of decay. This representation of the cycle of nature was brilliantly articulated by René Lalique (1860-1945), whose jewellery combined a number of distinct features which set his work apart from the vast majority of his contemporaries. Lalique possessed an extraordinarily fertile imagination. Once he had carefully studied the natural form in its own habitat – perhaps an insect such as a butterfly, a bird, a flower or a leaf – he would then interpret its essential characteristics into a spectacular pendant, comb or buckle startling in originality and technically incomparable, observing the minutest attention to detail in the setting and the materials. Plique-à-jour enamel was a particularly favoured medium, thus the wings of a dragonfly would contain a network of gauze-like *cloisons* or cells which were individually filled with a series of translucent glass panels in several subtle colours. Organic materials such as horn were reserved for hair combs which were sometimes stained or applied with compatible gems such as moonstones to suggest raindrops.

Impressive Spanish gold Art Nouveau butterfly bracelet by Carreras, c.1905, composed of four arched rectangular plaques each decorated with a colourful plique-à-jour enamelled butterfly on a frosted glass field further decorated with insects and foliage in shaded green enamel. Carreras, the longest established family of jewellers in Spain, was founded by Francesco d'Assis Carreras Duran.

Long gold Art Nouveau guard chain interspaced with a series of lozenge-shaped sections individually plique-à-jour and guilloché enamelled with stylised sprays of cherries.

Translucent polychrome enamel foliate spray gold pendant set with diamonds and pearls and a large Oriental pearl drop, c.1900.

Stylised gold Art Nouveau dragonfly brooch with diamond-set plique-à-jour enamelled wings, emerald cabochon thorax, diamond abdomen and ruby eyes, c.1900. To reinforce the sense of movement the wings of this charming brooch can be folded down enabling it to be worn as a pendant.

The human form was a popular and potent symbol for many Art Nouveau goldsmiths. The House of Vever was a dynasty of French jewellers which produced splendid botanical jewels sometimes incorporating the profile of a maiden in moulded glass. Vever designs are somewhat more reserved than Lalique's essentially flamboyant style and the settings are decidedly linear.

Philippe Wolfers (1858-1929) was a Belgian who designed a limited range of strangely evocative enamel and gem-set brooches and pendants incorporating the figure of a maiden in carved ivory. Lucien Gaillard often worked with horn, designing elegant combs of floral inspiration bearing a strong Japanese influence, while Alphonse Fouquet (1828-1911) and his son Georges (1862-1957) changed direction from the production of highly coloured neo-Renaissance jewellery to flamboyant and exotic avant-garde designs for theatrical figureheads such as Alphonse Mucha.

It has to be said that jewels by Wolfers, Fouquet and their contemporaries are, today, extremely rare and desperately expensive. Examples in pristine condition will easily fetch high five-figure prices while an important piece by René Lalique can achieve stellar prices. Nevertheless, inexpensive and pretty Art Nouveau jewellery does appear fairly regularly in the specialist retail and auction sectors, especially enamelled brooches, pendants, rings and accessories. Modest, unsigned and unattributed French gold brooches, silver pendants or horn hair combs will easily fetch high five-figure prices; in 2021 an ivory, horn, enamel and diamond comb fetched over $800,000 in Paris, although the addition of a few precious gems, pearls or plique-à-jour enamel will raise prices visibly. Condition is vital since the loss of enamel or a later repair is very difficult to rectify. Finally, do ensure that a piece which bears the label 'Art Nouveau' is genuine since large numbers of modern reproductions such as silver 'dragonfly' brooches, sets of buttons and photograph frames regularly appear at auction bearing rather 'non-committal' descriptions which mask their dubious origin.

Further reading

Pre-Raphaelite to Arts and Crafts Jewellery by Charlotte Gere and Geoffrey Munn (Antique Collectors' Club, 1996)

Jewelry & Metalwork in the Arts and Crafts Tradition by Elyse Zorn Karlin (Schiffer Publishing Ltd., 1993)

Art Nouveau Jewellery by Vivienne Becker (E.P. Dutton, 1985)

Tadema Gallery London. Jewellery from the 1860's to 1960's, B. Chadour-Sampson & S. Newell-Smith (Arnoldsche, 2021)

René Lalique. Exceptional Jewellery 1890-1912, Yvonne Brunhammer (Skira Editore, 2007)

Wiener Werkstätte Jewelry, Hatje Kantz (Neue Galerie, 2008)

Chapter 16

The Belle Époque: Early Platinum Jewellery and the 'Garland' Style

The restless, ever-changing profile of jewellery design in the 20th century was strongly influenced by the complex array of social, economic and artistic influences which characterised this turbulent era. Until the First World War several contrasting decorative themes ran concurrently and it was perfectly possible to find one jeweller selling a traditional stock of reliable but conservative diamond jewels – formal tiaras, star brooches and half hoop bangles – while his neighbour would specialise in the bold, daring themes of the Art Nouveau movement – brightly coloured enamel buckles, serpent bracelets and woodland diadems.

The term which was adopted to embrace the lighter, feminine designs of the Edwardian era in yet another contrasting expression of the craftsman's art was *Belle Époque*. Designers turned away from the heavy and predictable look of the Victorian era and began to create altogether lighter and more elegant pieces which were

Splendid platinum sapphire and diamond corsage brooch by Joseph Chaumet (1852–1928) with multiple swags, drops and 'Garland' style leaf decoration, c.1905. A veritable tour de force of Belle Époque corsage jewellery.

Pretty Edwardian platinum brooch set with brilliant-cut diamonds and emeralds with a pear-shaped diamond suspended below, c.1905. Note the way the colour of the emeralds in this elegant jewel are heightened by setting the stones in yellow gold.

Belle Époque diamond, platinum and Oriental pearl brooch/pendant on a diamond-set platinum chain, c.1905. Belle Époque jewellery was strongly influenced by many of the themes and inspirations which shaped the Art Nouveau movement such as the scrolling openwork 'whiplash' motif observed in this particular brooch.

Belle Époque diamond and platinum foliate pendant, c.1905. This piece exhibits two particular features of early 20th-century jewellery; an elegant naturalistic design where the diamonds are mounted in delicate millegrain collet settings.

clearly inspired by the delicate imagery of French rococo decoration from the end of the 18th century. Thus pretty shell and lattice motifs, swags, bows and hearts were seamlessly combined with charming naturalistic symbols such as sprays of leaves, flowerheads and trails of tendrils in a range of wonderfully feminine jewellery known as the *'Garland' style*.

As technically adept as craftsmen were during this period, such fine and intricate workmanship would have been impossible to achieve without the introduction of platinum, a brand new metal which both revolutionised

Belle Époque Oriental pearl, diamond and calibré ruby triple concentric hoop pendant with diamond tied ribbon bow surmount, c.1900.

Belle Époque diamond and platinum collar composed of two black velvet straps with applied diamond millegrain set cusps and edges extending from a diamond tied bow centrepiece with twin tassel finials, c.1907.

jewellery design and irrevocably changed how diamonds and gems were fashioned and retained within their settings. Unlike silver, platinum is substantially harder and stronger. This meant that precious stones, and diamonds in particular, could be mounted in unobtrusive claws or gripped in minute beaded lines and clusters known as *millegrain* settings. Platinum was therefore an ideal vehicle for 'Garland' jewellery in which tiny diamonds were placed into complex sprays of leaves or set in articulated swags, drops and latticework clusters.

The first quarter of the 20th century also saw significant advances in diamond cutting and polishing. The standard cut of the Victorian era was the old European brilliant – usually cushion in shape and with a tendency towards being thick and ill-proportioned. By the First World War several new and innovative cuts began to appear in English, French and Continental diamond jewellery including the marquise, the pendeloque, the lunette (half moon) and, of course, the round brilliant. Better proportions meant altogether more 'life' and 'sparkle'. Many diamonds used by prominent jewellers in the Belle Époque era were of a superior colour and clarity, another reason why early platinum jewellery is so highly sought today.

Belle Époque platinum and diamond tiara designed as a series of closely set vertical knife-edge bars applied with diamond wreath and quatrefoil motifs between diamond gallery borders, c.1905.

As well as fancy-shaped diamonds, coloured gems also began to be used far more extensively. Fine rubies from Burma, emeralds from Colombia and sapphires from Burma and Kashmir accompanied diamonds in a broad range of formal and everyday designs ranging

Edwardian emerald, platinum and diamond elongated pendant earrings with diamond bow tops and pear-shaped drops, c.1905.

Edwardian platinum and diamond jabot pin fashioned as an arrow with diamond swag chain connecting the two finials, c.1910. A jabot was often worn on a jacket or dress. One finial could be pulled off allowing the pin to be threaded through the material and secured by pushing the finial back on.

French Belle Époque platinum bracelet composed of a series of eight alternating diamond floral wreaths and laurel wreaths with calibré ruby baton connections, c.1905.

from elaborate collars and corsage ornaments to simple pendants and earrings.

Of all so-called 'precious' gems, the 'species' which is most closely associated with 'Garland' jewellery is the pearl. Subtle and understated, the neutral off-white, cream, pink and golden tones of this most elegant of gems perfectly complemented the flashy brilliance of diamonds. These were the days before cultured pearls irrevocably changed the industry. All the pearls used were of natural origin and thus highly prized for their beauty and rarity. Invariably smooth in lustre and found in a variety of interesting shapes such as compressed boutons, teardrops and strange baroque forms rather like bunches of grapes, pearls could be adapted into any number of designs. One of the most popular of these was the *sautoir*, a long necklace of interwoven seed pearl strands with tassel finials in pretty diamond and gem-set cap settings.

Rings conformed closely to the Belle Époque ideal. Pretty and understated, gems and diamonds were millegrain-set in target clusters, bows and hearts whilst their platinum mounts were further embellished with reeded decoration, engraved scrolls and even tiny rose diamonds in their galleries. Pendants and earrings were invariably composed of a round brilliant-cut diamond top stone supporting a larger pear-shaped diamond, Oriental pearl or precious stone drop. Designs were thus extremely simple but highly effective. The *negligée* pendant is typical of this genre where two gems are connected by either a platinum or white-gold rod and worn suspended from a simple matching trace chain. Brooches could range from the most basic bars set with a single stone or series of

Examples of early 20th-century platinum rings. Top row: Emerald cabochon and diamond cluster; marquise diamond and calibré ruby cluster; Oriental pearl in diamond flowerhead setting. Bottom row: sapphire and diamond double target cluster; Black opal and diamond oval cluster; elongated oval diamond three stone in a diamond cluster.

graduated gems to far more elaborate geometric shapes – roundels, squares, ovals and fans – in which the diamond frames are pierced with a delicate tracery to suggest gauze-like mesh, honeycombs and cobwebs. These superb brooches and pendants really were the finest examples of the craftsman's art since the mounts were sometimes composed of a series of tiny joints enabling the articulated jewel to be literally rolled or folded in half.

The demand for fine Belle Époque, Edwardian and early platinum jewellery has, frankly, never been higher and prime pieces, especially of French manufacture, will achieve top prices at auction or in the retail sector. Nevertheless, simple 'Garland' diamond pieces can still be bought relatively cheaply while secondary jewellery such as gold negligée pendants set with semi-precious stones, half pearl latticework brooches and simple diamond or gem-set bar brooches are still highly affordable and can make just as big an impact as costly 'formal' examples.

Further reading

Understanding Jewellery by David Bennett and Daniela Mascetti (Antique Collectors' Club, 1996)

Jewelry from Antiquity to the Present by Clare Phillips (Thames & Hudson, 1996)

Cartier 1900-1939 by Judy Rudoe (British Museum Press, 1997)

Chapter 17
Fabergé, Tiffany, Cartier and Their Contemporaries

Why Buy Signed Jewellery?

There is absolutely no doubt that a signature on a piece of well-made jewellery will enhance its value. In the case of some half a dozen celebrated international houses, this added premium can be quite considerable.

Manufacturers of luxury goods in general have always traded on the caché of their name and reputation. In some disciplines the difference in quality between the established product and its unattributed imitator can be purely negligible, demonstrating over and over again that a 'good name' conveys reassurance, style, social acceptability and old-fashioned snob appeal.

In the 19th century revivalist goldsmiths such as Castellani, Giuliano and Brogden routinely signed their jewellery with a house monogram. By the early 20th century Parisian jewellers such as Cartier, Boucheron and Chaumet not only signed their creations but engraved a unique serial number on the mount to prove authenticity and provide a 'library record' of the item's existence. Unfortunately, in a world fixated by good provenance, the evidence of a signature has given rise to the continuing and growing problem of fakes in which the addition of a spurious name can dramatically increase value. The problem is most deep rooted and widespread in the field of Fabergé where the sheer number of fakes on the market, occasionally proficient and frequently dreadful, has resulted in an ironic term being coined in the Fine Art lexicon – Fauxbergé.

So, why buy a clip by Cartier or bangle by Bulgari? The answer, quite simply, is reliability and superior craftsmanship. Raw materials such as diamonds, precious stones and their accompanying settings are carefully selected for their quality and consistency. Designs are bold, imaginative, exciting, thoroughly wearable and – a key asset in the world of jewellery – invariably timeless. Signed jewellery tends to be that much more expensive but the long-term commercial benefits may be considerable.

Peter Carl Fabergé

The life of this extraordinary goldsmith is well documented. Born on 30 May 1846, he attended business school in Dresden and subsequently visited Paris where he was heavily influenced by the abundance of neo-classical art

Opposite page: A fine and rare graduated two-row natural pearl necklace by Boucheron, ranging in size from 8.0mm to 2.6mm on an old-mine marquise-shaped diamond and platinum clasp, c.1910. Centre: Fine Cartier Burmese ruby ring, c.1905, the oval-shaped ruby weighing 3.30 carats on a platinum hoop with five diamonds set on each shoulder.

Fabergé two-colour gold cigarette case, c.1910, of rectangular oval section decorated with translucent yellow enamel on a wavy guilloché ground and set to the centre with an oval moss agate plaque set in a border of seed pearls; sapphire thumb push. Workmaster: Henrik Wigström.

Fabergé gold brooch mounted with two large purple sapphire cabochons in a border of seed pearls with a central line of small circular aquamarines, c.1905. Workmaster: August Hollming; '56' zolotnik stamp.

Fabergé silver-gilt rectangular box, c.1900, decorated with translucent strawberry-red enamel on a guilloché ground with twin gold laurel wreath bands and rose diamond-set thumb push. Workmaster: August Holmström. '88' zolotnik stamp.

Fabergé gold brooch, c.1905, of lozenge-shaped translucent lilac enamelled on a sunburst guilloché ground, edged in small diamonds and diamond tied bow surmount. Signed: 'Фаберже' (St. Petersburg); '56' zolotnik stamp.

Fabergé Siberian topaz and diamond brooch in the neo-classical taste, c.1900, in the original fitted hollywood box.

and architecture on display in the Louvre. At the age of twenty-four he took over control of his father's shop in St Petersburg and quickly gained a reputation for designing jewellery, silver and objets d'art of unparalleled elegance and originality. In 1884 he was commissioned by Tsar Alexander III to make the first Imperial Easter egg. This set the seal on a unique relationship between Fabergé and the Romanovs which was to continue right up to the cataclysmic events of the Bolshevik revolution in 1917. Indeed, Fabergé was fortunate to escape from Russia as a courier attached to the British Embassy. He died in Lausanne on 24 September 1920.

Fabergé's astonishing success was founded upon several critical factors. He was a brilliant marketing strategist and his relationship with the Imperial family opened many doors of influence throughout Europe. Perhaps his greatest success was expanding production to include purely decorative objets d'art – his so-called 'Objects of Fantasy' such as hardstone carvings, flower studies, toys and the celebrated Imperial Easter eggs. He made extensive use of translucent enamel recognising the importance of a medium which could decorate a large surface area and which often took the place of costly gemstones. He also perfected the technique of using several different colours of gold in his settings and favoured gems and hardstones which were indigenous

Important Fabergé gold parasol handle converted into a desk seal, c.1900, in the manner of Louis XVI of tapered cylindrical form decorated with three rose diamond-set latticework panels on an oyster-white enamelled guilloché ground, decorated with green and red enamelled foliate borders and wreaths set with half pearls, the cap finial set with a ruby cabochon in a pink enamelled surround repeated on the band above the base. Later added chalcedony seal stamp. Signed: 'Фаберже' (Fabergé). Workmaster: Michael Perchin: '56' zolotnik stamp.

Fabergé translucent lilac guilloché enamel, gold and diamond-set photograph frame. Fabergé frames often appear in interesting geometric shapes such as diamonds and six-pointed stars; the back covers are invariably cut from a sheet of ivory. Workmaster Michael Perchin, St Petersburg 1890-1895.

A group of Fabergé hardstone, enamel and jewelled egg pendants. Still fairly common today, miniature eggs offer collectors an accessible method of buying Russian jewellery at reasonable prices.

to Russia such as Siberian jade, rhodonite and lapis lazuli. Even the wood used in photograph frames and jewellery boxes was of Russian origin – palisander, Karelian birch and pale brown hollywood.

At the time of preparing this book the conflict between Russia and Ukraine has resulted in a range of sanctions being placed upon many foreign buyers of Russian Works of Art. This has inevitably resulted in a visible decline in Fabergé being consigned to international auction, the usual source of fresh material appearing on the market.

Needless to say, the uncertainty created by war and sanctions mean that prices of Fabergé have become far more subjective and difficult to predict with any degree of confidence. Nevertheless, it is still possible to buy modest brooches, small items of jewellery such as tiepins, cufflinks and miniature egg pendants in the salerooms, although condition is a crucial factor. Fakes can be difficult to spot, however. As a general guideline, look out for garish enamel colours which contain bubbles when examined under a lens, crude settings to gems, poor-quality goldwork and – a useful indicator for copies – makers' marks and assay stamps which are too obvious, too 'crisp' and too plentiful.

Tiffany and Jewellery in America

Extraordinarily versatile and original, Tiffany & Co. is rightly regarded as the leading pioneer of American jewellery and decorative arts since the 19th century. The firm was established by Charles Lewis Tiffany (1812-1902) in New York, initially specialising in giftware and stationery.

The stock was gradually expanded to include jewellery imported from Paris. The success of this operation led the firm to start designing and making its own distinctive jewels which, by the early 1900s, embraced a number of contrasting themes from traditional diamond and precious stone pieces in the fashionable 'Garland' style to bold and vibrant Art Nouveau floral studies and colourful enamelled symbolist jewellery mounted with unusual gemstones such as harlequin opal, fire opal and Montana sapphire.

On the death of C.L. Tiffany in 1902 the business was taken over by his son, Louis Comfort Tiffany (1848-1933), who developed many aspects of the decorative arts for which the company is celebrated today, most notably studio lamps, 'favrile' glass, ceramics, silver and metalware. In the 1950s several young and innovative craftsmen were commissioned to design their own jewellery for the company of which the most prominent was Jean Schlumberger, a Frenchman who introduced a range of chunky, enamelled gold bangles, earclips and rings exhibiting the famous Tiffany 'kiss' motif. This concept of independent artists developing their own range of ideas has continued right up to the present day with attractive and wearable jewellery designed by Paloma Picasso and Elsa Peretti now sold in Tiffany shops all over the world.

Tiffany is one of a group of prominent jewellers active in America from the early 1900s. Several of these long established firms, such as Oscar Heyman and Seaman Schepps of New York, are flourishing today. Each developed their own distinctive house style with the added ingredient of American flair and originality. Black, Starr & Frost produced elegant diamond jewellery in the European taste as far back as the 1850s, while another firm, J.E. Caldwell of Philadelphia, designed particularly pretty 'Belle Époque' platinum and gem-set pieces prized for their technical virtuosity.

The New York firm Marcus & Co. is closely associated with Art Nouveau enamel gold work. Unlike its European contemporaries, however, it chose to use plique-à-

Tiffany & Co. diamond chrysanthemum brooch with a cluster of Mississippi pearl petals, c.1910.

Tiffany & Co. platinum, diamond and graduated fancy-cut amethyst bow brooch, c.1925.

A Tiffany & Co. gold brooch designed as a winged cherub blaring a stylised puff of wind enamelled with the motto 'con amore' (with tenderness). A highly personal and romantic jewel, the mount is signed and engraved 'February 26 1893'.

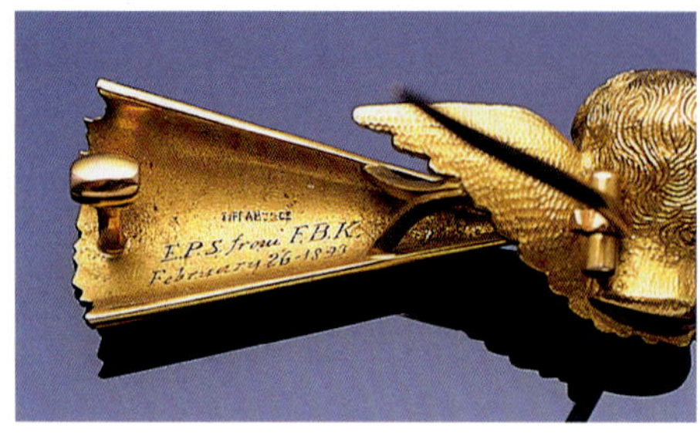

Reverse of the Tiffany brooch illustrating the Tiffany signature.

jour enamel in striking, dominant colours. This sense of confidence extended to its collection of Art Deco diamond jewellery which reflected the mood of innovation and flair in America between the wars.

Cartier, Van Cleef & Arpels and Boucheron

The progress of international jewellery from the end of the 19th century has, to quite a considerable extent, been driven by three Parisian firms which are recognised all over the world for the fantastic quality of their raw materials, their breathtaking imagination and the sheer brilliance of their designs. Each business has adapted its jewellery and accessories to keep ahead of the changing times and has pioneered advances in a broad range of skills from enamelling to the cutting and setting of gems. Ultimately all have played a major part in the way jewellery is worn today.

Cartier

The firm was founded in Paris in 1847 by Louis-François Cartier (1819-1904) and was subsequently taken over by his three grandsons Louis (1875-1942), Pierre (1878-1964) and Jacques (1884-1942) who each took responsibility for the development of the firm's operations in Paris, New York and London. The business was built up and consolidated by forging sound relationships with a host of important clients including European and international royalty, wealthy American financiers and industrialists, film stars and VIPs.

The great strength of Cartier was the firm's ability to introduce a wide and varied range of inspirations and themes into its jewellery designs, particularly during the

Exceptional Cartier Egyptian revival ruby and diamond pendant composed of a pavé diamond-set U-shaped pendant with stylised falcon head finials, the upper section set with a cluster of vari-size ruby cabochons and suspended at each side from a pair of black and red enamelled beads, mounted in platinum and gold and extending to a necklace (not shown) composed of alternating cylindrical and spherical onyx beads, c.1922-23.

Rare French Cartier 'montre bague navette' (navette-shaped) ring watch, c.1920, the dial bearing black Roman numerals, blued steel hands and visible balance within a rose-cut diamond bezel and diamond case.

years between the two world wars. Once Cartier had established itself as the leading manufacturer of jewellery in the 'Garland' style producing a constant flow of imposing diamond, platinum and pearl corsage ornaments, lavish collars, diadems and bandeaux, it turned its attention to exotic jewellery inspired by the art of Persia, ancient Egypt, India, Russia and China. Thus fine old Mughal gems were set in chic articulated Oriental diamond frames by the firm's Paris workshops, jewels in the Egyptian taste depicted pyramids, lotus flowers and 'Pharaonic' motifs fashioned from a combination of artfully set gems such as onyx, emerald and ruby, while Chinese and Japanese jewellery, clocks and accessories skilfully blended jet-black lacquer with a combination of coral, diamond and jade influenced by Oriental symbolism such as dragons, clouds and knotwork.

Fine Cartier diamond and platinum strap-work bracelet of Indo-Persian inspiration, c.1925.

Belle Époque French diamond and platinum bracelet by Boucheron of laurel leaf and foliate cluster design convertible to be worn as a bandeau hair ornament, c.1905.

Van Cleef & Arpels naturalistic platinum brooch in the japonaiserie taste. Made in 1927, this exquisite jewel is set with mirror-cut diamonds in the butterfly and individually polished and shaped emeralds and sapphires in the cornflower – elegance and technical virtuosity seamlessly combined.

Platinum brooch by Van Cleef & Arpels of tied bow design set with brilliant-cut diamonds and calibré-cut sapphires, c.1920.

Rare Van Cleef & Arpels French platinum and diamond bracelet watch, c.1930, the square dial below a single portrait-cut diamond cover.

Pair of French diamond architectural dress clips/hair clips by Van Cleef & Arpels, c.1930, of rectangular form with chevron finials set with brilliant-cut and baguette-cut diamonds.

By the 1930s the taste for Art Deco 'architectural' jewellery was in full swing and Cartier adapted its designs once again to create a stunning range of bold and original jewels in which gems were purposely cut, shaped and set to reinforce the sense of geometry and linear structure fashionable at the time. During the 1940s and 1950s the firm introduced a series of striking gold jewels inspired by such diverse themes as 'bicycle chains' and 'gaspipes'. In the 1970s the firm's 'Must de Cartier' range was introduced to create a line of affordable and wearable jewellery, wristwatches and accessories; indeed Cartier wristwatches such as the 'Panthère', 'Tank Française' and 'Pasha' are among the most popular models available on the market today.

Van Cleef & Arpels

The firm was established in Paris in 1898 when Alfred Van Cleef (1873-1938) formed an association with his two brothers-in-law Charles Arpels (1880-1951) and Julien Arpels (1884-1964).

Pair of French 18-carat gold entwined rope pattern earclips by Boucheron set with lines of rubies, sapphires, emeralds and brilliant-cut diamonds, c.1960.

Fine ring by Boucheron, c.1960, mounted with an elongated rectangular Kashmir sapphire weighing 4.97 carats on a broad platinum hoop with baguette-cut diamonds extending down the shoulders.

The technique with which Van Cleef & Arpels is most closely associated today is 'serti mysterieux' (invisible setting) in which rubies or sapphires are set in side-by-side formation with no apparent metal or mounting visible from the front. This sophisticated method involved chiselling grooves into the back of each individual stone and sliding them on to a series of gold or platinum rails. The technique made an enormous impact when it first appeared in 1935 and was used to great effect in brooches, bracelets and earclips of floral cluster and leaf design.

In the 1920s and 1930s the firm produced striking naturalistic and architectural jewels such as bracelets of 'Egyptian' influence inspired by the discovery of Tutankhamun's tomb in 1922 and, in the early 1940s, a range of distinctive broad gold bracelets and brooch clips composed of a series of honeycomb-shaped sections known as 'ludo hexagone' motifs. Like their celebrated contemporary Cartier, Van Cleef & Arpels moved with the times and by the 1960s the firm began to create a range of strongly chromatic jewellery set with contrasting gems such as polished emerald and ruby cabochons and diamonds in yellow-gold mounts.

Boucheron

After a fairly modest start at a small jewellery shop founded in 1858, Frédéric Boucheron (1830-1902) moved to far grander premises at 26 Place Vendôme, Paris. Much of Boucheron's early success was his reputation as a society jeweller supplying formal diamond jewels – tiaras, corsage brooches and elaborate collars – to brides, bridesmaids and their guests at formal wedding receptions held in the capital. Exactly like Cartier, Van Cleef & Arpels and other leading French jewellers such as Chaumet and Vever, Boucheron moved with the changing times and by the end of the 19th century was producing highly original pieces using innovative materials – for example, plique-à-jour enamel and gold combined with base metals. After Frédéric Boucheron died in 1902 the business was continued by his son Louis. In 1907 a shop was founded in London. Boucheron jewellery exhibits a distinctive style with a strong tendency towards formality, boldness and colour. Some of the firm's Art Deco jewellery – their range of carved hardstone flower jewellery, for instance – displays a marvellous imagination blended with exceptional technical skill.

Further reading

Jewelry in America, Martha Gandy Fales (Antique Collectors' Club, 1995)

Fabergé's Imperial Jewels, Géza von Habsburg and Marina Lopato (Fabergé Arts Foundation, 1993)

Fabergé in London, Kieran McCarthy (Antique Collectors' Club, 2017)

Cartier, Hans Nadelhoffer (Thames & Hudson, 1984)

Cartier 1900-1939, Judy Rudoe (British Museum Press, 1997)

The Art of Carl Fabergé, A. Kenneth Snowman (Faber & Faber, 1953)

The Master Jewellers, Edited by A. Kenneth Snowman (Thames & Hudson, 1990)

Russian Decorative Arts, Cynthia Coleman Sparke (Antique Collectors' Club, 2014)

Chapter 18
Art Deco and the Architectural Revolution

The catastrophic events of the First World War had a fairly devastating effect on art and artistic design in general; jewellery was certainly no exception. After 1918 it seemed singularly inappropriate and passé to wear delicate diamond 'Garland' sprays while Art Nouveau naturalistic enamels seemed firmly rooted in a time obliterated in the trenches of the Western Front.

A sense of restlessness and change was quickly spreading through Britain, Europe and America and it was inevitable that this would be articulated in new and daring artistic forms and shapes in absolute contrast to all the established formulae of the past. Another vitally important change was the sense of freedom and independence gained by women in society. During the war women had worked alongside men and for the first time ever had become the principal breadwinners while their husbands were away fighting at the Front. It soon became apparent that the values and attitudes of life before the war when helpless, fluttering ladies were adorned from head to foot in formal jewels to reinforce the concept of feminine perfection were well and truly over. An altogether more mature, businesslike woman now emerged favouring simple, uncluttered clothes and jewellery which was both practical and utilitarian in concept and design.

Pair of French platinum, diamond and 'invisibly set' sapphire earrings by Rubel Frères, c.1935, each mounted with a fanned spray of nine oval sapphires extending from lines of baguette-cut diamonds offset by arched sections of brilliant- and baguette-cut diamonds. The technique for setting gems such as sapphires and rubies without any visible claws or collets was first perfected by Van Cleef & Arpels in 1933. Known as 'mystery set' the effect was achieved by a delicate lattice of rails slotting into grooves cut in the pavilion of each individual gem which were then positioned in side-by-side formation. Technically hugely challenging, the process took hundreds of hours to complete. The sapphires in these remarkable earrings slot into a collet rather than a neighbouring stone and use screws on the backs enabling no fittings to be visible when worn.

Paris was still very much the epicentre of artistic inspiration and plans first proposed before the war were put into place to hold a major exhibition that could be a focal point for the diverse and often controversial ideas which were rapidly beginning to coalesce into one dominating style. In 1925 the rather grandly titled 'Exposition Internationale des Arts Décoratifs et Industriels Modernes' was opened in the centre of the city attracting several million visitors who came to admire furniture, sculpture, glass, ceramics, silver and particularly jewellery in which the principle common to all was 'new inspiration and real originality'. The exhibition made a huge cultural impact and gave its name to a movement which is synonymous today with elegance and chic – *Art Deco.*

Several different artistic concepts all contributed to Art Deco including Fauvism, Cubism and the early work of the Vienna Secessionists whose emphasis on minimal geometric lines was visibly apparent as far back as the start of the century. The simple, linear expression was quickly adopted by fashionable couturiers such as Coco Chanel and Elsa Schiaparelli who both launched a range of elegant, tailored suits for daywear which were smart and comfortable, in large part due to their considerably shorter hemlines. Evening gowns in silk and satin were incredibly sophisticated and figure-hugging; the *gamine*

French rectangular diamond plaque brooch millegrain set with brilliant-cut diamonds in pierced geometric formation within a border of small buff-top polished calibré sapphires, c.1925.

Elegant Art Deco articulated diamond and platinum earrings each suspending an oval-shaped Ceylon sapphire estimated to weigh 4.5 carats, c.1925.

French diamond epaulette-shaped platinum brooch pavé set with brilliant-cut diamonds and mounted with a polished Burmese sapphire with diamond baton fringe, c.1925.

look was in, accentuated by boyish figures and short, cropped hair. Unsurprisingly, long diamond earrings and ropes of pearls and sautoirs were particularly popular at this time.

In 1922 Howard Carter discovered the tomb of the Egyptian boy king Tutankhamun. This inspired a host of Parisian jewellers such as Cartier, Van Cleef & Arpels and Lacloche to create a range of 'Pharaonic' bracelets, brooches and clips set with solid clusters of emeralds, rubies, onyx and diamonds in a range of complex designs which included hieroglyphics, pyramids, scarabs and lotus flowers. This kind of jewellery is extremely rare today and commands staggeringly high prices at auction; a Lacloche or Cartier 'Egyptian' bracelet can easily fetch £500,000.

The idea of 'blocks' of colour strongly reinforced the Art Deco concept. Bold, decisive stones such as turquoise, chrysoprase, onyx and coral were cut into cubes, pyramids or batons and set against geometric clusters of 'white' diamonds which were mounted in 'architectural' three-dimensional platinum settings. Rock crystal was another important material. Inexpensive and plentiful, it could be cut and shaped into interesting angular shapes which looked sensational when mounted with onyx and diamonds in jewellery which was strongly monochromatic in appearance.

Unlike Arts and Crafts jewellery, large costly precious gems were certainly back in fashion during the 1920s.

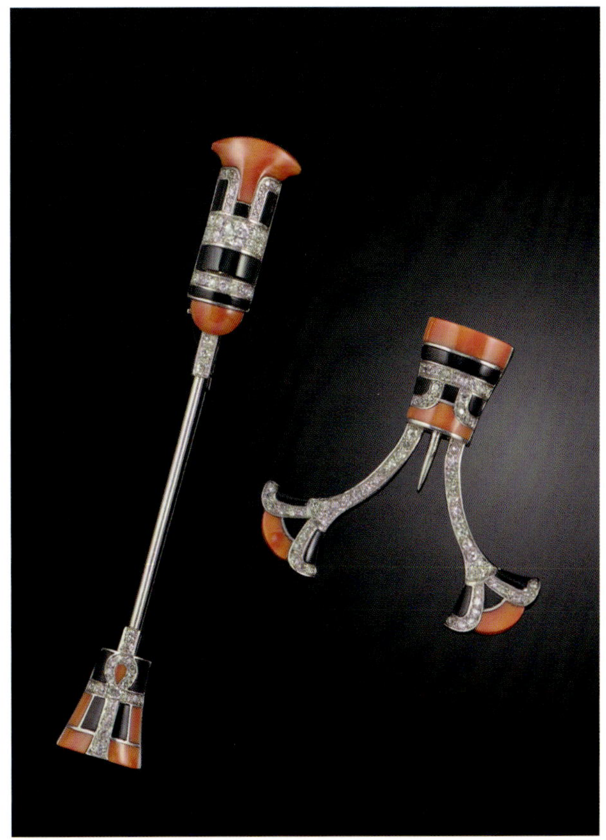

Art Deco platinum jabot pin/brooch by Cartier, c.1925, of Egyptian inspiration set with diamonds and coral and onyx sections in a stylised lotus leaf pattern, the finial with a similarly set Chi-Rho motif.

Art Deco platinum ring mounted with a square sugarloaf coral cabochon in an architectural setting of onyx and diamonds, c.1930.

Art Deco platinum drop earrings, c.1925, set with diamonds and slender calibré onyx batons with coral teardrops suspended below.

Burmese rubies and sapphires and Colombian emeralds were polished into sleek geometric shapes such as rectangular step-cuts, triangles and squares which were placed in architectural frames totally devoid of unnecessary embellishment or fussy engraving. Diamonds were cut into a shape which is closely associated with Art Deco jewellery – the *baguette*. The baguette-cut was ideal for slotting into geometric frames and contrasted perfectly with similarly shaped *calibré-cut* emeralds, rubies and sapphires. Brilliant-cut diamonds had, by the late 1920s, completely lost their irregular cushion-like Victorian proportions and could be set in regular lines or clusters which also accentuated the architectural ideal.

The profound success of Art Deco jewellery between the wars consolidated the reputation and growth of several international houses, among the best known of which are Cartier, Boucheron, Chaumet, Lacloche and Van Cleef & Arpels. These jewellers each had their own distinctive 'house style.' Van Cleef & Arpels, for example, pioneered the development of 'invisible settings' while Boucheron specialised in formal designs for the grand occasion and bold, angular jewels set with a combination of colourful hardstones in geometric formation. Cartier, probably the best-known jewellery house in the world today, constantly changed the direction of its output during the 1920s and 1930s producing a remarkable diversity of superb designs inspired by the art of China, Persia, India and Egypt. For example, their range of 'tutti frutti' jewellery – bracelets, clips and collars – consisted of old Mughal gems (emeralds, rubies and sapphires) which had formerly adorned splendid turbans and neck ornaments. These gems, carved into the

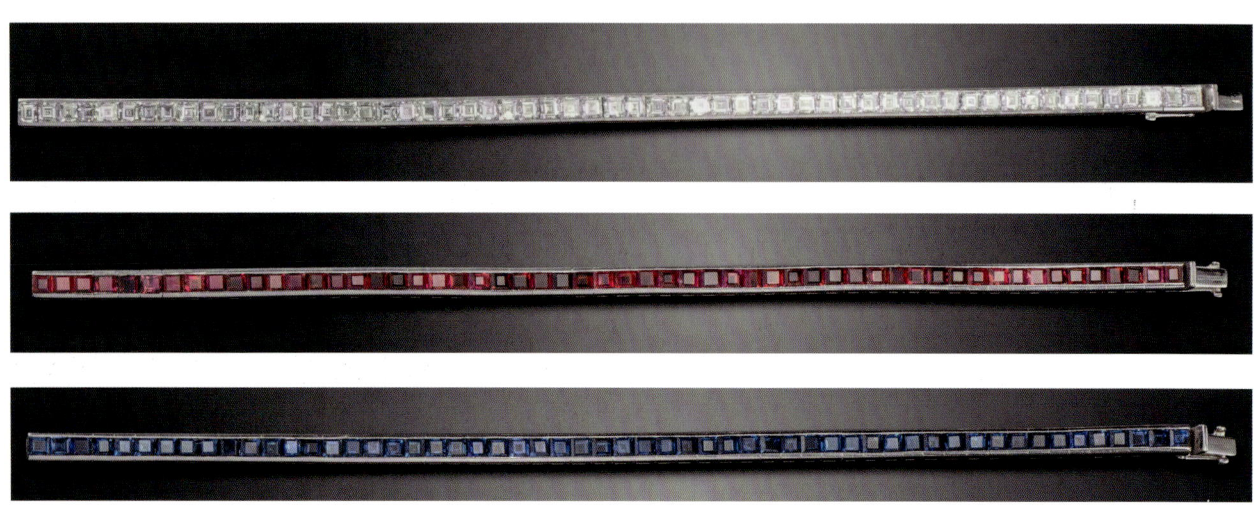

Three Art Deco platinum line bracelets each individually channel-set with a line of square-cut diamonds, rubies and sapphires.

Pair of 'Tutti-Frutti' platinum earclips of scrolling design set with brilliant- and baguette-cut diamonds and mounted with carved Indian emeralds and rubies, c.1945-50.

Art Deco 'Tutti-Frutti' platinum bracelet composed of four alternating clusters of carved Indian emeralds and rubies with diamond polka dot accents and between, four oblong baguette- and brilliant-cut diamond sections, c.1930.

shape of flowers and leaves, were then remounted in platinum and diamond settings in a wide range of designs such as *jardinières,* charming vase of flowers studies which recall the pretty 'garden' jewels of the 18th century except that, instead of Georgian diamonds, the little pots and stems were invariably decorated with black lacquer or lines of calibré onyx or emeralds.

Another important development was the expanding popularity of the wristwatch. From modest little gold or silver models by obscure Swiss manufacturers to fine diamond and precious gem-set examples by the big French houses, wristwatches had, by the early 1930s, totally superseded pocket watches. The angular shape of the watch head and bracelet were ideal for setting small brilliant- and baguette-cut diamonds in geometric formation while less expensive models were attached to black or grey silk cordette straps. Many of these examples are surprisingly inexpensive today, although a well-known name such as Cartier, Patek Philippe or Rolex will impact considerably on value.

The 1920s were vintage years for the bracelet, from

Art Deco 'Tutti-Frutti' platinum brooch, c.1930, of giardinetto design set throughout with brilliant-cut and baguette-cut diamonds and five large carved Indian emeralds and rubies with polished black onyx highlights and emerald cabochon finial.

French Art Deco 'Tutti-Frutti' platinum and diamond clip by Chaumet, c.1930, set with a cluster of carved emeralds, rubies and sapphires in an architectural frame.

French Art Deco platinum hoop ring by Mauboussin, c.1930, set with carved emeralds, rubies and sapphires and brilliant- and baguette-cut diamonds.

Rare American Art Deco propellor-shaped platinum brooch by Gillot & Co., c.1925, channel-set with a line of rectangular step-cut emeralds, sapphires and diamonds terminating in tapered rubies with similarly set calibré-cut lotus style finials and an outer border of small diamonds.

Working diagram of the Gerard Sandoz bracelet (see below).

pretty, narrow, fully articulated ribbons with bow-shaped centrepieces to complex multi gem-set Egyptian Revival straps. Line bracelets were especially popular, composed of a simple row of brilliant- or square-cut diamonds or diamonds in tandem with square onyx, emerald, ruby or sapphire. 1930s bracelets were altogether broader, heavier and more angular; many of these later styles can be rather mixed in quality combining brilliant baguette- and single-cut diamonds in repetitive scroll-like sections mounted in poorly finished white-gold frames.

The brooch, in a myriad of interesting forms, was a consistent Art Deco favourite. In common with bracelets earlier, 1920s brooches still hung on to the softer, gentler forms of the Belle Époque era and, although designs in the latter part of the decade clearly anticipated the geometry of the 1930s, they are generally speaking prettier and

French Art Deco gold bracelet by Gerard Sandoz, c.1925, composed of four circular carved jadeite plaques decorated with floral motifs alternating with four highly polished square gold plaques each centrally set with a prism of lapis lazuli between black enamel line sides. Together with its original gouache drawing. See working diagram (above).

Art Deco nephrite jade drum-shaped poudrier box by Cartier, c.1925, of Chinese inspiration, the body with four cylindrical onyx cuboid supports set with rose-cut diamonds resting upon red enamelled feet, the lid applied with a carved onyx and enamel surmount with polished rock crystal ring handle.

Chinese Art Deco carved jadeite pendant pierced with birds and foliage suspended from a platinum and diamond pagoda-form top, c.1925.

Art Deco pendant mounted with a carved and pierced oval jadeite plaque between twin coral batons with diamond-set onyx and black enamel highlights, c.1925.

Splendid Art Deco sautoir necklace by Rood, c.1930, mounted in platinum with square-cut emeralds, brilliant-cut and baguette-cut diamonds in architectural formation and suspending a similarly set key-shaped pendant. A quintessential piece of Art Deco, this impressive necklace can be dismantled to form a shorter necklace and a pair of bracelets (one of which is shown here). S.J. Rood was a leading family jeweller founded in 1873 and based in London's Burlington Arcade.

French Art Deco platinum and 18-carat gold double-clip brooch by Mauboussin, c.1935, each clip set with 14 square step-cut sapphires in an architectural frame of brilliant- and baguette-cut diamonds.

more imaginative. Sought-after designs included bows vividly contrasting diamonds with calibré-cut rubies or sapphires, epaulettes, fobs – usually articulated and set with small clusters of diamonds – ovals, cartouches, straps and hoops. Indeed, the hoop brooch was the quintessential Art Deco jewel composed of a large ring of onyx or rock crystal between diamond chevron sides. Novelties were also in fashion in the 1920s with sporting, racing and recreational subjects captured in gold or platinum. An interesting and fairly common method of wearing a simple brooch in the 1920s was the *sureté* or *jabot* pin in which the head of the jewel could be detached, the pin pushed through the garment and the head snapped back on the now-hidden shaft. Invariably fashioned as arrows or moulded glass buddhas, sureté pins are particularly collectable and relatively affordable today.

By the 1930s pretty pins and bows were superseded by all diamond-set architectural clips of which the most fashionable concept was the so-called double clip brooch. Composed of a pair of identical 'back-to-back' sections, each clip fastened on to a simple platinum or white-gold frame. Superior models contained a series of tiny pegs which slotted into receiving apertures. Double clip brooches could therefore be worn as a single jewel or dismantled to be attached to both lapels of a smart jacket. The natural extension of the double clip was the plaque brooch where geometric clusters of brilliant-, baguette- and single-cut diamonds were fashioned into a simple oblong or cartouche. Plaque brooches were extremely common before the war and of highly variable quality.

The 1920s and 1930s will always be associated with glamour, excess, fantastic parties, dancing, film stars and riotous fun. Cigarette cases, the ultimate fashion accessory, ranged from straightforward 9-carat gold or silver examples by Mappin & Webb or Asprey to highly colourful exotic creations by Cartier, Lacloche or Van Cleef & Arpels. These could be extraordinarily imaginative, decorated with enamel or set with hardstones such as lapis lazuli, jade and coral in a range of influences from Chinese to Persian and Egyptian. Smoking was, of course, socially acceptable at this time and, in addition, both men and women habitually used cigarette holders in a range of materials which included amber, polished gold, onyx and hardstone with rose-diamond fittings.

Women's accessories were in general use by the 1920s. Gold mesh evening bags were sometimes decorated with bold enamelling or set with lines of polished gems and diamonds while vanity cases in a variety of shapes and designs were frequently enamelled in pretty geometric patterns or coated in black lacquer. Sometimes these compacts were suspended from a tubular-shaped top section which doubled up as a lipstick holder – very messy at times when the contents leaked! Another highly fashionable accessory was the multi-purpose vanity case known as the *minaudière*. Patented by Van Cleef & Arpels, these useful receptacles contained compartments for cigarettes, powder, lipstick, comb, postage stamps and there was even space for a little watch head. Occasionally made from gold or silver and more commonly in white metal, French minaudières were sold in chic black suede wallets and perfectly complemented the sense of gaiety of the time.

Further reading

Antique and Twentieth Century Jewellery, Vivienne Becker (NAG Press, 1980)

Understanding Jewellery, David Bennett and Daniela Mascetti (Antique Collectors' Club, 1996)

Christie's Twentieth Century Jewellery, Sally Everitt and David Lancaster (Pavilion Books Ltd, 2002)

Art Deco Jewelry, Sylvie Raulet (Thames & Hudson, 2002)

Chapter 19

The 1940s and 1950s. Austerity, Creativity and Development of the 'Modern Style'

If the 1930s were synonymous with the bold angular shapes, striking colour combinations and the exuberant optimism which defined the Art Deco movement then, as far as jewellery design was concerned, the first five years of the 1940s could not have been more of a contrast. Never mind the sheer upheaval and economic chaos created by global conflict, essential precious metals such as gold and platinum became increasingly scarce and correspondingly expensive, while diamonds were siphoned out of the luxury jewellery sector and put to far more important use in the munitions industry for precision machinery, drill heads and optics.

In Nazi-occupied Europe much pre-war jewellery was seized and broken up for the stones and precious metal content, never to be seen again, while diamond and gem dealers, designer craftsmen and shopkeepers – many of whom were Jewish – perished in such death camps as Buchenwald, Bergen-Belsen and Auschwitz-Birkenau. This, inevitably, left a huge void, not only in the loss of manpower but also the wealth of knowledge, experience and technical know-how which had existed for generations before the outbreak of global conflict in 1939.

This is not to say that the jewellery industry faded away entirely during the cataclysmic war years. Jewellery certainly flourished in German-occupied Paris while in Britain, silver was available in limited amounts for inexpensive items such as Regimental brooches, and decorative bracelets. In America things went on pretty much as before, although after the war jewellery design fundamentally changed direction. There was still a flourishing market for 'architectural' diamond rings, brooches and bracelets but as the decade progressed the influence of Art Deco gave way to an altogether new and dynamic look known as the 'Modern Style'.

1940s gold bow brooch mounted with an emerald-cut blue topaz in a setting of circular-cut rubies and brilliant-cut diamonds on a polished gold ribbon frame.

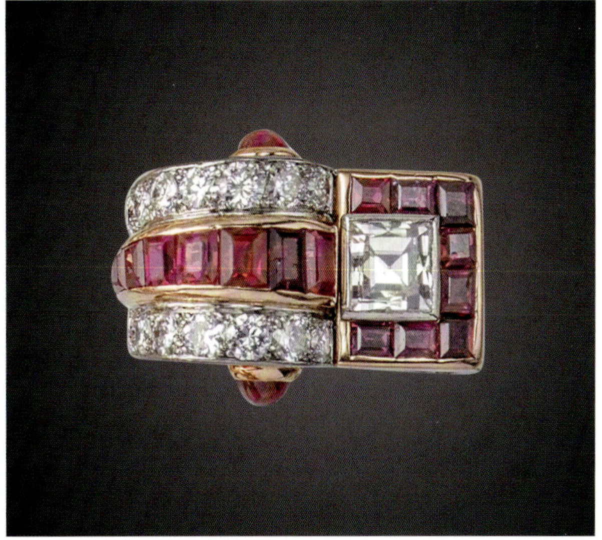

Retro-style 1940s ring mounted in gold and platinum of architectural construction set with a principal square-cut diamond, smaller brilliant-cut diamonds, cabochon-cut and calibré-cut rubies.

Pair of 1940s Van Cleef & Arpels French naturalistic gold earclips set with clusters of circular-cut rubies. Individually numbered together with the suffix 'CS' suggesting they were a special customised order.

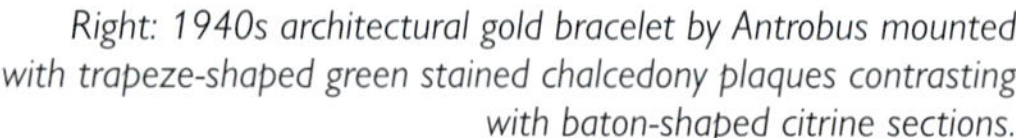

Right: 1940s architectural gold bracelet by Antrobus mounted with trapeze-shaped green stained chalcedony plaques contrasting with baton-shaped citrine sections.

A group of striking postwar gold jewels, c.1945–55, including a 'retro' collar mounted with vari-colour and vari-shape citrines and diamonds; an adjustable diamond-set 'gaspipe' collar, an asymmetric dress clip set with a cascade of citrines and a single large brown zircon, a pair of citrine sunburst earclips and a highly unusual gold, citrine and diamond 'organ pipe' bracelet by Michele Abate (1896–1981) suspending a line of conical drops with citrine cabochon finials.

1940s Bombe-style dress ring set with a principal round transitional-cut diamond on a pavé-set diamond and gold architectural mount.

1940s dress clip exhibiting an interesting combination of colours and shapes; the central emerald-cut green tourmaline effectively contrasting with fancy-cut dark brown citrines and diamonds.

1940s versatility and ingenuity: a gold dress ring of heavily fluted design set with batons of brilliant-cut diamonds and calibré-cut sapphires. The top of the ring is hinged at the side and opens to reveal a copper-colour watch face concealed within.

Unconventional, eye-catching and, frequently, downright eccentric this kind of jewellery seemed to be in perfect alignment with the restless desire for change following six years of strife and austerity and, ultimately, was to be adopted by all the leading international jewel houses. Instead of expensive (and difficult to source) precious gems, affordable – and colourful – semi-precious stones such as amethyst, zircon, tourmaline and peridot began to appear in bold, visually striking chunky gold dress rings, earrings, necklaces and oversized cuff bangles. Brooches were particularly suited to this new look for jewellery; a 1940s sculptural gold clip, for example, might be set with a large step-cut aquamarine in a semicircle of polished ruby cabochons; turquoises were found to be eminently compatible with sapphires or rubies while a particular favourite – used very effectively by Cartier – blended citrine of a warm golden-brown colour contrasting with citrine of a deeper, orangey hue. By artfully setting these stones in highly individual three-dimensional yellow-gold mounts a really dynamic effect could be achieved, and usually at a price far more affordable than diamonds, precious gems and platinum.

In 1951 the Festival of Britain, held on London's South Bank, proved to be the catalyst for a number of prominent London jewellery manufacturers to showcase a new range of innovative designs. Leading firms such as David Shackman and Sons, Stellman's, The Goldsmiths and Silversmiths Company and Garrard & Co. produced jewellery exhibiting a strong naturalistic influence – feathers, flowers, stylised birds and leaves. The settings themselves incorporated a range of interesting and dynamic features such as cylindrical batons, stirrups, nautical rope motifs and gems in three-dimensional clusters. The key elements of all this post-war jewellery was visual impact, individuality and effortless style. Necklaces and bracelets benefited particularly well from the addition of these new visual motifs, while the drive for industrial prosperity, underpinned by the exhibition itself, led to the creation of jewellery with a strong mechanical association such as the so-called 'gas-pipe' – a ribbed, snake-like flattened tube of gold often with gem-set finials.

Brooches were hugely popular during the 1950s and were to become a near-obligatory fashion accessory for at least the next twenty years. Often highly stylised and remarkably imaginative, a typical brooch clip of the '50's might be designed as a 'character in costume' – such as a ballerina wearing a jewelled tutu, a gem-set clown, a cowboy or a sporting subject such as a golfer or skier. Easy to wear and often relatively inexpensive they became witty and amusing conversation pieces, embracing a remarkably diverse range of subjects. Insects, birds and animals were particularly fashionable; dogs (especially poodles), 'winking' cats (known as '*chat malicieux*'), monkeys, owls and ladybirds; nothing, it seemed, was immune from the jewellery designer's creative imagination; needless to say, signed examples by leading manufacturers

1950s Cartier gold novelty beetle brooch with fluted coral thorax, lapis lazuli abdomen and emerald cabochon eyes signed 'Cartier London'.

French 1950s platinum and gold stylised ballerina brooch in the manner of Rubel Frères set with turquoise cabochons and brilliant-cut diamonds. This kind of novelty brooch proved extremely popular in the 1950s; examples by leading jewellers such as Van Cleef & Arpels are highly sought today with a correspondingly high value.

1950s gold 'propellor' brooch set with lines and clusters of graduated circular sapphires in a 'rotor' style frame. This interesting design incorporates the sort of strong industrial and mechanical elements often seen in jewellery of this period.

such as Cartier, Van Cleef & Arpels and Kutchinsky are highly sought today.

Perhaps unsurprisingly, it took a certain degree of confidence to carry off this type of look and for the more 'conventional' owner the most popular item of jewellery worn throughout the 1950s and beyond was the cultured pearl necklace, usually a graduated single row on a semi-precious gem-set clasp worn in the daytime or, a more elaborate three-row on a diamond clasp for more formal evening wear. Versatile, elegant and practical, the cultured pearl necklace was the 'must-have' accessory for a new generation of women many of whom, having gained a new

1950s French Boucheron gold wirework brooch naturalistically modelled as a feather and set with sapphires and diamonds.

Silver wirework torc collar suspending an abstract three-dimensional rectangular pendant. Designed and made by Alan Davie, c.1954.

Cartier gold, platinum, sapphire and diamond cockerel brooch. This beautifully observed piece captures all the essence and humour of the highest grade of 1950s figurative jewellery – even to the extent of setting tiny royal blue polka dots between the sapphires on the bird's breast. A veritable tour de force of the craftsman's art.

sense of freedom and independence during the war years, were going out to work for themselves. Many thousands of cultured pearl necklaces and bracelets were sold in this era of the cocktail party and the 'London season' although sadly, they are decidedly uncommercial today.

Generally speaking, diamond jewellery of the 1950s was recognisable for settings which suggested a less rigid, flowing 'organic' construction, exhibiting such features as scrolls, entwined ribbons, tied bows, drapes and floral cascades. Baguette-cut diamonds became a key component of much formal jewellery during this period; a typical double-clip brooch or necklace would often blend together both round brilliant-cut and baguette-cut diamonds, invariably set in asymmetric formation. Another significant development was that the settings used in the vast majority of formal diamond necklaces, bracelets and earrings were made out of 18-carat white-gold rather than platinum – the universal precious metal of the Art Deco period. Jewellery became increasingly adaptable in the '50s; hidden hook fittings would enable the wearer to dismantle the front section of a necklace and convert it into a separate pendant or brooch while another interesting feature of earrings in the 1950s was the so-called 'night and day' effect; a pair of modest diamond earclips worn during the day were transformed in the evening by attaching a line of baguette diamonds, gems

A fashion model photographed in 1953 wearing a classic three-row cultured pearl necklace, a pair of pearl and diamond earrings and a diamond spray brooch.

1950s formal wear; a diadem set with brilliant- and baguette-cut diamonds (convertible to be worn as a necklace or a brooch), 'night and day' earrings and an elaborate diamond necklace of asymmetric 'drape' design. This kind of diamond jewellery was popular in the era of cocktail parties and the kind of grand society balls which were held in the so-called 'London Season'.

9-carat gold jewellery in the early 1950s. Hard-wearing, stylish and adaptable, 9-carat gold had the great advantage of being affordable – an important feature at a time of rationing and bleak financial outlook.

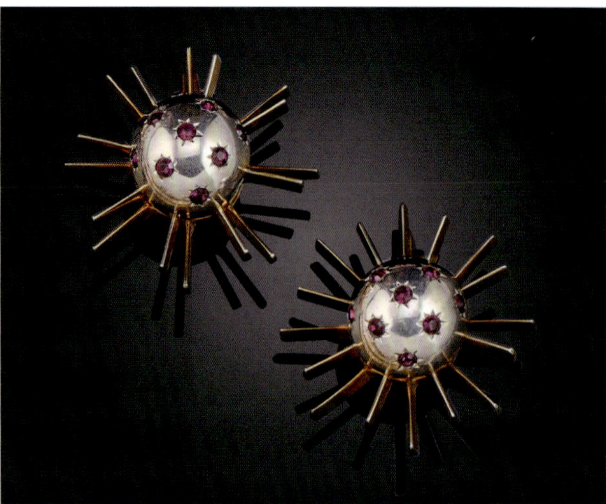

Pair of silver and gold earrings star-set with small circular garnets. Inspired by the Soviet Union's launch of Sputnik 1 on 4 October 1957.

or pearl suspension drops – an imaginative and versatile feature of jewellery in an era in which the echoes of wartime frugality still reverberated.

Accessories – wristwatches, cufflinks, powder compacts, lighters and cigarette cases – boomed in the post-war period. Jewelled watches were often incredibly stylish, more an article of jewellery than a timepiece. It became fashionable to conceal the movement by means of a sprung cover – so giving every appearance of a formal bracelet – while the watch case itself, often three-dimensional in construction, might be mounted at an asymmetrical angle and set with fancy-cut diamonds and colourful gems (rubies were particularly popular). The bracelets of these watches were just as interesting as the cases; tactile and chunky, examples made in the 1940s and 1950s were invariably fashioned from 18-carat gold and designed as ribbons of mesh, honeycomb-patterned straps, sinuous snake-like cords and articulated hinged panels.

A particularly notable accessory in this era of cocktail parties and 'The London Season' was the so-called *minaudière* – a rectangular multipurpose vanity case fashioned in gold, silver and metal (or a combination of all three) with several different compartments for the sort of practical essentials necessary for a grand evening out: cigarettes, lipstick, comb and mirror. Today, *minaudières* seem to be the perfect vehicle for conveying the sort of chic, up-to-the-minute fashion, fun and social viability which so many people craved after six long years of global war and austerity.

Further reading

International Exhibition of Modern Jewellery 1890-1961, (Worshipful Company of Goldsmiths, 1961)

Understanding Jewellery, David Bennett and Daniela Mascetti (Antique Collectors' Club, 1996)

Contemporary Jewellery and Silver Design, E.D.S. Bradford (Hazell, Watson & Viney, 1950)

Modern Jewellery. An International Survey 1890-1963, Graham Hughes (Studio Books, 1963)

Jewelry from Antiquity to Present, Clare Phillips (Thames & Hudson, 1996)

Chapter 20
The 1960s and 1970s. Experimentation and Development of 'The Designer Jewel'

In 1961 an important exhibition was organised by the Worshipful Company of Goldsmiths in association with the Victoria and Albert Museum. Called the 'International Exhibition of Modern Jewellery 1890-1961' it showcased many ravishing turn-of-the-century and later creations by well-established jewel houses such as Lalique, Fabergé, Chaumet and Bulgari as well as a broad range of modern and daringly innovative designer jewels by young up-and-coming British jewellers including David Thomas, Geoffrey Turk and John Donald. Also on display were a number of striking pieces by leading international craftsmen such as Stern, Jean Schlumberger and Verdura. It would be very interesting to turn the clock back and see just what members of the public made of some of the more exotic jewels on display. Pomodoro, for example, exhibited a massive and primitive looking cuff bracelet with applied molten decoration while a designer called John Paul Miller submitted a remarkable jewel fashioned as an octopus with lifelike tendrils extending from its shell. Gilbert Albert, a young and highly talented Swiss jeweller, loaned a splendid diamond collar in which the stones themselves were individually connected by a free-flowing series of asymmetrical rods.

In many ways, jewellery of the 1960s straddled two distinctly contrasting themes: the conventional look enshrined by the kind of traditional diamond rings, cultured pearl necklaces and formulaic brooches which had been sold by many high street retailers since the 1930s to the wildly experimental, abstract and visually arresting free-flowing forms which heralded an entirely new age of innovation and dynamic change. Needless to say, this wasn't only confined to the world of jewellery but

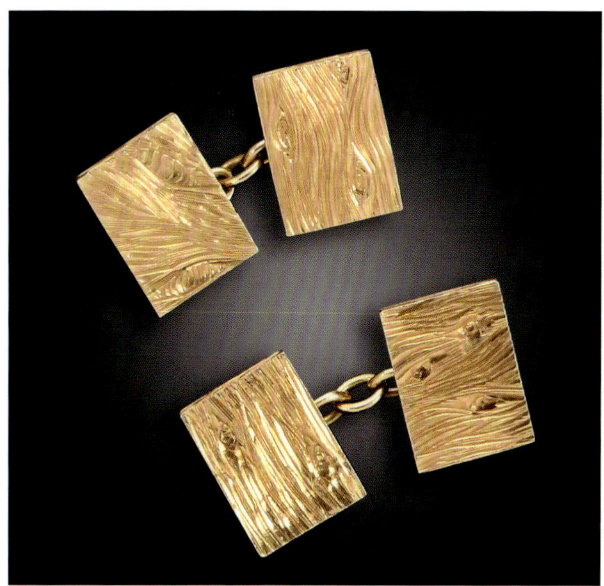

Pair of Boucheron textured bark-finish gold sleeve links. London, 1963.

Nanna and Jorgen Ditzel for Georg Jensen; Danish gold modernist architectural bangle bearing import marks for London 1961. A prime example of Scandinavian pared down simplicity characteristic of Jensen's creative work during this period

Cartier French gold collar of woven meshwork with crossover ribbon front and brilliant-cut diamond accents. Bearing later import hallmarks for London, 1961. A good example of the sort of highly wearable design in which Cartier excelled, ideal for the neckline of dresses and knitwear fashionable in the early 1960s.

Kutchinsky gold, ruby and diamond coiled wirework feather brooch and matching earrings, London 1963. Kutchinsky excelled in this kind of delicate naturalistic jewellery in the 1960s. Rubies and diamonds were always a popular choice as well as other interesting colour gem combinations such as rubies or sapphires blended with clusters of turquoises.

reverberated in just about every aspect of fashion, music, art and architecture.

These days, the craftsmen active in Britain in the early to mid 1960s are rightly seen as pioneers of the post-war revolution in jewellery construction and design, and their work is highly sought by dealers and collectors. One of the most celebrated today is Andrew Grima, who, from his unique slate-fronted premises in Jermyn Street off Piccadilly, sold a remarkably bold and dynamic range of sculptural gold jewels mounted with colourful semi-precious stones, baroque-shaped pearls and rough gem crystals. Using relatively inexpensive uncut and unpolished gems became a signature feature of several award-winning jewellers at this time. John Donald, for example, set large, eye-catching crystal and mineral specimens such as iron pyrites, rose quartz and idocrase in architectural and abstract gold frames while Charles de Temple, something of a maverick craftsman, specialised in 'wrapping' cultured pearls in chunky organic-looking gold mounts. All these designers shared one common feature: they were prepared to break the boundaries of what was considered 'traditional', creating daring and innovative jewels which, just

1960s 9-carat gold charm bracelet. It is difficult to overestimate just how popular charm bracelets were in the 1960s. Decidedly sentimental, jewellers caught on to the idea that new charms could be added to coincide with birthdays or, for example, a memorable holiday. Today they rarely sell for more than their value in gold.

Unusual 1960s gold and platinum brooch of 'bullet' design set with calibré sapphires, a coil of pavé-set diamonds and a further coil of polished gold.

John Donald 18-carat gold brooch composed of a series of polished and striated yellow- and white-gold cubes individually set with a brilliant-cut diamond. London, c.1963.

John Donald 18-carat gold, smoky quartz and diamond-set 'pyramids' brooch, c.1963. The use of rough gem crystals was a particular feature of modern designer jewellery in the '60s and '70s.

like so many aspects of the 'swinging sixties', were often deliberately made to astonish and provoke debate.

Needless to say, while all this designer-driven jewellery may very well have suited a more eclectic kind of buyer, for more mainstream customers in the 1960s the most accessible kind of jewellery available in the high street was fashioned from one material – 9-carat gold. Frequently mass produced in the Birmingham Jewellery Quarter, 9-carat was hard wearing and decidedly affordable. The 1960s was the era of the charm bracelet and quite literally thousands were churned out for a sentimental public wishing to commemorate a special birthday, Christmas or a holiday abroad. Today, 9-carat gold jewellery is incredibly common. It was liberally used in rings, necklaces, bracelets and earrings, and was frequently accompanied by inexpensive semi-precious gems such as garnet, citrine, turquoise and cultured pearl. Sadly, it rarely sells for more than its smelt value but with the record price of gold today even this can be surprisingly high.

By the early 1970s designers started to incorporate a range of new and innovative man-made materials into their jewellery – plastic, resin, titanium and acrylic – as well as natural, organic materials such as wood, stone, coral and ivory. Bold, colourful and versatile, the huge advantage of much of this eye-catching and highly original contemporary jewellery was that it could often be made –

Pair of unpolished pink tourmaline crystal and diamond earrings mounted in platinum and 18-carat gold by Andrew Grima, London 1963.

18-carat gold and platinum dress ring mounted with a large faceted topaz in a frame constructed from a series of oblong bars or 'matchsticks' in abstract formation by Andrew Grima, London 1968.

Modernist brooch by Louis Osman mounted with an interlocking 18-carat gold rectangular plaque riveted to a tablet of lapis lazuli and set with a synthetic emerald, c.1961.

French fluted coral, brilliant-cut diamond and 18-carat gold hinged bangle. By the early 1970s, coral had become one of the most popular organic materials to be used in decorative jewellery. Invariably extracted from the warm waters of the Mediterranean, 'precious coral' is known as corallium mobile or corallium rubrum.

1970s 18-carat gold abstract brooch by Charles de Temple set at random with brilliant-cut diamonds, circular green tourmalines and an unworked druzy quartz geode specimen. Note the reclining figure artfully located at the side of the frame.

Below: Kutchinsky diamond-set 18-carat gold fully articulated lattice-work bracelet with rope-twist detail, c.1972.

and retailed – at very affordable prices. Enamel also became a compatible and popular medium, especially when applied to inexpensive silver and silver-gilt jewellery. Two London establishments were largely responsible for raising interest in modern designer jewellery in the early to mid 1970s, providing a very useful platform for a wide range of talented young craftsmen to showcase their designs: Electrum Gallery situated in South Molton Street, and Cameo Corner in Museum Street, Bloomsbury. Many dynamic young craftsmen and craftswomen including celebrated names such as Gillian Packard, Wendy Ramshaw, Tom Scott, Ernest Blyth, Frances Beck and Ingeborg Bratman all benefited from the pioneering approach to contemporary jewellery design fostered by these two London shops.

Many top-of-the-range jewellers such as Cartier, Mauboussin, Van Cleef & Arpels and Tiffany developed their own range of distinctive 'high-end' jewellery for an increasingly discerning international clientele. It became popular in the 1970s to set diamonds in quite pronounced, abstract 'molten' gold mounts. Free-flowing, stylised jewels were decidedly in vogue. Clusters of contrasting gemstones, for example rubies and emeralds or sapphires and turquoises, were often set in white and yellow gold supplemented by small brilliant-cut diamond accents. To add to the overall effect many of these gems were polished *en cabochon* or even a combination of both the faceted and domed varieties. Earrings gained huge popularity as well as complete matching parures comprising a necklace, bracelet, brooch, earrings and dress ring. The 1970s were very much the era of coral jewellery and considerable natural reserves were depleted to supply the jewellery industry. In London, Kutchinsky specialised in the use of colourful hardstones, particularly malachite, tiger's eye, onyx and lapis lazuli which were mounted in striking molten and heavily textured gold settings as pendants on chunky matching gold chains. This fashion for 'blocks' of colour achieved particular popularity in the world of wristwatches where leading international firms including Piaget, Bueche Girod and Patek Philippe used coloured hardstones in their watch dials, sometimes setting a line of diamonds in the surrounding bezels on heavily textured 'brick pattern' bracelets.

Antique jewellery was still much misunderstood in the 1970s and really quite rare and valuable pieces could be purchased relatively cheaply. These were the days, of course, before the internet and there was frequently a serious lack of knowledge where old jewellery was concerned. Much that was available on the market could therefore be bought relatively cheaply – ironic when you consider just how finite a commodity antique jewellery actually is and how high prices have risen today. Cameo Corner, for example, boasted two large showcases in the main showroom crammed with Renaissance pendants, Georgian parures and Victorian earrings while a safe at the back of the shop was exclusively devoted to rare ancient gold artefacts such as Roman torc collars, fibulas and

Finnish gold and cultured pearl brooch by Lapponia, c.1970. The uncompromising, spare design of this piece perfectly evokes the fashion for powerful abstract modernist jewellery during this period of experimentation and change.

Kutchinsky gold 'waterlily' brooch set with brilliant-cut diamond stamens in a frame of textured petals. London, 1973.

Impressive abstract gold brooch/pendant by Andrew Grima mounted with a large unworked specimen of 'watermelon' tourmaline, the textured gold frame set with brilliant-cut diamond highlights. London, 1971.

Parure by George Weil comprising an 18-carat gold and amethyst diamond-set dress ring, bracelet and earclips. The combination of triangular-shaped gold sections and triangular-cut amethysts is a particularly effective feature of this suite made in London in 1976.

Italian three-colour gold flattened curb-link patten collar by Bulgari, set at intervals with brilliant-cut diamonds. By the 1970s leading international jewellery houses such as Bulgari were producing highly effective and wearable designs such as this collar which were often accompanied by a matching bracelet and earclips.

18-carat white-gold textured bracelet watch with lapis lazuli dial by John Donald, London 1971.

Bronze Age bangles. In 1974 this wonderful and unique stock was stolen in an armed robbery, never to be seen again. Crime has certainly had an important bearing upon the jewellery which people choose to keep. In the 1970s it was still relatively safe to own and wear, say, a valuable diamond ring or expensive wristwatch. Today, the genuine fear of criminal activity together with the fact that banks have closed their safe deposits to their customers and, tellingly, the impact of ever-rising insurance premiums mean that many people would rather choose to sell their jewellery than risk keeping it – all good reasons why so much jewellery has been sold at auction in recent years.

Further reading

International Exhibition of Modern Jewellery 1890-1961, (Worshipful Company of Goldsmiths, 1961)

Understanding Jewellery, David Bennett and Daniela Mascetti (Antique Collectors' Club, 1996)

Modern Jewellery. An International Survey 1890-1963, Graham Hughes (Studio Books, 1963)

Jewelry from Antiquity to Present, Clare Phillips (Thames & Hudson, 1996)

Modern British Jewellery Designers 1960-1980. A Collector's Guide, Mary Ann Wingfield (ACC Art Books, 2021)

Chapter 21
Before and After the Millennium

Jewellery in today's digital age has become a truly global commodity, bought by and sold to an increasingly knowledgeable and discerning network of international clients. Many leading retailers have established their individual brands in diverse locations all over the world, recognising that buyers in Taipei and Dubai are just as important as those from more 'traditional' centres such as London, Paris and New York. The pace of change has been truly staggering as, indeed, has the character and nature of the customers themselves. The sheer accessibility of jewellery-selling everywhere from the internet to international airports, from retail shops to auction houses has resulted in a new generation of sophisticated, well-informed buyers who demand and expect that the diamonds and gemstones which they are purchasing come from ethical and sustainable sources. Gone are the days when a notable gem could be sold without an independent grading report from a leading international laboratory; whether a near-colourless or fancy colour diamond, a fine ruby or sapphire, a report stating its specifications has become a crucial and obligatory accompaniment to the jewel itself. Auction houses have particularly benefited from the global reach of ever more sophisticated marketing and high-quality imagery; these days it is very rare indeed for a costly gem or obscure antique jewel to slip through the system undetected by the literally hundreds of buyers who continually trawl the internet for that elusive 'sleeper'– an item which nobody else has either seen or properly identified. Many salerooms in the UK have seen a marked increase in jewellery consignments and, due to the high price of gold today even quite modest 9-carat jewellery is fetching record sums. Antique jewellery, especially from the Georgian, Edwardian and Art Deco eras, has never been out of favour no doubt due to a greater awareness and appreciation of its beauty, wearability and individuality while the market for important fancy colour diamonds, Burmese rubies, Colombian emeralds and

18-carat gold and pavé-set diamond brooch by E. Wolfe & Co. realistically fashioned as a bird feeding its young. London, 1982.

14-carat gold brooch by Elizabeth Gage of square outline featuring a raised mountain goat motif representing the zodiac sign Capricorn, c.1980.

18-carat gold, cultured pearl and diamond necklace by Charles de Temple, c. 1985.

Kashmir sapphires and 'signed' jewellery by the leading houses continues to confound expectations.

The 1980s and 1990s saw a significant rise in buyers from the Middle East and Far East. Sotheby's first opened an office in Hong Kong in 1973 while Christie's held their first Hong Kong auction in 1986, both meeting the increasing demands of wealthy and aspirational Asia-Pacific buyers – many of whom were extremely knowledgeable about gems and diamonds. South Sea cultured pearls became hugely popular; necklaces and earrings were particularly prized by Far Eastern clients for their size, lustre, perfect sphericality and uniformity of colour. Even these gradually gave way in demand to pearls which were distinctly irregular or 'baroque' in shape; a very large number of these necklaces have appeared at auction over the past twenty years and inevitably, prices have dropped in line with the sheer quantity appearing on the market. Another gem which began to achieve record results has been Imperial jade where a necklace of highly translucent, well matched beads could fetch, quite literally, millions of

1980s 18-carat gold collar by Andrew Grima composed of integral sections of textured gold wire with a diamond line accent to the centre.

Gold and pavé diamond-set panther brooch with sapphire cabochon 'spots' and emerald eye, c.1980. A homage to Cartier's 'panthere' range of iconic jewels, this is a particularly animated and well made example although the maker is unknown.

Parure of 1980s gold collar, bangle and earrings. Bold, chunky and eye-catching, this jewellery exhibits a strong ethnic influence in its design.

dollars. Today, much of the low-quality jade that appears on the market is routinely treated to enhance its colour – which is why it is necessary to obtain an independent report confirming its origin.

If the buying habits of customers have changed, much of the 'affordable' jewellery available today has been made to reflect the expectations of an entire generation of new buyers, many of them young, aspirational and possessing disposable income. It goes without saying that social media has had an enormous influence upon the sort of jewellery people want and it is a simple fact of life that many people choose to wear jewellery which conforms to the popular prevailing fashion of the day, has been sourced from a high-profile designer or, better still, has been promoted by a celebrity or social media influencer. This means that a large proportion of new jewellery available today has lost much of its individuality in the drive to profit from a willing and credulous mass market. A cursory inspection of the modern jewellery department in a typical high-end retail store will thus often be a combination of expensive 'one-off' bespoke pieces by top international houses alongside a large number of stands selling rings, pendants, bracelets and earrings of a decidedly generic look which, although certainly attractive and wearable, does not differ greatly

'Meniscus' ring by Kevin Coates,1985. The cushion-shaped moonstone cabochon bezel demonstrates the 'meniscus' of the title; that of curving through tension of a liquid's surface against its mass. A sprite-like creature pulls, with hands which begin the shank, upon the moonstone through whose surface its face is pushed.

Modern round brilliant-cut diamond ring on platinum mount between baguette diamond shoulders.

Group of modern diamond and gem-set signet rings. By the 1980s many gems, particularly ruby, emerald and sapphire, were being artificially treated to improve their colour, clarity and overall appearance. Today, the vast majority of diamonds and gemstones which are bought and sold are accompanied by independent grading reports or a certificate from an internationally recognised laboratory. Gems which do not should thus be treated with extreme caution.

Tiffany & Co. modern 18-carat gold 'Bean' necklace designed by Elsa Peretti. Originally designed in 1974, the Peretti Bean motif is one of the most enduring and popular motifs in contemporary international jewellery.

Left: Modern emerald and diamond brooch in the Art Deco style. The continuing popularity of Edwardian and Art Deco jewellery has led to many copies being made, some of high quality and others decidedly substandard. Often manufactured in the Far East, settings and stones should be carefully examined before an expensive purchase is made.

Right: Gold ring stack by Wendy Ramshaw, c.2001. Ramshaw specialised in groups of several matching rings each bezel set with a polished gemstone such as moonstone, aquamarine and tourmaline. Housed on clear perspex ring stands they quickly became her signature branding.

in design or content from one jeweller to another.

Having said that, many jewellery designers and retailers have always tried to keep ahead of changing fashion and taste, and possibly the biggest impact to affect the market in recent years has been the production of so-called 'cultured' diamonds. Created inside a machine using extreme pressure and heat, laboratory-grown diamonds have actually been around for decades and when they began to appear in the early days of the 21st century they were fairly easy to identify, especially the 'fancy colour' varieties. However, in recent years many of the stones appearing on the market have proven to be virtually indistinguishable from their natural counterparts. Without doubt, cultured diamonds provide a sustainable and environmentally sound alternative to conventional diamonds and, just as important for a discerning public – particularly younger people – they are distinctly more affordable than natural diamonds. It is unlikely that the leading established international manufacturers and retailers will embrace this new material (at least in the short term) and turn away from using natural stones in their bespoke designs but cultured diamonds have

Gold shield-shaped brooch by Elizabeth Gage set with a pear-shaped pink tourmaline, a baroque pearl drop and surmounted by a Romano-British bronze figure of a horse, c.1994.

Bulgari gold stirrup ring mounted with a rotating disc pavé-set with a cluster of brilliant-cut diamonds, c.1990.

Cartier three-colour 18-carat gold 'Trinity' ring; a design classic, c.1980.

18-carat gold, baisse-taille enamel, diamond and sapphire brooch or hairpiece designed by Leo de Vroomen, c.1990.

Necklace of graduated South Sea cultured pearls, c.1990.

'Ondine' Brooch by Kevin Coates, 1995. The water sprite, Ondine, surfaces from a well of labradorite, ebony and inlaid mother-of-pearl bearing the pearl-soul which is her greatest gift.

certainly had a detrimental impact upon international diamond prices. Only time will tell whether confidence returns and buyers, at least in the mass market high street, turn back to buying traditional, natural diamonds or whether cultured, man-made diamonds are indeed the future of the UK jewellery industry.

Further reading

International Exhibition of Modern Jewellery 1890-1961, (Worshipful Company of Goldsmiths, 1961)

Kevin Coates. A Hidden Alchemy (Arnoldsche, 2008)

Understanding Jewellery, David Bennett and Daniela Mascetti (Antique Collectors' Club, 1996)

Popular Jewelry of the '60s, '70s and '80s, Roseann Ettinger (Schiffer, 1997)

Collect Contemporary Jewellery, Joanna Hardy (Thames & Hudson, 2012)

Jewelry from Antiquity to Present, Clare Phillips (Thames & Hudson, 1996)

Modern British Jewellery Designers 1960-1980. A Collector's Guide, Mary Ann Wingfield (ACC Art Books, 2021)

Selected Biographies

ABATE, Michele (1896-1981)
Michele Abate founded the family firm in Turin in 1920 specialising in dynamic Italian jewellery exhibiting its own highly individual and innovative style. The business is now located in the coastal city of Sanremo.

ANTROBUS
Founded by Philip Antrobus in 1815 the firm went on to become one of the leading London retail jewellery shops of the last century. In 1946 Antrobus was commissioned by Prince Philip of Greece to make Princess Elizabeth her diamond engagement ring and a diamond bracelet which the future Queen wore on her wedding day.

ASHBEE, Charles Robert (1863-1942)
One of the leading exponents of the English Arts and Crafts movement. Ashbee founded the Guild of Handicraft in 1888 and became its chief designer, specialising in silver, enamel and gem set necklaces, pendants and buckles of naturalistic inspiration such as peacocks, wild flowers and butterflies. In 1902 the Guild relocated from London to the Essex House Works in Chipping Campden, Gloucestershire, but closed in 1907 in the face of competition from Liberty & Co.

BOUCHERON, Frédéric (1830-1902)
French designer goldsmith specialising in fine diamond jewellery who founded his business on the Palais-Royal in Paris in 1858. In 1893 he relocated to Place Vendôme where the firm operates successfully today. Regularly exhibiting in France and America. The firm is celebrated for its bold and innovative designs from striking Art Deco brooches to elegant and wearable naturalistic themes fashionable today.

BOULTON, Matthew (1728-1809)
An industrialist and steam engineer who in 1762 diversified part of his considerable business into the manufacture of faceted steel jewellery, accessories and buckles at his Soho works located at Snow Hill, Birmingham. In 1773 Boulton entered into an arrangement with Josiah Wedgwood to supply cut-steel settings for neo-classical jasper cameos.

BROGDEN, John (active 1842-1884)
Designer goldsmith and retailer based at Henrietta Street, Covent Garden. Brogden specialised in several contrasting styles but is probably best known for the manufacture of architectural, classical and Assyrian-inspired jewellery using bright yellow-gold, hardstone cameos, enamel and pyrope garnet. His signature is JB in capitals in an oval cartouche.

BROWN, William (1748-1825)
and **Charles (1749-1795)**
Gem engravers specialising in neo-classical profiles who both exhibited at the Royal Academy.

BULGARI
Italian jewellery dynasty founded by Sotirio Bulgari in 1879 in Rome and subsequently located to the Via dei Condotti in 1905. Bulgari has been one of the most successful international jewellery retailers since the 1960s specialising in a combination of top-of-the-range special commissions and versatile easy-to-wear day jewels mounted with bold and colourful semi-precious polished gems or ancient coins.

BURCH, Edward (1730-1814)
Sculptor, gem engraver and Royal Academician who worked for both Josiah Wedgwood and James Tassie specialising in technically accomplished classical profiles.

BURGES, William (1827-1881)
Architect, designer and all-round polymath, much of Burges' output exhibited a strong Gothic Revivalist influence such as a fine gold pectoral cross and chain forming part of the Hull Grundy Collection at the British

Museum and the jewellery made for the wedding of his patron, the Marquis of Bute.

CARTIER

From its foundation in Paris in 1847, the name Cartier has been synonymous with superb jewellery, accessories, wristwatches and objets d'art. Established by Louis-François Cartier (1819-1904), the firm was subsequently taken over and expanded by his three grandsons Louis, Jacques and Pierre, each with responsibility for operating the salons located respectively in Paris, London and New York.

Cartier has never compromised the quality of its materials or the originality and execution of its designs. The firm was among the first to use platinum in intricate 'Belle Époque' diamond garland settings and by the 1920s and 1930s it was selling the finest jewels and accessories inspired by the art of India, Persia, the Orient, ancient Egypt and Russia to many of the world's most celebrated and distinguished clients.

CASTELLANI, Fortunato Pio (1794-1865)

Italian goldsmith and one of the leading interpreters of jewellery in the archaeological taste. Castellani mastered the skill of applying gold granular decoration on to many of his classical designs. This made a huge impact since the technique was thought to have been lost with the ancient Etruscans. To reinforce the integrity of the classical statement, he made extensive use of ancient coins, hardstone intaglios and scarabs in settings which took the form of amphoras, fibulas and *bullae,* a form of round ancient amulet. On Castellani's death, the business was continued by his sons Alessandro (1823-1883) and Augusto (1829-1914). The firm's mark is two overlapping letter 'Cs' in back to back formation.

CHILD & CHILD (active 1891-1915)

A firm of London silversmiths and jewellers owned by Walter and Harold Child specialising in attractive and reasonably priced gold, silver and silver-gilt jewels such as pendants, brooches and buckles. Recognisable for their stylised wing shapes, many of these pieces were translucent enamelled in turquoise blue and green and were sold in distinctive green leather cases. Their mark was a sunflower with the monogram 'CC'.

COATES, Kevin

Born in 1950, Dr Kevin Coates is rightly regarded today as one of Britain's pre-eminent goldsmiths and designer craftsmen. A true polymath – he is also a professional musician – he has won numerous international awards for his extraordinarily original and mystical jewellery, sculpture and objets d'art, all of which convey his remarkable imagination and unparalleled technical virtuosity.

COOPER, John Paul (1869-1933)

Arts and Crafts designer goldsmith who trained under Henry Wilson. After becoming head of metalwork at the Birmingham School of Art he left to start his own business. Using his favoured medium of 15-carat gold, John Paul Cooper soon mastered the technique of cloisonné and champlevé enamelling and produced hundreds of items of jewellery and accessories set with coloured gems or a range of unusual organic materials. Much of his output was heavily influenced by the work of Henry Wilson.

DAVIE, Alan (1920-2014)

A Scottish-born artist, jazz musician, teacher and craftsman active in the post-war period, Davie's jewellery was sold at leading retail stores such as Harrods and Asprey. He designed and made the jewellery worn by Vivien Leigh in the play *Antony and Cleopatra* in 1951.

DE TEMPLE, Charles (1929-2019)

Reputed to be the son of Tom Mix, the American silent movie film actor, Charles de Temple's life and career was just as unconventional as his remarkable jewellery. Following a spell at Ringling's Circus and a range of dead-end jobs he began to make jewellery and by the 1950s had opened a shop in New York. In the 1960s he moved to London and became one of the most important figures in the post-war designer jewellery movement.

DE VROOMEN, Leo (1941-2025)

Working alongside his wife and fellow designer Ginnie, Dutch goldsmith Leo de Vroomen is best known for his dynamic and highly wearable sculptural jewels often set with bold colourful gemstones or decorated with subtle shades of coloured translucent enamel. He qualified as a Master Goldsmith in Switzerland and settled in London in

1965 where he went on to win the prestigious De Beers Diamonds International Award in 1974.

DONALD, John (1928-2023)
A leading British jewellery designer who was particularly active in the 1960s and 1970s, John Donald's small retail studio located at 120 Cheapside in the City of London was well known to a wide range of corporate and private clients (including Princess Margaret) all of whom recognised and appreciated his innovative, experimental and highly individual style.

DUNLOP, Sibyl (1889-1968)
Scottish-born Arts and Crafts designer and retailer who trained in Brussels and opened a shop in Kensington Church Street specialising in silver jewellery mounted with gems and hardstones in characteristically understated colours. The fact that many of her designs involved gems set in naturalistic and geometric cluster formation led to frequent confusion with the very similar work of another jeweller, Dorrie Nossiter.

FABERGÉ, Peter Carl (1846-1920)
Unrivalled Russian designer goldsmith. After serving an apprenticeship in Frankfurt and visiting several European cities, Fabergé returned to Russia and in 1870 took over control of the family business. In 1882 the firm showed at the Moscow Pan Russian Exhibition where it won the Gold Medal. His reputation spread rapidly and in 1884 Tsar Alexander III commissioned the first Imperial Easter egg designed in plain white enamel and opening to reveal a 'surprise' – a miniature gold hen containing a jewelled crown within its body. In the same year Fabergé was awarded the Royal Warrant. Imperial patronage sealed his success and he won important commissions from diverse distinguished customers including several European and Oriental ruling families. Apart from shops in four Russian cities, he opened a salon in London's Bond Street selling his incomparable jewels, accessories and 'objects of fantasy'. The war years saw a gradual decline in Fabergé's fortunes and the firm was ultimately closed down by the Bolsheviks in 1918. Fabergé managed to escape to Lausanne where he died in 1920.

Fabergé's phenomenal success was in no small part down to his decision to expand his business from the manufacture of purely functional items to the production of decorative and ornamental objets d'art embracing a broad range of exquisite articles such as hardstone carvings, flower studies in rock crystal pots and, of course, the fifty-seven Imperial Easter eggs. He employed a team of highly skilled workmasters, each with their own particular speciality. Fabergé's use of translucent enamel and gold applied in several different colours was simply incomparable, combining supreme good taste with flawless attention to detail and technical mastery of the medium. His association with the Imperial Family simply adds to the potency of the Fabergé legend.

FAHRNER, Theodor (1859-1919)
German jewellery designer who anticipated the geometric, linear forms of the Art Deco period with his range of 'Affordable Art Jewellery' in silver, enamel and panels of hardstone set in borders of marcasite.

FALIZE, Alexis (1811-1898)
and his son **Lucien (1839-1897)**
specialised in highly colourful cloisonné enamel jewellery of Japanese and Persian inspiration such as their range of flat disc-shaped pendants depicting Oriental birds and flowers.

FOUQUET, Georges (1862-1957)
Art Nouveau goldsmith celebrated for his bold and powerful designs incorporating diamonds, gems and plique-à-jour enamel. His best known work was a fabulous enamel snake bracelet designed by Alphonse Mucha for the actress Sarah Bernhardt.

FROMENT-MEURICE, François-Désiré (1802-1855)
Parisian jeweller who pioneered designs inspired by Gothic and Renaissance art known as the *style cathédrale*.

GAGE, Elizabeth
Born in 1937, Elizabeth Gage MBE is one of Britain's most successful and enduring jewellery designers. She originally trained at the Chelsea School of Art and the Sir John Cass College and in 1972 won the De Beers Diamonds International Award. She is well known today for her range of 'Zodiac' rings and bespoke jewels incorporating ancient artefacts, coins and rare gems.

GASKIN, Arthur (1862-1928)
and his wife **Georgina (1866-1934)**
Goldsmiths and silversmiths producing exceptional Arts and Crafts silver and gem-set jewellery. Closely associated with William Morris and the Pre-Raphaelites, Gaskin jewellery is strongly naturalistic favouring colourful clusters of cabochon-cut gems in leaf and tendril settings.

GIULIANO, Carlo (1831-1895)
Leading figure in 19th-century classical and Renaissance Revival jewellery celebrated for his accomplished use of enamel. Born in Naples, Giuliano served his apprenticeship with Castellani before setting up a workshop in London and his own retail premises in Piccadilly in 1874. His 'art jewellery' is notable for its originality and understated elegance, using subtle gemstones such as tourmaline, zircon, hessonite, garnet and Ceylon sapphire which blended together extremely well in compatible gold settings, and were embellished with intricate enamelling and often further enamelled and engraved on the backs.

After his death the business was continued by his two sons, Carlo and Arthur, who designed equally distinctive jewels such as necklaces, bracelets and brooches characteristic for their use of monochrome enamel. Carlo Giuliano's mark is the monogram 'CG' in an oval cartouche and 'C & AG' after 1896.

GRIMA, Andrew (1921-2007)
Contemporary jeweller and craftsman using bold and unusual uncut crystals or coloured gems such as aquamarine, topaz and pink beryl in striking textured gold mounts. Grima pioneered daring abstract forms in the 1960s and 1970s and his work is highly collectable today. His signature is 'Grima' or 'AG.'

HORNER, Charles Henry (1837-1896)
Early 20th-century Halifax silversmith producing inexpensive but strongly defined enamel and silver jewellery, especially pendants, brooches and hatpins in naturalistic and Celtic themes. His monogram 'CH' is invariably accompanied by a Chester Assay Office hallmark.

JENSEN, Georg (1866-1935)
Danish silversmith and goldsmith well known for striking and wearable jewellery largely inspired by nature defined in sculptured, semi-abstract forms. Jensen's sound business acumen and marketing skills have meant that the firm flourishes successfully today. Designs are individually numbered, include gold as well as silver and sometimes incorporate polished gems and hardstones such as lapis lazuli, moonstone and garnet. Pieces are signed in full or with the monogram 'GJ' in a circle of dots.

KNOX, Archibald (1864-1933)
Goldsmith, silversmith and designer of Arts and Crafts jewellery. He produced numerous designs for Liberty & Co. bearing a strong Celtic influence decorated with enamel and set with gems typical of the genre such as opal, moonstone, turquoise and blister pearl in what became known as the Liberty 'Cymric' range.

KUTCHINSKY (established 1893)
London-based jewellers active today and prominent in the 1960s and 1970s for fine diamond jewellery including abstract gold pieces set with interesting combinations of gemstones and pendants mounted with discs of hardstone such as malachite and tiger's eye.

LALIQUE, René (1860-1945)
Renowned Parisian goldsmith with incomparable technique and a gifted imagination. One of the leading representatives of the Art Nouveau movement which spread through Europe at the end of the 19th century, Lalique created visionary jewels in gold, silver and even unusual metals such as aluminium, many of which were decorated with plique-à-jour enamel, fine coloured gems or moulded glass plaques. Lalique's appreciation and application of the natural form was represented by many intriguing and evocative themes which combined several contrasting motifs within the single jewel such as insects, flowers – both flourishing and decaying – and the female nude figure. The overall effect was unfailingly sensuous, harmonious and fantastic.

LIBERTY & CO.
Founded by Arthur Lasenby Liberty (1843-1917), Liberty & Co. of Regent Street, London championed the cause of the Arts and Crafts movement by commissioning several of its leading designers such as Archibald Knox, Arthur Gaskin and Jessie M. King to produce affordable

and wearable jewels for the firm's 'Cymric' range. The commercial needs of the company were incompatible with the artistic integrity of C.R. Ashbee, however, but Liberty was crucial to the development of Art jewellery in England, bringing the work of small individual craftsmen to the attention of the wider public.

MARCHANT, Nathaniel (1739-1816)
Gem engraver who enjoyed considerable success in his lifetime carrying out commissions for many prominent families and politicians such as William Pitt and Earl Spencer.

MELILLO, Giacinto (1846-1915)
Gifted Neapolitan goldsmith who took over the running of Castellani's workshop in 1870. Heavily influenced by classical and 'archaeological' themes, Melillo is probably best known for his Etruscan-style gold jewellery fashioned as winged cherubs, lions and cornucopias decorated with minute granulation and twisted wirework.

MURPHY, Henry George (1884-1939)
Harry Murphy trained under Henry Wilson as a silversmith and goldsmith where he gained considerable experience working with metals and decorative enamel. After a period spent in Berlin with Emil Lettré, he returned to England and set up his own shop in Weymouth Street, London, known as the Falcon Studio. Murphy was an accomplished draughtsman and designer in several diverse media and his output exhibits a range of influences from Gothic and Renaissance to Art Deco. He was also a gifted teacher. His signature, 'HGM', is accompanied by a falcon crest.

MURRLE BENNETT & CO.
(active 1884-1914)
Firm of goldsmiths and silversmiths founded by Ernest Murrle, a German-born jeweller who entered into partnership with a Mr Bennett in 1884. Creative in the Arts and Crafts medium, the firm worked closely with Arthur Liberty who offered an ideal shop window for the company's elegant and wearable necklaces, brooches and pendants frequently set with blister pearls and semi-precious stones such as turquoise matrix. The firm's signature is 'MB' or 'MB & Co.'

OSMAN, Louis (1914-1996)
Louis Osman studied at the Bartlett School of Architecture and the Slade. He is probably most celebrated for designing and making the gold coronet worn by the future King Charles at his investiture in 1969. Working from his studio at Canons Ashby in Northamptonshire his output embraced silverware, sculptural works of art and a range of dynamic jewellery which has become highly collectible today.

OVED, Mosheh (active 1903-1953)
Founder of Cameo Corner, the celebrated Bloomsbury antique jewellers, Mosheh Oved was a near-penniless Polish Jew who, on arriving in London, persevered to build up an incomparable stock of rare jewels and a list of clients which included Queen Mary and Rudolph Valentino. Together with his common-law wife, Sah, he also designed and made a range of silver and gold rings fashioned into the shape of animals and birds notable for their sensitivity.

PHILLIPS, Robert (1810-1881)
'Phillips of Cockspur Street' was established in 1846 and specialised in the manufacture of archaeological and Renaissance Revival jewellery embellished with fine enamel and compatible gems in high-quality gold settings such as coral fringe necklaces, intricate enamel pendants and Assyrian-style diadems. Phillips was also important for his early encouragement and sponsorship of Carlo Giuliano. Upon the death of Robert Phillips, the business was continued by his son Alfred. Their jewellery is marked with a stylised Prince of Wales feather in a lozenge border.

PICHLER, Giovanni (1734-1791)
and half-brother **Luigi (1773-1854)**
Italian gem engravers specialising in fine interpretations of classical subjects and profiles which are sometimes found in late 18th-century hardstone rings and necklaces. Their signature was inscribed in Greek capitals.

PINCHBECK, Christopher (1670-1732)
Fleet Street watchmaker who perfected the technique of combining an alloy of copper and zinc to produce a versatile metal which successfully imitated gold. The material should not be confused with cheaper and inferior gilt metal of later manufacture.

RAMSDEN & CARR

Omar Ramsden (1873-1939) and Alwyn Carr (1872-1940) were leading figures of the English Arts and Crafts movement. After meeting at the Sheffield School of Art, they subsequently formed a successful partnership in London from 1898 to 1919 producing silverware, silver jewellery and enamels.

RAMSHAW, Wendy (1939-2018)

Wendy Ramshaw is best known today for her 'ring stacks'– sets of several integral matching rings individually set with a polished gemstone mounted on a sculptural cylindrical Perspex stand. As well as using gold and silver her jewellery incorporates a range of contrasting media including stoneware, porcelain, feathers and glass.

RUBEL FRÈRES

Founded in 1915 by Hungarian brothers Jean and Robert, Rubel Frères established their workshop in Paris and quickly gained a reputation for creating jewellery of high technical virtuosity for leading jewellers situated in the Place Vendôme, most notably Van Cleef & Arpels. Rubel Frères are best known today for their range of incomparable ballerina and dancer brooches.

SAULINI, Tommaso (1793-1864) and his son Luigi (1819-1883)

Italian hardstone and shell cameo engravers and portrait sculptors notable for the fine detail and accuracy of their work, much of which was signed T. Saulini F. or L. Saulini F.

STREETER, Edwin (1834-1923)

An important figure in the late Victorian London retail jewellery sector, Edwin Streeter was an excavator and dealer in gems from around the world who set up in business in Conduit Street in 1867 and subsequently in Bond Street. He produced regular colour catalogues of his stock which today give us a better understanding of original prices and what was fashionable in the 1890s.

TASSIE, James (1735-1799)

Scottish discoverer of a technique in which real hardstone cameos and intaglios were cast and faithfully copied in paste glass. Using a sulphur-based mould, Tassie produced a compound which could be coloured or colourless and transparent or opaque. They were enormously popular in the 1770s; indeed a set of several thousands was commissioned by the Empress of Russia.

TIFFANY, Charles Lewis (1812-1902) and Louis Comfort (1848-1933)

Leading American jewellery designers and retailers. After initial success in the stationery and giftware business, C.L. Tiffany diversified into the design and manufacture of jewellery and silver first in New York and subsequently in Paris and London. Adept in a broad range of fine and applied arts, the firm has consistently produced elegant jewellery whether in the Belle Époque 'Garland' taste, Art Nouveau and Deco or Post War and Modernist styles. Today, Tiffany & Co. is one of the world's leading brand names for up-to-the-minute gold and silver jewellery and giftware.

VAN CLEEF & ARPELS

A leading firm of French jewellery designers and manufacturers active since 1898 when the firm was founded by Alfred Van Cleef and his two brothers-in-law Charles and Julien Arpels. Among their most successful accomplishments was the technique of 'invisibly setting' gems such as rubies and sapphires into striking platinum and gold jewellery such as the petals of flower spray brooches. The firm is internationally known today for its distinctive jewellery, wristwatches, accessories and perfumes.

VEVER, MAISON

Founded by Paul Vever in 1821 and continued by his two sons Paul (1851-1915) and Henri (1854-1942), Maison Vever produced elegant and often understated Art Nouveau gold and enamel jewellery. Henri was also the author of a definitive three-volume history of 19th-century French jewellery.

WEIL, George (born 1938)

Born in Vienna in 1938 George Weil managed to escape with his family to England just before the war. He trained at Saint Martin's School of Art and by the late 1960s and early 1970s was designing gold jewellery at his Hatton Garden premises of a distinctly abstract, sculptural form, sometimes set with unworked crystal specimens embellished with small diamond and gem accents.

WIESE, Jules (1818-1890)
and his son **Louis (1852-1923)**

The Wieses have gained particular recognition in recent years for their distinctive and faithful interpretation of jewellery in the Gothic taste. Jules trained in the Froment-Meurice workshops before establishing his own business in 1865. The firm used simple polished cabochons of gems such as ruby and Ceylon sapphire as well as ancient coins in mounts which were hammered and left intentionally simplistic to suggest a medieval appearance. The signature, occasionally used, was 'JW' with a star above.

WILSON, Henry (1864-1934)

Important figurehead of English Arts and Crafts jewellery, both as an innovative designer and a mentor to other goldsmiths such as Harry Murphy and John Paul Cooper. Wilson taught at the Central School and Royal College of Arts and was strongly influenced by medieval and ecclesiastical imagery. Much of his work was decorated with colourful enamel, such as his celebrated 'Diana' tiara studded with gems and cylinders of rock crystal.

WINSTON, Harry (1896-1978)

New York entrepreneurial jeweller. The key to Harry Winston's phenomenal success was to buy 'unfashionable' estate jewellery, break out the stones and remodel them into new and stylish settings which gained immediate popularity with a wealthy New York and international clientele. The appositely named 'King of Diamonds' handled many of the rarest and most important diamonds and precious gems during his lifetime, even donating incomparable stones such as the Hope Diamond to the Smithsonian Institution in Washington.

E. WOLFE & CO.

Established in 1850 by Johan Jacob Wolfe, E. Wolfe & Co. quickly established itself as a leading manufacturing jeweller, receiving notable commissions in the early 1900s from several European royal families. The firm flourishes today from its Hatton Garden premises supplying many of the leading retail shops in London and beyond with fine bespoke jewellery.

Jewellery Compendium

1. VALUATIONS

Valuations can be a highly subjective matter where assessments vary considerably depending upon the type of item involved, its rarity, design and composition and even the location where it is examined. Unfortunately, not all valuers are as experienced as others which is why it is important to employ the services of a qualified specialist with a proven track record who has handled similar jewellery to your own. In my opinion, there is absolutely no point in taking a Fabergé frame or Boucheron bracelet to a high street jeweller selling modern manufactured gold, watches and giftware while many auction houses are surprisingly ill-equipped to advise accurate, up-to-date values on fine and rare diamonds, objets d'art and antique jewels.

Jewellery valuers in the U.K. are encouraged to undertake a two-year diploma course in Gemmology ultimately gaining fellowship of the Gemmological Association (F.G.A.). A further year's study of diamonds leads to the Gem-A Diamond Diploma (D.G.A.). A large number of leading shops are affiliated to either the National Association of Jewellers (N.A.J.) or the Jewellery Valuers Association (J.V.A.) which provide in-depth courses and seminars for its members, teaching the essentials of good valuation practice as well as much of the technical data necessary to do their job properly.

In an increasingly litigious world, the importance of a detailed, comprehensive valuation with accompanying digital photography cannot be overstated. A document which states accurate grading of diamonds, country of origin, quality and authenticity of coloured gems, the age of antique jewels and diverse aspects of weight, condition, repairs and defects will not only enable you to replace a loss with another item as near to the original as possible but may also help to prove legal title in the event of recovery.

What Type of Valuation Do I Need?

The majority of jewellery valuations are provided for insurance purposes. Generally speaking, this involves theoretical replacement of a loss in the retail sector with an item of equivalent design, quality, condition and value to the original. A piece of jewellery purchased, say, at Cartier or Tiffany & Co. will undoubtedly have a different 'mark-up' from another bought from a dealer in 'the Trade' which is why it is crucial to establish precisely where any replacement would take place. Similarly, certain types of antique jewellery – Castellani, Lalique or Fabergé for example – may only be available from highly specialised shops and dealers in the London West End sector or even overseas, underlining once again the importance of getting professional advice from the right people.

Probate valuations are provided upon goods which form part of the estate of a deceased person and are based upon the price which the item might reasonably be expected to fetch if sold on the open market at time of death. Open Market values correspond to the price the item would be likely to fetch at auction and are thus lower than retail insurance levels. Other types of valuation include Capital Gains Tax, Family Division and Divorce (sometimes rather acrimonious with a degree of tact and diplomacy recommended). Post Loss Assessment is provided as a retrospective opinion for items lost but where no previous valuation may exist.

How Much Should I Pay?

Some valuers still calculate their charges based upon a set percentage of the total value of their customer's property. Personally, I believe this method is somewhat unethical and may be open to abuse; also, there is always the question hanging in the air that assessment has been made on the high side to obtain a bigger fee. The fair and proper approach adopted by the majority of shops, valuers and auction houses today is to levy a fee according to how long it takes to do the job. This is usually a set hourly rate plus VAT and may involve an additional expense for subsequent research. Whichever method is used, do establish at the outset a formal charging structure as well as the credentials of the valuer.

2. FAKES, FORGERIES AND ENHANCEMENTS

Jewellery, just like every other artistic endeavour, has suffered more than its fair share of faking and forgery. The problem is not a recent one either. From early times brass and gilded metal have masqueraded as gold while glass and imitation stones have been effective substitutes for diamonds and precious gems for centuries. Jewellery panders to the very worst of man's baser instincts adding spice and intrigue to the more prosaic attractions on offer. Greed is a very potent ingredient in the myth of jewellery, often resulting in conflict and financial calamity. Here is a list, by no means exhaustive, of some of the more common pitfalls encountered on a regular basis in the world of gems and jewellery.

(i) *Gems.* It is possible today to synthesise, enhance, radiate, improve and alter the appearance of practically every species of gem in the world today.

Diamonds are imitated by a whole range of colourless gems, some crude and obvious and others technically outstanding. Flawed diamonds are sometimes lasered to remove carbon defects while fancy coloured diamonds can be enhanced to change or intensify colour. When purchasing a diamond, do ensure it is accompanied by a certificate from a leading international laboratory to establish authenticity. An active and complex problem for the diamond industry today is the number of cultured diamonds flooding the market. When they first appeared it was fairly easy to tell the difference between natural diamonds and the lab-grown variety. However, recent improvements in the production, composition and appearance of cultured diamonds mean they are now virtually indistinguishable from their natural counterparts. It is therefore extremely important to obtain documentary evidence of the veracity of a diamond; individual stones sold today invariably exhibit a unique serial number lasered on to their girdles, which will correspond with a certificate submitted by a leading international gem laboratory such as the Gemological Institute of America (G.I.A.).

Cultured diamonds are sold on the basis of being affordable, conflict-free, ethically sourced and environmentally friendly while 'real' diamonds, particularly those which are colourless and flawless are incredibly rare, cut from crystals which are millions of years old and are considerably more expensive than the lab-grown variety. How all this will affect the market for antique and secondhand diamond jewellery in the future remains to be seen. One thing is clear, however: cultured diamonds are here to stay.

Rubies and sapphires have been synthesised since the 1920s and many Art Deco jewels are set with these man-made gems. View any calibré or baton-cut gems with suspicion, especially when set in cocktail watches, bracelets and clips. In the same way, ensure that any modern rubies and sapphires purchased in the Far East are accompanied by an independent certificate of authenticity.

Of all precious gems, emerald is probably the one which has been the most extensively enhanced. A certificate is therefore essential, particularly for modern emeralds of 'good' colour.

Opals are enhanced and strengthened in colour by cementing layers above and below the genuine material known as either doublets or triplets.

Aquamarines are imitated by synthetic blue spinels while cheap colour-changing synthetic corundums have been sold as valuable alexandrite since the 1950s.

Glass has been an effective substitute for costly gems since the Middle Ages. Glass – or paste – is softer than real gemstones, indicated by abrasions and 'moulded' facets on the surface. Often containing bubbles and swirls, glass is a poor conductor of heat and is therefore warm to the touch. Eighteenth-century paste jewellery can be remarkably deceptive, so close inspection of Georgian rings and brooches is recommended. Finally, do examine foil-backed stones – particularly sapphire, ruby and pink topaz – with great care. Your precious ruby might just be foiled rock crystal.

(ii) *Jewellery.* Treat all 'signed' jewellery with a measured degree of caution. The exploitation of fake Fabergé has become so widespread as to give rise to the term 'Fauxbergé'. Similarly, all the well-known names – Cartier, Van Cleef & Arpels, Tiffany and Bulgari – have all been extensively faked. Some of these are so downright awful that the signatures are spelt incorrectly.

Fake 'signed' jewels – and indeed fake period jewellery in general – always lack the quality, patina and integrity of their genuine counterparts. Settings are badly finished while gems are inferior and diamonds are often flawed. Much of the 'Art Deco'-style jewellery sold today is made in the Far East to a superior standard, but the diamonds are perfectly proportioned modern cuts and the coloured gems exhibit a machine-like consistency. Nineteenth-century revivalist jewellery is both faked in its entirety and is forged by adding a spurious signature to the setting. A false Castellani or Giuliano cartouche is usually crude and soft-soldered in lead but superior examples have fooled many.

The quality of much contemporary plique-à-jour enamel is extremely good resulting in some exceptionally clever 'Art Nouveau' fakes such as butterflies and figurative brooches. If in doubt, check with an expert in the field.

Eighteenth and early 19th-century jewellery is particularly desirable today which means that plenty of fakes abound. Watch out for 'Georgian' gold belcher link muff chains – the modern copies are heavier and not so delicate as the originals. Other 'Regency' fakes include twin heart rings, Giardinetti rings, rose diamond earrings in settings which are just too crisp to be original and message jewellery such as 'regard' rings and lockets.

(iii) *Wristwatches.* Wristwatches are probably faked more comprehensively than just about any other commodity in the luxury goods market and the better the name, the more likely the fake. Manufacturers such as Cartier and Rolex are constantly on their guard for fake copies of Tank watches and Oyster Chronometers and we have all seen those amazing pictures of phoney watches being crushed under a steamroller. Always ensure you purchase a watch from a totally reliable source and check it is supplied with the original box and guarantee.

Finally, as a general rule of thumb do check the sales ticket carefully. Fakes and forgeries are usually sold at prices which are by no means cheap but which are just too good to be true if the article were genuine. Always obtain a receipt which gives a clear and unequivocal statement of age and origin. If buying from an auction house the same rule applies, although it is wise to bear in mind the well-known phrase used extensively in this business – *caveat emptor* – buyer beware.

3. CLEANING, RESTORATION AND REPAIRS

A clumsy and crude repair to a good quality antique jewel will ruin its integrity and may seriously affect its value. The problem is not so widespread nowadays, probably because jewellers and their customers have a greater awareness of the importance of prime condition, in which repairs and conversions are only undertaken as a last resort. Nevertheless, 'historical' modifications are depressingly commonplace in which original fittings, pins and loops have been removed, makers' marks deleted, hallmarks chopped out of Victorian rings, roller catches attached to antique brooches, ill-matching gems and modern diamonds insensitively set in antique frames and, last but certainly not least, ugly lead solder used in place of discreet gold.

The fact of the matter is that regardless of how skilled the repair or conversion, an experienced valuer can always tell. So, unless you intend to keep the piece 'in the family' for perpetuity, give the matter considerable thought first. Buyers of antique jewellery are just like buyers of old paintings, ceramics and furniture. They want material which is untouched, preferably unrestored and which last saw the inside of a jewellers on the day of original purchase.

Having said all that, there is no point in locking your brooch or bracelet away in a drawer unworn and neglected for years simply because it is unfashionable and difficult to wear. The key is to seek the right advice from a qualified jeweller and preferably one with an excellent local reputation. A good starting point is to check that the shop is a member of the National Association of Jewellers (N.A.J.). This means that you have recourse to a higher authority – a kind of 'jewellery ombudsman' – should you be dissatisfied with the service you receive.

Many well-established jewellers, particularly in Central London, are not affiliated to the N.A.G. but still offer excellent workshop facilities. It is usually worthwhile checking with B.A.D.A. (the British Antique Dealers' Association) or L.A.P.A.D.A. (the Association of Art & Antiques Dealers) for a list of current members.

Jewellery repairs and conversions can be extremely expensive so do ensure that you obtain a written estimate before the work takes place. No matter how competent the jeweller, some aspects of restoration work are inadvisable. Examples include rare works of art such as Fabergé, early jewellery, enamel, gold filigree and mosaics. Nevertheless, some modifications may actually enhance value. These include converting small uncommercial Victorian cluster brooches into necklace clasps, polishing the worn and abraded surfaces on antique coloured gems, refoiling period gems where the original tinfoil has deteriorated and replacing discoloured and unsightly pearls and turquoises with new specimens which match the originals.

Cleaning

Just like repairs, cleaning should be approached with great care. Many antique gems and jewels should only be handled by experienced restorers while pearls are especially vulnerable. Nevertheless, you can make a huge difference to the appearance of your own gold and silver jewellery – and rings in particular – by soaking an old toothbrush in warm water, applying a few drops of washing-up liquid and gently brushing behind and around the setting with small circular motions to dislodge dust and dirt. Avoid soap which dries to leave white deposits and dry thoroughly with kitchen paper. This method is excellent for diamonds, rubies, sapphires and semi-precious dress rings such as aquamarine, citrine and amethyst in open back settings. It is unsuitable for porous or fragile gems such as emerald, pearl, opal and turquoise. One last point – put the plug in the sink!

Above: Eighteenth-century diamond brooch.

Above, right: The back of the same brooch showing an appalling hotchpotch of bungled repairs.

Acknowledgements

In this new extended edition of my 2003 book *Starting to Collect Antique Jewellery* the vast majority of images have been sourced from the Jewellery Department of Woolley and Wallis, the Salisbury Fine Art Auctioneers. I am indebted to Associate Director Marielle Whiting for her kindness and generosity in allowing access to ten years of fine jewellery catalogues from which many of the illustrations are taken, as well as Jacob Carpenter for his patience and good humour in the administration of all the images. Jewellery photography is never easy, and thanks must therefore be extended to Woolley and Wallis's indefatigable photographer, Richard Valencia, for his sheer professionalism and unfailing technical skill.

I am grateful to Mia Jackson, Curator of Decorative Arts at Waddesdon Manor, for permission to use images of Renaissance pendants and the Museum of London for images of jewellery from the Cheapside Hoard'. I am indebted to the following for giving their permission to use images in 'Collecting Jewellery' which first appeared in 'Starting to Collect Antique Jewellery'; Jonathan Norton (S.J. Phillips), Stephen Burton (Hancocks), Mark Evans (Bentley and Skinner), Kieran McCarthy (Wartski), Sheldon Shapiro, Sandra Cronan and Olivia Gerrish. Images of jewellery in the three new chapters have also been provided by Eleni Bide, Librarian, and Hannah Causton, Collections Officer at The Goldsmiths' Company, Frances Noble, Director of Jewellery at Noonan's Auctioneers of Mayfair and John Joseph and photographer Alexa Dickel at Gray's. Thanks, also, to Messrs Garrards for their kind permission to use three photographs from the Goldsmiths and Silversmiths 1953 publication 'Finer Gifts' and finally, my particular thanks to Dr Kevin Coates, some of whose unique and remarkable jewels I am privileged to showcase in this new book.

My grateful thanks to Andrew Whittaker and James Smith of ACC Art Books for commissioning *Collecting Jewellery* and to my editor, Sue Bennett, for all her help and advice in the book's production.

Finally, none of this would have been possible without the continuing support and encouragement of my wife, Patricia, to whom *Collecting Jewellery* is dedicated.

Index

Page numbers in **bold** indicate illustrations and/or captions

About the Author

John Benjamin began his career in 1972 at Cameo Corner, the Bloomsbury antique jewellers specialising in rare and historic jewellery from ancient Greece to the 19th century. In 1976 he joined Phillips the Auctioneers as a cataloguer and valuer ultimately becoming International Director of Jewellery responsible for the auction programme in London and Geneva. In 1999 he left Phillips to set up on his own as an independent jewellery consultant.

A lecturer, writer and broadcaster he has lectured all over the world on a range of jewellery-related topics and for 32 years was a regular contributor on BBC Television's ever popular *Antiques Roadshow*. He is a Fellow of the Gemmological Association, a Fellow of the Society of Antiquaries, a Freeman of the Worshipful Company of Goldsmiths and a Court Assistant to the Worshipful Company of Arts Scholars. In 2021 he was appointed Honorary Jewellery Advisor to the National Trust.

John is co-author with Paul Atterbury of *The Jewellery and Silver of H.G. Murphy*, also published by ACC Art Books.

Image Credits

The Antique Jewellery Company (courtesy Olivia Gerrish): 30 (bottom right), 119 (bottom), 122 (right); Bentley & Skinner: 76 (bottom centre), 126, 128, 156 (right); Bridgeman Images: 104 (Private collection / Photo © The Fine Art Society, London, UK / Bridgeman Images); Kevin Coates: 185 (bottom right); Sandra Cronan: 63 (bottom left, bottom right); Garrard: 173 (top right, bottom), 174 (left); The Goldsmiths' Company (Photographer: Clarissa Bruce): 178 (top centre, top right, bottom row), 183 (bottom left); The Goldsmiths' Company (Photographer: Richard Valencia): 185 (bottom left); Hancocks (courtesy Stephen Burton): 76 (bottom right), 147 (left); Brian and Lynn Holmes: 58 (bottom), 62 (right); John Jesse: 123, 133 (top left); John Joseph and Alexa Dickel: 171, 178 (top left), 182 (bottom right); © London Museum: 43, 70 (left), 71 (top left, top centre); Linda Morgan: 116; Noonans Mayfair: 177, 180 (bottom row), 182 (top), 185 (top centre, top right); S. J. Phillips: 41 (top left), 44 (top left, top centre), 54 (left), 76 (top left), 77, 83 (bottom), 99 (top left, top right), 100 (top left), 125 (top right), 127 (bottom); Private collection: 86 (top centre, top right); Mrs Sylvia Quenet-Chute: 158 (top left, top right); Ginny Redington Dawes: 87 (bottom), 90 (top left); Satoe: 37 (bottom right); Shapiro & Co.: 142 (left); Spectrum Antiques: 37 (bottom left); Waddesdon Image Library, Mike Fear: 42 (left, right); Wartski Ltd: 157 (left); Woolley & Wallis: 2, 8, 11, 12 (right), 13–17, 18 (bottom right, top left, top right), 19, 20 (top left, bottom left, bottom right), 21–23, 24 (left), 25–29, 30 (left, top right), 31, 32, 33 (right), 34–36, 37 (top), 38–40, 41 (top right, bottom left, bottom centre, bottom right), 44 (top right, bottom row), 45–53, 55–57, 58 (top left), 60, 61, 62 (left, centre), 64 (centre right, bottom left, bottom right), 65–70 (centre, right), 71 (top right, bottom row), 72 (centre, right), 73 (centre, bottom), 74, 75, 76 (top right, bottom left), 78, 79 (centre, bottom), 80–82, 83 (top left, top right), 84, 85, 86 (top left, bottom), 87 (top), 90 (top right, centre, bottom), 91–93, 94, 95–97, 98 (top centre, top right, bottom row), 99 (bottom row), 100 (bottom row), 101 (bottom row), 102, 103, 105, 106, 107 (top left, top right), 108–110, 111 (top left, top right), 113, 114, 117, 118, 119 (top, centre), 120, 121, 122 (left), 124, 125 (top left, bottom), 127 (top left, top right), 129, 130, 132, 133 (top right, bottom), 134–141, 142 (right), 143–146, 147 (right), 148–153, 154 (top row), 155, 156 (left), 157 (right), 158 (bottom), 159–169, 170 (top left, top right), 172, 174 (right), 175, 176, 179, 180 (top row), 181, 182 (bottom left), 184, 185 (top left)

Front cover: Kutchinsky gold, ruby and diamond coiled wirework feather brooch, 1963. Private collection / Jon Stokes

Back cover: (Top left) Late Victorian diamond bee brooch, c.1890. (See page 22); (Bottom left) Pendant/brooch studded with turquoises with similarly set heart and key suspension drops, c.1825. (See page 101); (Centre) 19th-century Italian Etruscan revival gold ram's head bangle, c.1860. (See page 106); (Top right) Fine cornelian intaglio depicting Mercury with caduceus attribute, probably 1st–2nd century A.D. (See page 40); (Bottom right) Regency diamond brooch fashioned as a spray of dog rose, c.1825. (See page 93)

Frontispiece: Impressive Victorian fully articulated diamond corsage brooch, c.1880. (See page 92)

Parts of the text and some images previously published in *Starting to Collect Antique Jewellery* (Antique Collectors' Club, 2003)

ISBN: 978 1 78884 347 8

A CIP catalogue record for this book is available from the British Library

The author and publisher gratefully acknowledge the permission granted to reproduce the copyright material in this book. Every effort has been made to trace copyright holders and to obtain their permission for the use of copyright material. The publisher apologises for any errors or omissions in the text and would be grateful if notified of any corrections that should be incorporated in future reprints or editions of this book.

Editor: Sue Bennett
Designers: Steve Farrow, Mariona Vilarós Capella
Reprographics Manager: Corban Wilkin

EU GPSR Authorised Representative:
Easy Access System Europe Oü, 16879218
Address: Mustamäe tee 50, 10621 Tallinn, Estonia
Email: gpsr@easproject.com Tel: +358 40 500 3575

Printed in China by C&C Offset Printing Co. Ltd
for ACC Art Books Ltd, Woodbridge, Suffolk, UK

www.accartbooks.com